WHITEY'S
CAREER CASE
THE INSULIN MURDERS

HAROLD W. WHITE

ISBN: 1463706499
ISBN-13: 9781463706494

Dedication

This book is dedicated to my partner Marty Deiro, may he rest in peace, and to all the old 187 P.C. Bull Dogs of the Los Angeles County Sheriff's Department Homicide Bureau. They know how it feels to get their teeth into a difficult homicide investigation. *They never let go!*

Acknowledgments

First I would like to thank my wife, Mary, who lived through this whole project as she struggled through my notorious handwriting in typing the original manuscript. It was no picnic for her to put up with my mood swings as I relived the entire investigation for the thousandth time.

Next, Retired Division Chief John Graham, who read the manuscript, made valuable suggestions and offered sound advice about the entire project.

Jack Richardson, my editor-in-chief, made the manuscript flow better.

Mary Nieswender, reporter for the *Long Beach Press-Telegram*, whose accurate reporting and friendship I will never forget.

Last, but not least, is "Ask Judy" Mahoney, who pulled this whole project together by many revisions and her expertise.

"For he who avenges murder cares for the helpless. He does not ignore the cries of those who suffer."

Psalm 9:12

Holy Bible, New Living Translation

CONTENTS

WILLIAM DALE ARCHERD
AKA James Lynn Arden

Marriages and Victims

MARRIAGES

NAME	DATE	PLACE
Odessa Halloway Baker	8 May 1930	Magnum, OK
Eleanor Marcella Russell	8 June 1935	Yuma, AZ
Dorothea Ford Henes	27 June 1949	Reno, NV
Annulled	14 May 1956	Reno, NV
Zella Austin Winders	15 May 1956	Las Vegas, NV
Died	25 July 1956	Covina, CA
Juanita Elisabeth Plum	10 March 1958	Las Vegas, NV
Died	13 March 1958	Las Vegas, NV
Gladys Teresa Stewart	4 October 1958	La Habra, CA
Remarried	22 May 1959	La Habra, CA
Divorced	29 October 1965	Las Vegas, NV
Mary Brinker Post	18 April 1965	Ontario, CA
Remarried	12 November 1965	Riverside, CA
Died	3 November 1966	Pomona, CA

Victims

NAME	DATE OF DEATH	PLACE
William Edward Jones	12 October 1947	Fontana, CA
Zella Austin Archerd	25 July 1956	Covina, CA
Juanita Plum Archerd	13 March 1958	Las Vegas, NV
Frank Lawrence Stewart	17 March 1960	Las Vegas, NV
Burney Kirk Archerd	2 September 1961	Long Beach, CA
Mary Brinker Post Archerd	3 November 1966	Pomona, CA

1
Archerd: "AGAIN!!"

"Whitey, this is Walsh." He didn't stop to take a breath. "Ron Martin was having lunch at the Alhambra Elks Club this noon when Al Stewart told him that Archerd had lost another wife." Captain George Walsh, former lieutenant in the Homicide Bureau of the Los Angeles County Sheriff's Department, now captain at Altadena Station, and my old boss. Lieutenant Martin was a former homicide investigator, and had been familiar with the Archerd investigation since 1956.

"Jeeesus Christ, George, think that rotten bastard could've murdered her, too?" I was mad, but not surprised.

"Don't know, Whitey. Ron's right here." There was silence and then I heard Martin's strident voice.

"Whitey, Al Stewart, manager of the Alhambra Elks Club, told me that Archerd's wife was involved in a minor traffic accident a few days ago and had died of her injuries."

"It looks as if Gladys didn't believe us when we told her that she'd be next," I interrupted.

"It wasn't Gladys; she's still working at the Elks Club. Archerd divorced her and married another woman. Stewart got his information from Gladys."

"Know anything about this other woman, what her name is, where she lived, where she died?"

"Only other information is that they lived in San Bernardino County. Stewart didn't want to be pressed, but said he would keep his ears open. Wish I had more information."

"Thanks a lot, Ron. Keep me posted if you hear anything more. I'll do some checking and see what I can come up with," I said.

Damn. That crafty son-of-a-bitch has killed another wife sure as hell, and we won't be able to prove this one either, unless we get lucky. In all my twenty years of law enforcement I had never felt so utterly frustrated. It's a hell of a helpless feeling to know that a psychopath like William Dale Archerd can kill so many people, to know how he kills and why, but not be able to come up with a criminal cause of death in order to prove murder. It was at this point that I decided Archerd's crime spree had gone on long enough. I was going to nail him if it took the rest of my career to do it.

The ever-increasing murder rate, manpower shortages, and current civil unrest in the Los Angeles of the 1960s left little time to devote to any one particular case. I decided I'd make time.

I rechecked my notes and found the last entry dated 5/18/66: "Info from CII. Archerd arrested this date by Pomona police department on the charge of driving under the influence of drugs."

I called Pomona P.D. "Mooney, would you please check your report of 5/18/66 on the arrest of William Dale Archerd, a.k.a. James Lynn Arden, and give me his home address and next of kin?"

Shortly, Mooney returned. "Next of kin: Mary Brinker Post Arden, home address 15715 San Jose Avenue, Chino." "Put a copy of your report in the mail for me, and thanks."

I was puzzled when the San Bernardino Coroner's Office had no record of Mary Brinker Post Arden's death. Allegedly, she had died of injuries from an auto accident that occurred in San Bernardino County. I didn't believe it. I grabbed my notebook and headed downstairs to the Coroner's office.

Phil Schwartzberg, the duty Deputy Coroner, was on the phone when I walked in. He waved and pointed to a chair. When he finished his conversation he turned and said, "What can I do for you today, Whitey?"

"Phil, you remember that Archerd character we've been trying to nail for years?"

"How could I forget him? Don't tell me he's killed *another* wife?"

"That's what I'd like to know. Would you check your files and see if you have a record of death on Mary Brinker Post Arden Archerd?"

Phil was on his way to the files even before I had finished. He spun that big Wheeldex around to the A's, ran his finger down the list of names and pulled out a card.

"Yep, here it is. It says she died at Pomona Valley Hospital, possibly from injuries received in a traffic accident November 3, 1966 in Montclair."

My heart pumped a couple of extra beats as I realized that she had, in fact, died in Los Angeles County, and any responsibility for the investigation of her death would be ours. "Do you know who did the autopsy and whether the cause of death has been established?" I asked.

"Doctor Miller did the post-mortem, and the cause of death hasn't been established. The lab report isn't in yet, but I'll give you a copy of the preliminary report."

"Phil, would you flag that card so that if anyone inquires about her death I can be notified?"

"Sure, Whitey, anything I can do to help you nail that devil. Good luck."

I took the stairs back to the third floor, three at a time. Maybe, just maybe, this would be the break we had been looking for since 1956 when Sergeant Harry Andre first suspected Archerd of killing Zella, Archerd's fourth wife. Harry was just as frustrated then as I was now. Then came the death of Archerd's fifth wife, Juanita, in 1958 and Frank Stewart, Gladys' ex-husband, in 1960 when Sergeant Dick Humphreys had the case. He couldn't do anything with it either. But I knew I could do it, with a little luck and a lot of hard work.

I went into Captain Al Etzel's office to tell him what I had just learned. "Pelon, Archerd has killed another wife sure as hell," I said as I sat down.

"The hell you say!" Then he added, "And knock off that Pelon shit." (*Pelon* means bald in Spanish, but not many people outside the Homicide Bureau dared to use that nickname.)

I told him about my conversation with Walsh and Martin, and added what I had learned since.

"Whitey, I don't want to spoil anything for you, but you know you're next up on the lieutenants list. Have you any suggestion for someone to take over for you?"

Oh Christ. In my excitement I had forgotten about my promotion. I would almost give up that promotion if I could put Archerd away forever.

"Dammit, Al, I know more about that slimy bastard than anyone, including himself. Walt Thornton and I worked up a good case on Archerd when he killed his fifteen-year-old nephew back in 1961. All we had was circumstantial evidence then, and the District Attorney felt it wasn't strong enough to file a murder charge. If this case is handled properly, I think we can file a complaint using similar acts in the deaths of Zella, Juanita, Frank Stewart, Burney, and maybe that Jones fellow in 1947. Isn't there any way you can keep me here to at least supervise the investigation?"

"We're trying to get an extra item for another homicide lieutenant, but it doesn't look too good. I want you to bring this case up to date as soon as possible and start clearing all your other cases, so you can leave with a clean slate." Just like being kicked in the teeth, I sat back stunned.

"How many does this make, Whitey?" Etzel asked.

"Well, there's three wives, a nephew, Gladys' ex-husband, and Jones, the one that our witness Dorothea told us about back in 1957."

"I want you to write a memo to the boss about this latest death; then make another, listing all the victims with as much information as you have. Might be that we can generate some action from the corner pocket." He picked up another crime report to indicate the conversation was over.

That last remark lifted my hopes a little. I set about preparing the memos the captain had requested.

I didn't sleep well that night, wondering if Archerd would get away with this murder as he had with all the others. I was at the office early the next morning. As I walked in I saw Roy Collins reared back in Captain Etzel's chair with his feet on the desk. He was snoring loudly. I shook him gently, and then stepped back to avoid the roundhouse swing I knew was coming. His backhand grazed my ear as it flew by.

"White, you son of a bitch, don't ever do that to me!"

"What's the matter, Roy, have a bad night?"

"Yeah, I just got in about an hour ago. This crazy bastard shot his wife in the side with a shotgun using double-ought buckshot, then stuck it in his mouth and blew his damned head off.

I had worked several cases with Roy and still had one pending: a case where a nation-wide cat burglar had killed his female accomplice, dumped her body on a fire trail in the mountains up near Monrovia, then poured five gallons of sulfuric acid over her body. The suspect, James Jones Bradford, was still at large. We sat drinking a stale cup of coffee. "Roy, do you feel like bringing that Bradford case up to date today? The captain gave me orders to bring everything I'm involved in up to date before I'm promoted."

"Promoted! White, you wouldn't make a pimple on a good lieutenant's ass! Naw, I'm too bushed; let's do it Monday. I have court that day anyway."

Just then Jane Sawai, our head secretary, walked in. "Did I awaken you this morning when I came in, Sergeant Collins?"

"No, not this morning Janie, but you have the last three mornings. Can't you come in a half hour late like all the other girls instead of an hour early?"

"Janie, don't let that old redhead get to you. He just got up on the wrong side of the desk this morning."

"He doesn't bother me, Sergeant White; I know his bark is worse than his bite."

Baby Jane, as we called her, was a tiny Japanese girl who was cute as well as an extremely competent supervising stenographer. She was highly thought of by everyone in Homicide.

Phil Schwartzberg came up about ten o'clock and handed me a copy of the coroner's protocol.

"You didn't have to bring it up, Phil. I could have come after it."

Phil sighed and made a face. "I had to get out of that zoo for a while. A fellow can take only so much violence and death."

I scanned the report rapidly. "Phil, if you weren't so damned ugly I'd kiss you. Do you realize that this is the first time we've had a cause of death consistent with our suspicions in this whole Archerd affair?"

On the last day of December I sat at my desk throwing away old reports and getting my personal things together. I had been told earlier in the week that I was to report to Lakewood Station at midnight January 2. My promotion had come through. God knows we could use the money, with a son in his senior year of college and a daughter thinking of marriage. I should have been happy about it, but I could only feel sorely disappointed. I knew that if Archerd wasn't stopped now, there might never be another chance.

Just before noon, a tall, rather handsome man in his late thirties came into the office, and asked for me.

"My name is Richard Saint Francis Post. The coroners' office referred me to you about the death of my mother. I don't quite understand why the Homicide Bureau is involved when it's obvious that she died as the result of a traffic accident."

"I'm Sergeant White, Mister Post. I asked the coroner to refer anyone inquiring about her death to me. Sit down and I'll tell you all about it." Then I told him what our suspicions were and what our investigation had uncovered so far.

"I just can't believe it! I never dreamed there was any suspicion of murder. This is incredible. In her letters, my mother seemed to be so happy with Jim. Why in God's name would he want to kill her?"

"I'm not quite sure myself. In all the other cases it seems the motive was either money or to rid himself of a problem. Perhaps in this case it was both. That's one reason I wanted to talk to you. Could there have been any money left to him as the result of her death?"

"Not much, if any. She lived on her salary as a publicity agent for Claremont College and a small pension left to her by my father; also a tiny royalty she received from a book she had written several years ago. Surely that's not enough to kill her for."

"Sometimes it doesn't take a lot of money for a motive to kill. Is there anyone else I should talk to who might shed some light on a possible motive?"

"My sister, Anya. She was here for the funeral and helped Jim dispose of Mother's things. Perhaps she can tell you something. Then there's Father Evan Williams, her rector. She was very close to him, since my father was also an Episcopal priest."

He wrote down their names and addresses. "You can be assured of our utmost cooperation in this investigation, Sergeant."

"Mister Post, from this point on, I won't be the investigator. Today is my last day. I'm being promoted and transferred to another assignment."

"I'm sorry to hear that. I mean I'm sorry that you will not be able to carry on with the investigation. You obviously know more about this case than anyone. Would it help if I requested that you be assigned full time?" he asked, fidgeting with his horn-rimmed glasses.

"I don't know; I've never heard of it being done in this office. We're understaffed as it is. Since the Watts riots and all the unrest caused by the anti-Vietnam activities, the hippie cults and the Black Panthers, all law enforcement agencies are spread pitifully thin," I told him.

He picked up his briefcase and started for the door, then turned and said, "If you need me, I'll be at my sister's house in Pennsylvania until late January. After that you can contact me at the American Embassy in Maseru, Lesotho." He walked briskly out of the office.

What a hell of a shock that must have been for him, coming all the way here from Africa, thinking his mother had died in a traffic accident, to learn that she had been murdered. I finished cleaning out my desk, but my mind was focused on Archerd. I felt the case could be proved. An investigator should be assigned full time, and I knew I was the one with all the information and the feel needed for the case. Why the hell couldn't they see that? I wondered what would happen, who they would assign. Finally, I slammed my briefcase on my desk. It's not my worry any more.

"The hell it isn't!"

2
The Promotion

For the next few weeks I tried to focus all my attention to reacquainting myself with patrol procedures and administration of the early morning watch at Lakewood Station, but my thoughts kept returning to the Archerd case. I was afraid they'd let it die and he'd kill another unsuspecting wife. I still hadn't given up on feeling that someday I would finally get that rotten bastard.

At Lakewood Station I was the new kid on the block. As such, it was my fate to be assigned as Watch Commander on the early morning shift. Captain Paul Strohman greeted me with a sly smile that I believe hid a desire to laugh up his sleeve for being so lucky as to have one of the 'Big Dicks from Downtown' working patrol. It seemed he got a perverted sense of enjoyment out of telling me that I was at the bottom of the totem pole.

He and his 'gopher,' Sergeant 'Catfish' Johnson, conspired against me so that I would buy the coffee by losing at their game of pitching pennies to a crack in the floor. Little did he know that I had seldom bought coffee by losing a coin toss. In fact, I had been taught by the best, Lieutenant Hal Marlow, who had an office right next door. He should be in the Hall of Fame of Penny Pitchers. Hal later served several years as Under Sheriff.

Captain Strohman, or "Stump" as we called him, told me that I would spend a couple weeks working the day shift until I got the hang of things. As it turned out, I don't think I worked more than four or five day shifts, as I had several homicide cases in court.

However, by the time I had been there three weeks I did get to know the district pretty well. My memories of the Lakewood Station area were of alfalfa and bean fields with sheep grazing on the stubble. Now, in the late sixties, it was wall-to-wall houses and business districts from the ocean to the mountains.

I never worked there long enough to have my brand new uniform cleaned. Stump wouldn't let me forget the time I never worked for him. Every time I would see him he would say, "You are the guy that worked for me for *three weeks* one day." Later on, when we were both captains, we worked on some special projects together. He eventually made Chief before he retired.

I was interrupted at briefing one morning by a call from Roy Collins. "Whitey, James Bradford has been arrested in Detroit. I'm working on the extradition now. This trip is going to be a bitch, though. We've got to go by way of North Carolina to talk to the victim's 'Auntie.' Be down here about ten, tomorrow morning, so we can pick up our travel money and reservations. Pack your bag; we'll be gone four or five days."

Bradford was a nationwide cat burglar who killed his girlfriend. Her body had been found about five miles above Glendora, lying right in the middle of a fire access road running along a hogback ridge at approximately the two-thousand-foot level. She was lying on her back, and it appeared that her clothes were partially burned off.

The autopsy showed that she had been hit in the head, possibly with a ball peen hammer, leaving about three quarters of an inch depression. Her skin was stiff and rigid, similar to weather-worn leather. Her fingers were curled into fists and had to be removed and soaked in a photographic solution for several days before they were pliable enough to fingerprint.

We had Cliff Cromp, our rotund, cherubic-faced criminalist, come and look at the body. His first statement was, "Looks like she took a bath in sulfuric acid."

Then we took Cromp out to the crime scene and showed him where she had been found. He nosed around the scene for about forty-five minutes and came up with the O-ring seal from the lid of a five gallon container of sulfuric acid. From that O-ring he was able to tell us the company that had made that batch of acid, when it was made, and where it was shipped to one of a dozen companies that sold acid to swimming pool maintenance companies. We were able to locate the right company within a few days.

Cromp explained the reason her skin was so leathery. For sulfuric acid to become active, it had to mix with a little water, so the natural late night and early morning mists prevalent in the area were sufficient to cause skin to become tanned like leather. If there had been a heavy rain, most of the acid would have washed away and the tanning effect would not have been as severe. She was identified as Betty Peace, a twenty-three-year-old black woman born in Durham, North Carolina. Her next of kin was her auntie who had raised her from a baby. This information came from an arrest report from Los Angeles Police Department.

We contacted the auntie by phone. She told us she had just seen our victim about a month ago when she and her boyfriend, James Jones Bradford, had come by in a brand new Buick Wildcat. They were all togged out in brand new expensive clothes and new hairdos. Bradford had a fifty dollar hair process and Betty had her hair done up in "one-a-them brand new styles."

She said, "James just called here askin' where Betty was. Sed she'd got mad and left him and that he hadn't seen her in two, three weeks. I wasn't surprised, 'cause Betty tole me she was goin' leave him. What happened to my baby, anyhow?"

We had to tell her that Betty was dead; also that if Bradford called back to find out where he was calling from.

We checked CII for any record of James Jones Bradford and located a local address where his wife lived with their eleven-year-old son. Mrs. Bradford was a nice, well-adjusted lady suffering from sickle-cell anemia. She told us she hadn't seen James for some time; the last time she saw him was when he came by one day driving his new Buick and wanted her to drop him off at Los Angeles International Airport. She didn't know where he was going.

With her permission we searched the car and found the plastic seal that covered the neck of a five gallon jug of sulfuric acid, and a sales receipt from the pool supply company. We put out a nationwide broadcast for James Jones Bradford.

I didn't have clothes that could withstand Detroit's winter. I called my wife, Midge, and asked her to go to May Company and buy me a pair of thermal underwear. She said, "Ralph just came in. I'll have him go down and pick some up for you." Ralph and Evalynn Gannaway had shared an old green farmhouse with us in Bellflower back in 1946 during the time that housing was hard to come by for returning servicemen. We had been close friends ever since.

When I got home there were two packages waiting for me: two bottoms but no tops. I called Ralph and said,

"Ralph, you dipstick, you bought two bottoms and no tops. Would you go down and get me two tops?" Ralph was a good sport about it; in about an hour he was back with two thermal tops.

Roy and I checked in at the Jack Tar Hotel in Raleigh later that night with a bottle of Jim Beam. The Chief of Detectives from the Raleigh Police Department woke us the next morning and took us to his favorite restaurant for breakfast where we had hush puppies, grits and ham with lots of black coffee.

There was four inches of snow in Raleigh and it looked as if it was going to snow all day. We met Betty Peace's auntie about ten o'clock. She was a short, slightly overweight, black lady about sixty years old. Roy and I both liked her immediately. She was a lovely, God-fearing Baptist, eager to help us in any way she could.

She told us what Betty had told her. Betty and James traveled constantly across the country, stopping at only the best motels and hotels. James would break into the rooms of his marks and take nothing but cash, credit cards and driver's license from the occupants while they were sleeping. Of course, the victim never knew he had been robbed until he went to settle his hotel bill. By this time James was in the next state, using the credit cards to buy expensive jewelry and clothing. While he was trying on clothes and keeping the proprietor busy, Betty would steal expensive items of clothing and jewelry and stuff them into her pantyhose, "them whatchacallem underwear that fitchatite." She said James and Betty would repeat the same action every night as they drove across the country. Betty also told her aunt that when she told James she wanted to quit being a thief, he had told Betty, "Bitch, you ever leave me, I'll kill you."

"I think that's just what happened. She quit, and he killed her."

Of course this conversation was tape recorded with Auntie's permission. Statement reporter Harry Tolmach transcribed the tape. He grabbed me as I came into the office a few days later and said, "Whitey, what in hell is a fitchatite?" I had to tell him that it referred to pantyhose or leotards that fit tight!

Roy and I caught the early morning flight from Raleigh-Durham to Washington, D.C. We were the only passengers on that plush old flagship, so we rode all the way to DC in the lounge, pampered by the stewardesses.

From DC we flew to Detroit. I think there were only a dozen or so passengers. One of them was a self-important county commissioner. He loved to talk. Roy and I were tired and tried to sleep, but were polite to him. We told him a little bit about our case and our assignment to Homicide Bureau. We may have embellished it a tad for clarity. About a week later, we were notified that we had just received a commendation from the County Commissioner of some Ohio county!

Detroit had a foot of snow on the ground, and it was still snowing with a steady wind blowing. We checked into the Cadillac Hotel. The next morning we went to the county jail and asked to see James Jones Bradford. We were told that Mister Bradford was with visitors at the moment. Immediately we were suspicious – Bradford was getting privileges? In rather strong language, we made it known that if James wasn't with his attorney, we would like to see him immediately.

That shook up the jailer. He took us back to Bradford's cell. The visitors were Jones' new girlfriend and her mother. There he stood in his fifty-dollar hair process, wearing his four hundred dollar suit and one hundred twenty-five dollar shoes, and he looked like he was ready to go out on the town. Roy and I got the picture right away. James was spending his stolen cash pretty lavishly. We spoiled his party when we told James that he was going back with us to Los Angeles in the morning. The two ladies couldn't get out of there fast enough.

We weren't surprised the next morning when the deputy assigned to drive us to the airport said, "I don't know if the roads are open enough to get to the airport." We made it in fifteen minutes.

We sat James Jones Bradford between us on the plane. He tried to make conversation, but we ignored him. A little later he said, "How much money you fellows make a year?"

"Enough," I told him.

"Sheeit, man! I make thirty, forty thousand a year and don't ever pay no taxes!"

Roy looked straight at him. "James, from now on you ain't makin' nothin'. You're goin' to the gas chamber."

James whined, "Sergeant, I don't want to die!"

"You should've thought of that before you killed Betty Peace."

He didn't have another word to say the rest of the trip.

Eventually James Bradford was sentenced to die in the gas chamber. His sentence was commuted to life imprisonment, probably due to the anti-death penalty movement, and the large number of prisoners on death row awaiting results of their many appeals before the Supreme Court.

All the time Bradford was in the county jail, until he was sentenced and sent to San Quentin, he sent Roy kites (letters) telling him about the guilt of one of his cellmates. He was always ratting on someone. None of his information was any good. His plea was always, "Sergeant, I don't want to die."

I'll bet he's walking the streets of Los Angeles right now. Of all the cases I investigated, none of the defendants has ever been executed. Whether or not the death penalty is a deterrent to the commission of murder is a subject that will be argued long after I'm dead and gone. During the sixties there was a lot of pressure to do away with the death penalty entirely. This has resulted in a huge backlog of inmates who have filed to have their cases heard before the U.S. Supreme Court. I can't remember when the last person was executed in the state of California. Doesn't anyone care about the victims of capital crimes?

3
Back On The Case

The morning after returning from Detroit I ran into Acting Chief of Detectives Kenny Irving on the third floor of the Hall of Justice.

"Well, if it isn't old William Dale." He'd been calling me that ever since I raised so much hell about the death of Archerd's nephew. "I've been doing a lot of thinking about this Archerd case and I've decided to see if I can borrow you from the Patrol Division to try and resolve it." Grinning, he took a long pull on his ever-present cigarette.

"That's music to dance by, Chief! I've been worried about what was happening to the case ever since I left. I have a feeling things are about to turn in our favor, and we're going to put that dude in the gas chamber where he belongs." I didn't even try to hide my excitement.

"I knew you would like having another crack at that character." He puffed again on his cigarette and headed for his office.

White, the ball's in your court now. You've got to deliver. I was flushed with excitement and could feel my heart beating rapidly. I was already planning my next move to sink Archerd.

Three weeks later I was loaned back to the Detective Division and assigned full time to investigate the Archerd murders. I knew I was under the gun and would be expected to uncover all the facts necessary to either prove our suspicions or forevermore keep quiet about the "Archerd Case." I also knew that if pathology in general, and the coroner's office specifically, had not developed the necessary means to establish a specific cause of death in each case, all my effort would be lost.

God, what a disturbing thought! I shuddered, realizing the responsibility I was about to undertake. Even so, I accepted that responsibility with renewed enthusiasm. Somehow I knew that all the pieces of the puzzle were about to fall into place.

Captain Etzel and I walked into Chief Irving's office as he was putting on his coat. "Don't sit down; Joe Carr is waiting for us," he said, nervously puffing on his cigarette.

We rode the elevator up to the sixth floor, walked down the hall to a door where the frosted glass panel read 'JOE CARR CHIEF TRIALS DEPUTY.' The receptionist held the swinging half-door open. "Go right in, Chief. Mister Carr is expecting you."

"Good morning, fellows. This meeting seems like a rerun of days past. The same cast of characters, the same problem with a new victim." He waved us to a row of chairs already arranged in a neat arc in front of his desk. He continued, "As I recall, in the past we haven't been able to establish a criminal cause of death. Can we do that at this stage?"

Chief Irving said, "Whitey has an idea or two." He nodded to me. "Tell them, Whitey."

"Joe, what I had in mind was trying to see if we could build a circumstantial case using common plan, scheme and design as a basis. As you know from our talks in the past, all the victims died of the same symptoms."

"Hold it a minute, Whitey." Carr stretched his lanky six foot-three inch frame, adjusted his glasses, walked to the door and told his secretary, "Honey, bring in a fresh pot of coffee; we're going to be here for some time. And ask Jim Shea to come in, please."

I was glad to see Deputy District Attorney Shea sit in on this, as he had helped me with difficult cases in the past. I told them that right now we had a total of six victims who had died of similar causes. I started from the first death that we knew about, which was actually Archerd's second victim. We learned about victim number one, Robert Jones (later identified as William Edward Jones), while death of the second victim, Zella Winders Archerd, was being investigated.

Dorothea, Archerd's wife since 1949, told investigators that Archerd had married Zella May 15, 1956, one day after he had had his marriage to Dorothea annulled. Dorothea was one pissed-off ex-wife, and she wanted blood! She further told Harry Andre, the investigator of Zella's death, that she was sure Archerd killed Zella and Robert Jones by injecting them with insulin. She and Archerd were avid mystery fans and were always fantasizing about how to commit the perfect murder. Archerd had worked on the insulin shock ward at Camarillo State Hospital where insulin was used to treat schizophrenics. He knew insulin was a normal body hormone produced by the pancreas and would not be suspected as a lethal agent. At this time we had no further information on Robert Jones, victim number one.

Archerd met Zella Winders when he called on her to sell her folding doors she wanted installed in her house. She had just divorced her husband and was awarded some cash and the house as her share of the divorce settlement. In a matter of weeks, Archerd talked Zella into selling her house and moving into his house, which was a rental. Proceeds from the sale amounted to ten thousand one hundred eighty-seven dollars, which was promptly deposited into their joint account July 13, 1956. From this account Archerd bought a new Thunderbird, which he proudly showed off to his friends. By the middle of July this bank account was almost depleted.

Zella was so madly in love with Archerd that she wrote to several of her friends, telling them of their great love affair. She liked to boast about having an 'almost-doctor' in the house, alluding to Archerd's claim he had to drop out of medical school just before graduating.

What a snow job. The closest he ever got to becoming a doctor was an aid man for Kaiser Steel at their iron mine off Highway 66 near Kelso, California; and he was a 'bed pan jockey' at Camarillo State Hospital, where it was his job to monitor patients who had been injected with insulin and keep the doctors and nurses advised of their condition. This is where he learned that patients overdosing on insulin would go into a coma and sometimes have grand mal seizures.

By the time I got to this point, I had their complete attention. I continued to brief them on our entire investigation. With the information from Dorothea, Andre cranked up his investigation a few notches. He didn't fall for the story Archerd had told him:

Archerd and Zella had gone to dinner. On their return Zella went to bed and was about asleep when Archerd went in and told her not to look, as he was being held at gun point and being robbed. Archerd then put a pillowcase over Zella's head. The "robber" told them he was going to inject them so they would be sedated and unable to call for help until after the robber was gone. Archerd said he was told to drop his trousers and was given two injections. Zella, who was in her nightgown lying on her bed, was also injected in the buttocks twice. The robbers allegedly took Archerd's watch and six hundred dollars cash, then left. Shortly thereafter Zella started twitching and moaning, then went into what Archerd called grand mal seizures.

The following morning he called Doctor Chambers, who came to the house and examined Zella. He noted two needle marks in her left buttocks. Zella was still in a coma. Chambers told Archerd to get her to a hospital as soon as possible. Archerd refused, telling him his wife was deathly afraid of hospitals.

"At least get someone in here to take care of her. If she gets any worse, call me," Doctor Chambers said.

Archerd called Velma Rosenaw, a practical nurse, to clean Zella up and change bedclothes before Archerd went to work. He called Zella's daughter, Darlene Lopez, then called Doctor Chambers again. Chambers showed up and examined the patient again. He found four needle marks on the patient's buttocks; by that time Zella was deceased.

Sergeant Art Gillette, Narcotics Bureau; Larry Picano, Robbery Detail; and Harry Andre, Homicide Bureau, meticulously searched the entire house. Only one hypodermic needle was found. However, the search of a vacant lot next door yielded one vial labeled NPH-U80 insulin manufactured by Eli Lilly Company. These two items were marked for identification and retained for any future prosecution.

On July 16, 1956 an autopsy was performed on the body of Zella Archerd at eleven-fifteen a.m. at the Los Angeles County Coroner's Mortuary. Death was ascribed as terminal bronchopneumonia due to coma of undetermined origin. There was no way known at that time to determine that death was caused by an injection of insulin. Fortunately, several microscopic slides of brain, pancreas and other tissue were held for future study.

Sergeant Andre had put in untold hours and consumed numerous bottles of Maalox before he was promoted and transferred to another assignment. He did, however, leave copious notes and reports that would prove to be very beneficial to any future investigator undertaking the task of trying to prove death caused by multiple injections of insulin.

I went on and described the other murders we knew Archerd had committed. The first one chronologically was the death of "Robert Jones" in 1947. Dorothea told us that Jones had molested a twelve-year-old babysitter and was facing a charge of statutory rape. He had asked Archerd to help him out. Archerd told Jones, "I'll take care of everything."

He had Jones fake a minor traffic accident, after which Jones was admitted to Pomona Valley Hospital with a concussion. Archerd had the family move Jones to the Kaiser Hospital in Fontana, where he suddenly died. This was about all we knew of the Jones affair at that time, as we could find no record of the traffic accident or death of a Robert Jones. He was later found to be William Edward Jones.

In 1956 came victim number two, Zella Winders Archerd.

The next death was that of Juanita Plum Archerd. Archerd started living with Juanita in January 1957. While living with her there were two separate house fires. They collected over fourteen thousand dollars from Juanita's insurance, which was more than a cop's annual income at that time. Her divorce from Myron Plum had been finalized May 5, 1957; Archerd married Juanita March 10, 1958, in Las Vegas, Nevada.

Three days later Juanita died at the Money Marie Motel in Las Vegas. The coroner attributed her death to an accidental self-administered overdose of barbiturates. Archerd described her condition as having some sort of seizure.

Using the name of James Lynn Arden, Archerd married Gladys Stewart in Las Vegas October 4, 1958. On May 28, 1959 he remarried Gladys under the name of William Dale Archerd.

Gladys' ex-husband, Frank Stewart, died March 17, 1960, at Southern Nevada Memorial Hospital, allegedly from injuries received from slipping on a banana peel in the men's restroom at McCarran Airport in Las Vegas. Similar seizures were noted on his hospital chart. There was also one dilated eye and one pinpointed eye.

Frank Stewart had flown to Las Vegas with Archerd, who took out about two hundred thousand dollars flight insurance on Stewart. There were three policies: one beneficiary was Jenny May Archerd, Archerd's mother, another was William Dale Archerd, and the third Gladys Archerd. Archerd filed suit to recover the insurance money, but the company claimed no one had any insurable interest. The case never came to trial. There was also a suit, filed by Stewart's daughters, alleging negligence on the part of McCarran Airport.

On August 2, 1960, Archerd set fire to Phillip and Stella Morin's car. He conspired with Stella to set the fire after she had driven Archerd's car to Las Vegas for him, while he and Stewart flew to Las Vegas. Stella collected the insurance money.

On October 10, 1960, Archerd and Stella conspired in a phony hit-and-run accident. Archerd dropped Stella off at the home of a man who had advertised a car for sale. Stella was to take the car to her mechanic and bring it back. She actually met Archerd on a street in Altadena where he bent the antenna and wiped some dust off the front fender. They abandoned the car. Stella drove home and Archerd filed a hit-and-run accident report. Archerd ended up in a

hospital with one eye dilated, complaining of a severe headache. He filed a civil suit against the owner of the car.

The next incident was the alleged hit-and-run accident
in Bellflower. Burney Kirk Archerd, Archerd's fifteen-year-
old nephew, was allegedly hit by a red pickup truck. Burney
was admitted to Long Beach Memorial Hospital with one
eye dilated, a severe headache and a bruised hip. He died
eleven days later, after suffering grand mal seizures and a
low blood sugar attack.

"You know all about that, Joe. Captain Etzel, Lieutenant
Walsh, Sergeant Thornton and I presented all those facts to
you back in 1961," I said.

"Yeah, I remember, Whitey. Now what about this latest
victim? Do you have anything new that would help us put
this character away?"

"Yeah, Joe, I think we are about to have a change of luck.
This latest victim is Mary Brinker Post Arden Archerd. She
was the widow of an Episcopal priest, and at the time of
her death she was assistant publicity director of Claremont
Colleges in La Verne. She married Archerd in April 1965.
Archerd moved into her home in Chino. The marriage was
contentious from the start, probably because Archerd was
still married to Gladys, whom he later divorced, in October
1965. He then re-married Mary, but things just didn't work
out. They eventually filed for bankruptcy, and Archerd left
her. Mary was desperately in love with Archerd and tried
everything she knew to locate him and bring him back. She
wrote mushy love letters to him and mailed them to their
attorney and anyone else they knew. No luck.

"Then it was Mary's fate on October 28, 1966, when she
drove home to lunch. On the way back to her office she
rear-ended another car and suffered a bruised nose and
black eyes. She sent another flurry of letters to anyone
Archerd might know. In the next couple of days, lo and
behold, 'Jim' came home. Three days later Mary died in

Pomona Valley Hospital from low blood sugar complicated by grand mal seizures. We had a good autopsy of this victim and a good chance of proving he killed her with multiple injections of insulin."

Joe Carr held up his hand. "Stop right there, Whitey. Let me talk to Buck." Buck Compton was the chief deputy district attorney.

Joe got on the phone and said a few words, then said to all of us, "Let's go up to Buck's office. He wants to see all of you anyway. We've been keeping him abreast of this situation all along."

We all rode the elevator up to the sixth floor where we were promptly ushered into the chief deputy district attorney's office. Buck Compton was a six-foot, two hundred twenty-pound, ex-Los Angeles Police Department detective in his mid-forties with thinning sandy hair. It was not hard to imagine that he had been a First Lieutenant in the 101st Airborne Division. He was wounded in the Battle of the Bulge, for which he was awarded the Silver Star and Purple Heart.

Buck was reared back in his swivel chair nursing his Sherlock Holmes pipe. He said, "Joe, I know enough about that case to know you wouldn't all be here if what you have wasn't pretty close to being ready to go."

Carr jumped right in. "Whitey, tell the boss what you have in mind."

I didn't need the prompting. "Mister Compton, this bastard has been killing people since 1947, and no one has been able to do a thing about it. I think with a little help and a lot of luck we can make a great circumstantial evidence case against Archerd. I'd like to have a good deputy district attorney work with me on this case. If we go to trial, it would be a one-shot deal; we'll probably never get another chance at him."

"How long do you think it would take to wrap it up, Whitey?"

"Well, we have lots of ground to cover and around four hundred witnesses to locate and re-interview. I think a minimum of six months would be a good guess."

He whistled under his breath. "I suppose you already have someone in mind for this job, Joe. Otherwise you wouldn't be here."

Carr said, "Jim and I have tentatively agreed that since Ray Daniels has somewhat of a medical background, he would be a good choice. He's just finishing up with a case and will be free in a few days. Ray, as you know, wrote the voir dire manual for prosecutors to use when examining psychiatrists and other medical doctors." This referred to the examination of jurors who are sworn to speak the truth.

Compton replied, "You know that I am starting a special section with several select prosecutors who will specialize in complicated medico-legal cases." He suggested a different deputy district attorney, but Shea disagreed with him.

There was a decided chill in the air after the rather heated "discussion" between Compton and Shea. Compton wanted his medico-legal team involved, since it was his baby. Shea, who worked closely with his prosecutors and knew that Daniels was eminently more qualified than the DDA that Compton had named, stuck to his guns and finally won the argument. Ray Daniels was our man.

I was gratified that Jim Shea, a scrappy prosecutor, wanted to make sure this case was handled properly. Shea was a slender, five-foot-nine-inch, hundred fifty-pound Irishman who had spent nine years as a vice cop with LAPD; during that time he received his law degree.

Daniels was skeptical about his chances of successfully prosecuting. What bothered him was his fear that Archerd would walk up behind him and inject him with insulin. Shea successfully allayed Daniels' fear and convinced him that he was the man to prosecute the case.

Jim and Ray met with the coroner, who thought himself the world's greatest pathologist. In my opinion he was a bombastic, self-important person who never valued anyone else's opinion on anything. At this meeting the coroner felt that Shea and Daniels were wasting his valuable time, and attempted to brush them off with as little conversation as possible.

Daniels would have none of it, however. "Doctor, I just have three small questions to ask you."

The coroner condescended to answer Daniels' questions. Of course one question led to another, and the conversation lingered on. The coroner was obviously irked, and finally admitted to Daniels that he had little or no knowledge of insulin and its effects on the human body. It was obvious that they would not get a lot of help from him.

That conversation was instrumental in convincing Daniels, with his medical knowledge, that he was the man to handle the prosecution. Plus, he wanted the challenge of breaking new ground in the medico-legal arena.

4
The Team: White, Deiro, and Daniels

At the same time Daniels was assigned to the case, Deputy Marty Deiro, a six-foot-two-inch ex-Navy heavyweight-boxing champion, was also assigned to assist our team. I had heard of Marty but had never met him. All the things I heard were good, including his reputation for being cool in the face of danger. One story was that he stopped a potential riot out in Topanga Canyon one night with one eight-inch punch to the jaw of the ringleader, who was holding a gun on him at the time. I learned later that the dude didn't wake up for a couple of days. I couldn't help but think, *What an imposing pair, with my six foot, two-hundred twenty-five pound frame, thinning white hair and a pronounced red birthmark on my nose, along with Marty's two hundred and forty pounds. We might scare the hell out of most anybody.* Really we were a couple of pussy cats.

Marty and I hit it off right away. With all my years as an investigator, my worst shortcoming was the art of keeping

paperwork up to date and in a manner that information
could easily be retrieved. Marty proved to be an expert
at this, and quickly set about putting the Archerd files in
order.

"Marty, up to now I've only scratched the surface in this
investigation. Now it's up to us to start digging and have as
much information as we can by the time Ray Daniels shows
up to help us," I told him after we had finished reviewing all
the reports and notes that had been collected.

"You just point the way and we'll get 'er done." I think
he had already caught the fever that had been building in
me for the past few years.

"The first thing we'll do is talk to everyone we can who
knew Mary Brinker Post Arden. We'll start out by inter-
viewing her family doctor. He's the one who treated her
after she was in the wreck and also in the hospital," I told
him.

Marty picked up his briefcase, threw in several new
notebooks, extra pens, a twelve-foot steel tape, a flashlight
and a lot of other things. I noticed when he opened it up
that there was a clean shirt, a pair of drawers and a pair of
socks. "You planning on spending the night somewhere,
Marty?" I asked him.

"Hell, I heard about you, White. They tell me you never
know when to go home, and I can't stand to wear underwear and socks more than two or three days at a time," he
laughed.

We drove out the San Bernardino Freeway heading for
Claremont. At Doctor Smilkstein's office we had to wait
about a half hour while he finished meeting his last patient
for the morning. We had told his nurse that we wanted to
see him about Mrs. Arden Archerd. She had the medical
file ready when we were ushered into his office. On the
walls and scattered about the office were several articles of
obvious Asian origin. He was quick to notice my interest

and stated, "Those are art objects I picked up in Vietnam during my visits there."

"Oh, are you a medical officer in the Army?" I asked.

"No, I belong to a medical group that volunteers our services to the civilians of Vietnam. I've been there twice for three months at a time. It's unbelievable, the lack of medical facilities in that country," he replied. He then directed us to chairs arranged in front of his desk. "My nurse tells me that you are interested in Mrs. Arden. What can I do to help you?"

"Doctor, we have reason to believe that Mrs. Arden did not die from injuries she received in a traffic accident. In fact, we believe that she was murdered by her husband."

He looked at me with astonishment through the palest blue eyes I have ever seen. "I can't believe that. I have treated them both at one time or another. They seemed to be so happy together. I can't believe Jim would do a thing like that. True, he is a little strange, but murder?"

"I know it's hard to believe, Doctor, but we have very strong evidence that causes us to believe that he did kill her."

He picked up her medical file and scanned it rapidly. "You know, I don't believe the injuries she suffered in that traffic accident were the cause of death, or even contributed to it. She was in my office immediately after the accident and her injuries were very minor. I treated her for a small laceration on the bridge of her nose and a slight contusion on her right cheek, prescribed a mild sedative and some sleeping pills, and sent her home. Her biggest worry was how she'd look going to work the next morning."

"When did you see her next, and what was her condition?"

"On November 2, at the hospital. Doctor Muzineks saw her on admission to the emergency room and called me. She was in deep coma, and the EEG showed no sign of cortical activity, which indicated she was near death. The lack of cortical activity usually signifies severe brain damage. There is no way I can account for that type of brain damage unless something happened after I saw her in my office. Frankly, gentlemen, I don't understand it," he replied incredulously.

"Do you have an opinion as to her cause of death at this time, Doctor?" I asked.

"I'm not sure at this point, since I haven't seen the coroner's report. For my own information, I will review her hospital records."

I handed him a copy of the report. "Doctor, would you call me in a few days so we can talk more about this?"

"I'm in the Los Angeles County USC Medical Center every Thursday. If you'll meet me there at ten o'clock Thursday morning, I should have some answers for you," he answered.

"That's fine, Doctor. We'll see you next Thursday," I said as we got up to leave.

"Lieutenant, I have a personal interest in this case. As well as being a patient of mine, Mary and I knew each other well over five years. You can count on my cooperation."

Marty and I made our way over to Claremont College where we located the publicity director, a Mister Zaner Faust. Mister Faust told us that he had known Mary for several years and that they had worked together on the *Newtown Bee* back in Connecticut. Mr. and Mrs. Faust often saw Mary socially; in fact they had stood up for her when she married Archerd. They didn't think too much of him, as he was too slick, but they tolerated him for Mary's sake. I showed him a mug shot of Archerd and he said, "Yes, that's Jim all right. Does that mean he's a criminal?"

"He's served some prison time in the past, but that has nothing to do with this case. When was the last time you saw Mary?" I asked.

"I saw her the morning before the accident. I didn't see her alive again. We were supposed to have dinner with her the next night, but she called and said she didn't want anyone to see her in that condition."

"Was Jim at home when she called?"

"No, she and Jim had been having some trouble. Mary caught Jim at some gal's house last August over in Alhambra. Ever since then he's had the habit of taking off for a few weeks at a time. That reminds me–on the phone she said she had been desperately trying to find him. She wanted him to know about the accident," he replied.

"Do you know of anyone that saw her after the accident and before she was admitted to the hospital?" I asked.

"Just Paul Lewis – he was a close friend of hers before she married Jim – and the Fields, who live across the street from Mary and Jim." He took a pad and wrote Lewis' address and phone number down and handed it to me.

"Thank you, Mister Faust; we'll probably want to talk further with you. By the way, do you know whether Mary carried any insurance through the college?" I asked.

"I'm sure she did. You should check with the personnel department."

We found the Fields' residence nestled among trees at the edge of the Los Seranos Golf Course. Mr. and Mrs. Fields, a couple in their early sixties, were eager to talk to us. They had known Mary for over five years and liked and respected her. They neighbored a lot with her before she married Jim, but less frequently since then, although when either couple was gone from home any length of time the other couple would look after their animals and homes.

Without asking, Mrs. Fields went to the kitchen and brought out a plate of freshly baked chocolate chip cookies, my favorite, and some good strong black coffee. She obviously felt this interview was going to last a while. She was right.

After gaining all the background information about the Ardens I could, I zeroed in on the time from the accident to her death.

"Mister Fields, when did you first see Mary following the accident?"

"I didn't see her at all the day of the accident. She came over the next day. She wanted me to take her to the post office. While we were downtown, she bought a fifth of whiskey."

"How did she look the day you took her to the post office? Was there any difference in her appearance from the last time you saw her?"

"Outside of a skinned nose and a couple black eyes, she looked okay to me. She still sounded like the same old Mary, still complaining about Jim not being home."

Mrs. Fields interrupted, "She's been complaining about that for several months now. She even complained about it in the letters she wrote when we were on vacation. Said he came back and stayed three or four days, then left again."

I redirected my questions to Mister Fields. "Did she have anything else to say on that trip to the post office?"

"Oh, yeah! She said she was going to call her lawyer and have him find Jim and bring him home."

"When did you see her after that?"

"I think it was Monday. I took her down to get a loan car. She told me that Jim had called last night from San Jose and was coming home. I just dropped her off at the garage and came on home. We didn't see her the next day at all, but we did the following day."

"Tell me about it."

Agitated that her husband wasn't getting to the point fast enough, Mrs. Fields interrupted. "We were just coming from the store and were driving by their house when Jim waved us down. He showed us some colored pictures of the wreck and Mary's bruised face. They looked awful!"

I no longer directed my questions to either of them. It was obvious that Mrs. Fields was going to do the answering anyway.

"Was Mary with him?"

"Yes, she was. The swelling had gone down some and the discoloration was almost gone."

"When was the next time you saw Mary?"

"Well, it was about eight o'clock the next morning. Art and I were having breakfast. Jim came over all dressed up. He had a suit on and a tie, shoes all shined up. He said he needed some help, that Mary kept him awake most all night, groaning and thrashing around. Said he couldn't wake her up this morning."

I just let her keep talking. "I asked him if he'd called an ambulance, said he had. Art and I went over with him and there she was, lying in bed, pink slobber running out of her mouth. Her tongue was sticking out of her mouth about an inch and a half. Looked like she'd bit it. She'd wet the bed, too."

Marty sat on the couch sipping coffee and making notes. Mrs. Fields got up and poured more coffee, then continued, "The ambulance finally got there and the attendant came in, took one look at her and asked Jim if her eyes always looked like that. Jim said he didn't know. Then the attendant asked if she was taking any medication and Jim took a bottle out of his pocket and handed it to him. The ambulance took off with Mary. Jim followed in his car. That's the last time we saw her alive." She sighed as if to say, "Well, I've got that off my chest!"

Back in the car heading for Pomona Valley Hospital, I could hardly keep from floor-boarding it. "Marty, it's all beginning to fit. We've got her in good condition late in the evening and by his own words to the Fields, he was with her all night. I can't wait until I've seen that hospital admission sheet!"

"Yeah, I could see you getting itchy when Mrs. Fields was telling about how Archerd came over, then how she found Mary. From what I know so far, it's beginning to look good," he replied.

At the Pomona Valley Hospital we were able to see the patient's admission record as well as her history from admission to death. It was obvious that I would need help in interpreting most of it, but we were able to determine that the husband had supplied some background of her condition at least twelve hours prior to admission.

"Husband states patient had possibly a drink and a sleeping pill before retiring. He heard a noise during the night, went to her bedroom and observed a possible convulsive episode."

We were also able to determine that on admission her blood sugar level was 50 mg percent. She had been administered glucose intravenously and in spite of this, the next day it was 36 mg percent. Both percentages were far below normal. The nurse's notes indicated that the husband was with her for at least five minutes of each hour.

It was impossible to hide my excitement when I told Marty, "We've got him with her all night before her admission to the hospital and a good deal of time with her after she was in intensive care. Her convulsions and extreme low blood sugar are documented. These symptoms match the symptoms documented in the nephew's case and with one of his other wives. This will go a long way in helping us prove a circumstantial case."

"Yeah, Whitey, I agree with you there, but I also agree with Joe Carr that we really need just a little bit of direct evidence."

That was going to be easier said than done. In the case of the nephew we thought we were going to come up with some direct evidence when we shipped his tissue to the Eli Lilly Labs in Indiana, but due to poor packaging, all the tissue putrefied. Maybe we would have better luck this time. I remembered the disappointment I felt back in 1962.

On the way back to the Hall of Justice I made mental notes of what we were going to do the next day. The first thing was to call the Eli Lilly Labs in Indiana. The next was to make a progress report to the boss. I hoped that Ray Daniels would be available so we could really get rolling.

By the time I dropped Marty off at his car, it was dark. I had forgotten to call my wife, Midge. It seemed I forgot to call her when I was going to be late, or was way out in the boonies where there were no phones. Either way, she didn't like it too well. I couldn't help feeling guilty about it. When I walked in the house, Midge was on the phone. "The Gannaways want to go out to dinner. Are you up to it?"

"Sure, I'd like that. I feel like celebrating a little anyway. Let's go to the Tallywhacker." That was our pet name for the Tally Ho, a nice restaurant and bar.

"They will be over in a few minutes," she said as she hung up. "Where have you been? I've been waiting for you to call!"

"I'll tell you all about it at dinner, and then I won't have to repeat it."

The Gannaways had shared my frustrations when I was investigating the death of Archerd's nephew. I knew they would be interested in being brought up to date on this current investigation.

I thought I detected a tear in the corner of Midge's eye. She can't be that upset about my being a couple hours late, I thought. She came over, put her arms around me and squeezed. "Jan just told me that she and Lonnie are planning on being married in June," she said tearfully.

Damn! Everything was happening at once. My little girl was getting ready to fly the nest, and Van would be graduating from college. Jan would be moving to Chicago when Lonnie entered dental college at Loyola, and Van would be going to Vietnam. I thought of all the good times we had had together as a family, exploring the tide pools along the beach, picnicking in Silverado Canyon, tobogganing in the snow, and all the other things a well-adjusted family does. I thought how pretty Jan was the night she was installed as Worthy Advisor in Rainbow Girls, and the flawless speech she made at the National Assembly in Long Beach. I remembered the time she refused to kiss me when I let her off at school. "Daddy, I'm too big for that now."

Van was still playing baseball at Long Beach State. Every chance I got I would steal an afternoon to catch one of his games. I had coached his ball teams from the time he was eight until he was in high school. I remembered the time he almost cut his foot off starting the lawn mower, and the time he and Mike Wrona, both sixteen at the time, decided they were going to whip my ass. The boys had forgotten that I wrestled in Junior College. I think that the match of the century lasted all of two minutes, and they found out that they had to grow a few more years.

All that reminiscing stopped when we heard the Gannaway's car in the driveway. We each wiped away a tear or two, then greeted Ralph and Evalynn.

Five o'clock came mighty early, especially since Ralph kept the waiter busy bringing highballs all night. When we finally finished dinner it was nearly closing time, and I was in no condition to drive home. Ralph helped Midge get me into bed, but I had managed to set the alarm. I wanted to get to the office early so I could call Eli Lilly as soon as they opened. A cold shower and a shave helped clear my head somewhat. By the time I got to the office I felt a little better.

I found Collins in the coffee room, red-eyed and harassed. Apparently, he had been out working all night. He greeted me with his usual, "Hello, Dipshit, don't you ever sleep?" I poured a cup of coffee and sat down.

"I've got to make an early call back east or I would have come in late this morning. That damned Gannaway did it to me again."

"Yeah, you look like you've been rid hard and put in the barn wet," he chuckled.

I placed the call to Eli Lilly and told them what I had in mind. They remembered the fiasco with the tissue from the nephew and were interested in our current investigation. After they heard me out, they told me that there was a new procedure to test for the presence of certain substances in body tissue, a procedure called radioimmunoassay. A pathologist at UCLA Medical Center, Doctor Edward Arquilla, could perform this test for us.

My heart pumped furiously. I could hardly wait for Marty to get in so I could tell him the news. I didn't want to feel too optimistic, though. I had been disappointed too many times before. But somehow I knew we were about to rack up our first real solid evidence needed to convict my old nemesis, William Dale Archerd, a.k.a. James Lynn Arden.

Marty came in about seven-thirty a.m. When I told him what I had learned he jabbed me playfully on my shoulder, knocking me half way across the room. "Ke-e-rist! White, it looks like things are about to go our way now!"

"Damn, Marty, now I know why you were Pacific Fleet champ! With a punch like that, you could have been world champ," I complained as I rubbed my shoulder.

* * *

5
Put Up or Shut Up

We were ready for Daniels when he came in. "I've been talking to Jim Shea and Joe Carr all morning about this case. From what I know now, we have a hell of a lot of work to do before I can tell if we are going to have a case or not. Frankly, I'm skeptical. I don't like these circumstantial cases," he told us matter-of-factly.

I knew that it was "put up or shut up" time. Here was a no-nonsense, straight-from-the-shoulder sort of guy, even if he stood only five-foot-seven in his elevator shoes. I soon learned that Daniels came from good Irish stock, had been raised in Providence, Rhode Island, and had made it the hard way. In fact, he worked his way through pre-med and law school as a brick mason. In spite of his slight stature, he was built like a brick wall.

"We do have a little more information than when we talked with Shea and Carr," I told him. "We learned just this morning that there is a new process that can help us in determining the presence of certain substances present in body tissue and that the man with the knowledge is right here at UCLA."

"What I'd like to do is take all the information you have with me so I can get a better picture of this whole case."

Marty quickly gathered up an extra copy of all our reports, put them in a folder and handed them to Daniels.

"We have an appointment tomorrow at the USC Medical Center with Doctor Smilkstein. We'd like you to go with us," I said.

"Good! I'll be here at nine a.m. See you." He quickly left the office.

"Marty, how in hell is he going to get through all that stuff by tomorrow?"

"I don't know, Whitey. Maybe he has a photographic memory," he said dryly.

The next day Daniels walked in the office at nine o'clock sharp. It was soon evident that whether or not he got through all that stuff was not important. He had an uncanny grasp for facts and surprised us with his knowledge of the case.

"Look, we know all these people died of similar symptoms. We also know that he was close at hand when each of them died and that he stood to gain something from the death of each one. You know and I know that we have no proof of any criminal cause of death. So far, all we have is a set of facts that look suspicious as hell. Granted, it is a very strong suspicion, but we need more than that. So let's get to work."

"Doctor Miller has agreed to meet with us at the same time we see Doctor Smilkstein," I told Daniels. Doctor Miller had done the autopsy on Mary.

"That's fine. I wanted to talk to him anyway. Let's go."

We met in the cafeteria on the tenth floor of the old Los Angeles County Hospital. Doctor Smilkstein had reviewed Mary's hospital charts, and Doctor Miller had brought along a copy of his autopsy report. Briefly, I explained to them that we had been investigating the deaths of six people closely connected with William Dale Archerd, and that we suspected him of killing each one with an injection or injections of insulin.

Doctors Smilkstein and Miller had consulted with each other for some time when Daniels asked, "Now that you both have had an opportunity to examine the hospital records and the autopsy report, do you have any opinion as to Mrs. Arden's cause of death?"

Doctor Miller answered, "In my opinion, Mrs. Arden died of acute interstitial and intro alveolar pneumonitis due to hypoglycemic shock, probably caused by an injection or injections of insulin."

"I agree with Doctor Miller. However, I am at a loss as to why her blood sugar and spinal sugar continued to decline, even though she was given glucose, plasma and isolites as well as other liquids," Doctor Smilkstein said.

"Is it possible that she was given an injection of insulin prior to her admission and additional injection or injections after admission, causing the steady decline of her blood sugar and spinal sugar?" Daniels asked Doctor Smilkstein.

"That is most likely what happened, but I can assure you that at no time was insulin authorized by me or any other doctor following her admission to the hospital."

"I'm not suggesting that at all, Doctor. I see by the hospital chart that Mister Arden was with her at least five minutes out of every hour for some time. He was the only person other than the nurses in intensive care near her, from admission until death. Could it be possible that he injected Mrs. Arden while the nurse was busy?"

Doctor Miller broke in, "Mister Daniels, the only puncture marks I recall finding anywhere on the body of Mrs. Arden were in the cubital fossa of the arms. This indicated

to me that she was receiving intravenous injections at various times."

Daniels then asked, "Doctor Smilkstein, isn't it sometimes a practice when a patient is being fed intravenously and additional medication is needed, that this medication is injected into the tube rather than subcutaneously?"

"Yes, that is a very common practice. That would also explain why Doctor Miller never found any other puncture marks on the body," he replied.

As we got up to leave, Daniels said, "Doctor Miller, Doctor Smilkstein, I want to thank both of you for your help in this matter. You'll be hearing from us."

"I'm only too happy to be of any help possible. You already know that Mary – Mrs. Arden – was a close personal friend," Doctor Smilkstein stated.

"I, too, am prepared to help you any way I can, Mister Daniels," Doctor Miller added.

We were walking toward the door when Daniels turned and asked Doctor Miller, "Did you save any tissue samples from the autopsy?"

"Yes, I saved all the usual tissue samples, including the brain and pancreas. They have been preserved and can be examined any time."

By this time I was glad that Daniels had been assigned to assist us in this investigation. It was evident that he already had a firm grasp on all the facts we had uncovered so far, and I could sense his enthusiasm growing by the minute. I poked Marty in the ribs and he answered with a wink. We both knew that Daniels was now hooked, and that the three of us could direct all our energies toward building a case against that evil psychopath.

On the way back to the Hall of Justice, Daniels said, "We've got to have a place to work. We can't work in that zoo of yours; there's too much distraction, and my office is too small. Anyway, Marty fills it up all by himself."

By the time Marty and I had finished our brown bag lunches, Daniels was on the phone. "Whitey, I've got us a room. If you and Marty will move those files up here, I'll get some desks moved in and a phone hooked up."

By five o'clock that afternoon we were in business. The room was so small you couldn't cuss a cat without getting any hair in your teeth. It must have been used originally for a broom closet. We were on the fifth floor, just down the hall from the duplicating and collating room which proved advantageous in the months to come.

Marty and I made a point of meeting at seven thirty every morning in the third floor coffee room of the Hall of Justice. We would review what we had done the day before and make notes of things we planned to do. We intended to be one step ahead of Daniels all the time. Most of the time we succeeded.

We also had to keep "Pelon" informed of any progress. Each time I would brief him, I would lay out everything we had done and what we intended to do in the future. I was always prepared to answer any questions he might have; that is, I hoped I could. It never failed though; he would ask questions until he found one I couldn't answer. Only then would he be happy. This kept up for a few weeks until he finally said, "Whitey, damn it, I don't have time to listen to all this bullshit! I know you are doing a good job. From now on, just give me a little memo every Monday, so I can keep the boss off my ass."

At this point we had never been able to pin down any information on the death of a possible victim that Dorothea Archerd had told Harry Andre about back in 1956. I gave Marty all the information I had on it and told him to see what he could come up with. Daniels and I had an appointment to see Doctor Edward Arquilla at the UCLA Medical Center.

We had a time finding the doctor's office. The Medical Center building covers several acres and consists of several wings connected with a maze of aisles and corridors. I guess there was some sort of order to it, but I was never able to find it. Each time I went out there I had to search for his office all over again.

I was surprised when I first saw Doctor Arquilla. I expected to find a stodgy old bald-headed sourpuss. Instead, here was an off the cuff, relaxed, friendly man in his mid-to-late forties, with an athletic build and suntanned. He was squeezing a handball, changing hands from time to time as he greeted us. "What can I do for you fellows?" he asked as he waved us to a seat.

I told him the story that we were to tell many times in the coming months. In fact, I got so I could recite it word for word in my sleep. Later, when we would try to enlist the aid of medical and scientific experts, Daniels would say, "Whitey, it's your turn to tell it."

I would say, "No, it's your turn."

I would soon learn that all so-called experts weren't as easy to convince that we were really on to something. Doctor Arquilla was a medical research scientist who could think outside the box, unlike other experts we had talked to. We had scarcely finished telling our story and our suspicions when Doctor Arquilla asked, "Do you have any brain tissue of any of the victims?"

I saw Daniels sit up straight and move to the edge of his chair. We both knew that here was a man that saw a challenge and welcomed a chance to become involved in our investigation.

"I know that we have some tissue from the latest victim and possibly from the fifteen-year-old nephew," I told him.

"I don't want to get your hopes up too much, and I won't promise anything. If you can get as much tissue from each victim as possible, I'll be able to tell you more about it," he said.

I already knew what Daniels was going to say before he said it. "Lieutenant White will bring you the tissue first thing tomorrow."

On our way back to the office, Daniels gave me detailed instructions as how to handle the tissue. "Have the lab technician date and initial each container in your presence, sign a receipt for it and get a copy. When you deliver it to the doctor, repeat the same process."

I snapped, "Dammit, Ray, I've been handling evidence for twenty years! I know how to maintain the chain of possession."

"Whitey, I didn't mean anything by that. I just don't want anything to go wrong," he apologized. That wasn't the last time there would be flare-ups between us during the next year and a half. By this time we were both so emotionally involved with the case that relations would become strained at times. After all, we were spending more time with each other than we were with our wives.

It didn't take long for me to cool down; we were soon talking excitedly, speculating as to what Doctor Arquilla would find. "I think Arquilla is going to be the key to this whole investigation. What he finds from examining that tissue will either make or break the case," Daniels said.

"My hope was that he will find something that will confirm that at least Mary Arden was killed by injections of insulin," I told him.

Marty met us just as we were walking into the Hall of Justice. "I've got something here on Archerd, but I haven't been able to identify the 1947 victim," he said, handing me a copy of the Kaiser steel mill newspaper and a photocopy of Archerd's employment record as an aid man at the mill.

"Keep at it, Marty, and find out all you can about Archerd's job at the hospital; who he worked with, where he lived at the time and anything else you can come up with. Also check the nurses' registry to see if you can locate Dorothea. We're going to have to talk to her pretty soon."

The coroner's lab called late the next afternoon and said the tissue samples were ready. I then called Doctor Arquilla and asked how late he would be there. I wanted to deliver the tissue to him personally in order to keep the chain of possession as short as possible. He said he would be there until about five. Just time to make it, I thought. As I headed out the Santa Monica Freeway, it started raining. *That's all I need, rain and rush hour traffic,* I thought as I inched my way along the slippery, jammed freeway. *Another cold supper.* I couldn't remember the last time the family had sat down to dinner together.

I delivered the tissue specimens to Doctor Arquilla just as he was about to leave for the day. He was in a hurry to get home and so was I; there was little conversation between us. I left as soon as the proper receipts were signed and headed back down the freeways toward home in Paramount. It took me over an hour and a half to get home. Looking back, that was a good thing. It gave me a chance to review in my mind what had transpired from the time I became involved in the Archerd investigation up to the present.

I began thinking about the death of Archerd's nephew, Burney, how hard Walt Thornton and I worked on that case, and how disappointed we were that we couldn't dig up enough solid evidence to put William Dale Archerd away for killing him. I ran that whole scenario over in my mind several times on the slow drive home. I could visualize a slide show of different scenes in the various stages of our investigation.

It is strange how clearly I could remember in detail the things that were depicted in it. I remembered telling someone a few years back, "You only remember the unsolved ones." I guess that's why that slide show was so vivid in my mind.

As I was about to pull into my driveway, I recalled the early days of my law enforcement career. I was fortunate to have chosen such a career.

It had stopped raining.

6
How I Got There

I first became acquainted with the old Hall of Justice in 1952. I had just finished four years as a patrol deputy at Norwalk station and a year of duty with the United States Air Force in Korea. That was followed by two years as a sergeant in charge of the day shift at Biscailuz Center. At that time it was a detention facility for fifteen and sixteen year-old juvenile offenders awaiting placement in a state operated correction facility.

I was glad to escape Biscailuz; I was rapidly forming the opinion that all teenage boys were smart-ass jerks. My son was going to be a teenager soon, and I wanted to greet those years with an open mind with no preconceived opinions of teenage boys. Don't get me wrong; those two years were a valuable experience. I learned a lot about our Corrections Division and worked with many good people that I was proud to have known in later years.

The old Hall of Justice has been called a lot of names in the past: "The Gray Bar Hotel" was by far the most popular. It housed the coroner, district attorney, Superior Courts, the tax collector and the Sheriff's Department headquarters, plus the county jail, which occupied the top five floors. Originally designed to house eighteen hundred inmates, it eventually housed more than twice that number. One floor was reserved for female prisoners. The jail was constructed with lots of steel and reinforced concrete. All that extra weight from the steel doors and bars on the cells on the top floors of the building eventually led to its temporary demise, even though it had withstood several earthquakes over the years.

I still remember the beautiful lobby with its huge chandeliers, tan granite-paneled walls and polished brass handrails along the stairways. There was a bank of elevators along the north wall and two jail elevators on the south wall. If those abandoned halls could talk, they would tell us tales about the incarceration of movie actors Errol Flynn and Robert Mitchum, Caryl Chessman (the red light bandit), the Manson family and other notable criminals such as Sirhan Sirhan and William Dale Archerd.

The 1994 earthquake caused so much damage that the grand old building had to be closed, ostensibly for the last time. It still sits there at the corner of Temple and Broadway, a mere shadow of her former self, and she still looks rather majestic, even in her emptiness. The present sheriff, Lee Baca, is trying to have the old Hall restored to her original beauty, so he can bring his scattered units home from their many locations. Many old retirees, myself included, hope the sheriff is successful.

The next four years I worked with some outstanding investigators. I learned a lot from each one about the art of commercial auto theft investigation – that is, stealing cars for profit. The thief would buy a total wreck from an insurance company, steal a car of the same make and model, then sell the stolen car using the total wreck's registration and pink slip. It wasn't uncommon to recover fifteen or twenty stolen cars in one investigation. On one occasion we recovered about twenty newly registered automobiles, a stack of four hundred counterfeit pink slips and over one hundred thousand dollars in counterfeit twenty-dollar bills. The hardest part of an investigation of commercial auto theft was teaching the prosecutor the technicalities of that type of case. It seems that auto theft, in the eyes of a district attorney at that time, ranked right up there with spitting on the sidewalk. Hence, those cases were assigned to the most inexperienced prosecutor. After about four years of frustration, I'd about had a belly full if it. But this is where I learned the technique of collecting and preserving evidence, as well as the use of scientific experts outside my sphere of knowledge, which proved to be advantageous to me when I became involved in the Archerd investigation.

One day Lieutenant Charles McGowan, a.k.a. "Boston Blackie," stuck his head in the door and beckoned me out into the hall. I walked up to him and asked, "What's up, Charlie?"

"Whitey, how would you like to work homicide?" I couldn't reply quickly enough. *This isn't happening! I never thought I would have the chance to work homicide!* I sputtered, "Charley, you've got to be kidding!"

"No, Whitey, this is for real. We are getting two new items on the next budget. You are the first person I thought of, since I have known you over ten years and have seen some of your work."

Blackie really was from Boston. He had the map of Ireland for a face and the Boston dialect to go with it. He said, "Keep it under your hat for a while; it'll take a few days to go up the ladder. I'll let you know."

It wasn't more than a week later that the transfer came through. I was about to become a big Homicide Detective!

Claude Human was the other recruit to fill the new items. Claude was another product of Missouri and he had the same Midwest twang that I did. We both took a lot of ribbing from the rest of the crew. We didn't mind, though; we knew we could carry our own weight.

I was assigned a desk that had an extra-large blotter atop it. I wondered about that and looked under it. Right near the left edge was an obvious bullet hole with the bullet still in it. I asked Lieutenant McGowan, "Whose desk am I taking?"

"That was Spike Waldrip's desk," Blackie replied. "Why?"

I said, "That doesn't surprise me. I remember parking beside him one day and saw a big hole in the roof of his car. I asked him what happened, and he said, 'Aw, Whitey, I went huntin',' and made the mistake of puttin' my dog in the back seat with my shotgun. We were comin' across a rough field; he caught his paw in the trigger, and Boom! That was it. Scared the hell out of me.'"

A week or so later I happened to park by him again and he was driving a new car. "Spike, you haven't shot this one yet, have you?"

"Yep, sure did. I was just finishing up a suicide, and in clearing the gun I shot it right into the transmission. Killed it deader 'n hell!"

McGowan said, "That's what happened here. Same scenario, different location." Spike wasn't too careful with firearms.

When I first got to homicide in 1957, things were really busy. It was during the time the El Segundo police officers were killed; Dick Carroll and Ray Hopkinson were assigned that case. Claude Everley and Jack Lawton were working the Auction City kidnapping of an eleven-year-old girl, Harry Andre was working the Zella Archerd case, and several other high profile cases were ongoing.

The El Segundo police officer killings were solved in 2003. This was made possible by two separate groups: the Homicide Bureau of the 1950s and the current group of young, dedicated "cold case" investigators. July 22, 1957, two teenage couples were parked in a lover's lane. A lone gunman approached their car, robbed the foursome, taking what little money the boys had and a watch from one of the girls. He then raped one of the girls. While fleeing the scene in a stolen 1949 Ford he ran a red light and was stopped by El Segundo police officers Milton Curtis and Richard Phillips. He shot the officers, fled the scene and was never identified until January 2003.

Sergeants Dick Carol and Ray Hopkinson worked the case hard for several years. They had partial prints of the suspect taken from the stolen car he had abandoned. They ran the prints through CII and FBI files with no luck.

A gun was found buried in a back yard in El Segundo. It had been purchased at a Sears store in New Orleans a few days before the robbery/homicide occurred, and proved to be the weapon that killed the two police officers. Through all the years I worked homicide, someone was still working on that case. Finally, in 2003, Los Angeles County Sheriff's Homicide Bureau submitted the partial prints to the FBI's new fingerprint database and struck gold. They were able to identify 69-year-old Gerald Mason of Columbia, South Carolina, as the killer. Nearly forty-six years later, this case was finally solved.

The Auction City kidnapping involved eleven-year-old Stella Darlene Nolan. Sergeants Claude Everley and Jack Lawton worked this case. On one occasion, I assisted Everley in bringing in a suspect and interrogating him. Everley was convinced that we had the right suspect but we couldn't prove it. Several years later our suspect committed a similar murder. During that investigation the suspect "copped out" to the kidnapping of the Nolan girl. He led investigators to the over-cross of the I-5 freeway in Norwalk, where he had buried the Nolan girl after he had violated her.

I have forgotten the name of the suspect, as I had very little to do with the investigation.

About this time I was introduced to Zella Archerd and her husband, William Dale Archerd, a.k.a. James Lynn Arden. Harry Andre, who was assigned the Zella Archerd case, was incensed, irate, pissed-off and downright obsessed with the case. He was always ready to talk to anyone about "his" case. We had hardly met when he handed me the investigators copy of the "Blue Book." This was a book with itemized and indexed pages that contained every report ever written about the case in question. This was done as an aid to the investigator as well as the prosecutor. We usually made four copies: one for the investigator, one for the prosecutor, one for the defense and one for the file. By this time discovery motions were the rule for the defense. It was simpler to make a copy for the defense at the outset rather than have the court order it.

At any rate, Andre handed me the book and said, "Take this and study it; maybe you could offer some ideas that we haven't thought of." *Me, have an idea about a homicide case? I just got here!* It's safe to say that I would read and re-read that little Blue Book many times in the next ten years.

Andre did a good job of investigation and tried really hard to make a case proving that Archerd did murder Zella Winders Archerd by injecting her with lethal doses of insulin. His investigation was well documented in the Blue Book. Unfortunately, at that time, it was not possible to prove a criminal cause of death by injecting insulin into the body of a human being.

Andre was the first to develop information that Zella could have been killed by lethal injections of insulin. He did this by contacting Ted Nissen, who was a parole agent for the State of California and had worked at San Quentin prison at the time Archerd was serving time for selling narcotics. It was Nissen's job to censor inmates' incoming and outgoing mail. Nissen became familiar with Archerd and Dorothea, Archerd's wife at that time. He kept tabs on them long after Archerd's parole was up.

Dorothea wasn't happy about Archerd divorcing her. As soon as she heard of Zella's death she contacted Nissen. He, in turn, told Andre that Dorothea had told him that she was sure Archerd had given Zella a fatal dose of insulin. Andre had long conversations with both Nissen and Dorothea; as a result he was convinced that Archerd had indeed murdered Zella.

Nissen was of further help to Andre when he presented him with Archerd's cumulative summary from San Quentin. A 'cum sum' documents every step of an inmate's activities from the time he is charged with a crime through his imprisonment, parole and release. From this cum sum Andre learned that during Archerd's periodic reviews he was given several psychological and psychiatric examinations. In brief, these examinations allowed that Archerd was an intelligent, but uneducated, shallow individual, with a strong neurotic condition characterized by numerous somatic tensions and a character disorder. He lacked fundamental honesty and ruggedness of character, was essentially shallow, changeable and not to be trusted in the presence of narcotics.

This cum sum was a valuable tool that contained many leads for Andre to pursue. Eventually, he was promoted and transferred to Norwalk station. His investigation was turned over to Sergeant Dick Humphreys, who followed up on Andre's leads. Claude Everley, Andre's original partner, had already transferred to the Aero Bureau, where he piloted one of the department's helicopters.

Humphreys pursued the case vigorously and investigated two more deaths that were attributed to Archerd. Both of those deaths occurred in Las Vegas and were out of our jurisdiction. The first was in 1958 when Archerd and Juanita Plum Archerd were on their honeymoon. The next was in 1960 when Frank Stewart, the ex-husband of Archerd's next wife, Gladys, died allegedly from head injuries he received during a slip-and-fall on a banana peel in the men's restroom at McCarran Airport in Las Vegas.

In 1961, Burney Kirk Archerd was allegedly the victim of a hit-and-run. He died eleven days later, following constant visits from dear old Uncle William Dale Archerd. This is when I officially entered the Archerd investigation.

Burney Kirk Archerd, male Caucasian, fifteen years of age, of Long Beach, California, was admitted to the Long Beach Memorial Hospital. He arrived at the emergency room about four-thirty p.m. August 21, 1961, brought in by his uncle, William D. Archerd, of Monterey Park, California. Mister Archerd signed the admission slip as authorizing person. Burney died at ten twenty-five a.m. September 2. The next morning I received the first report, via county mail, reporting the death of the victim. I was about half way through the report when Lieutenant Harry Andre called me from Norwalk station.

"Whitey, did you see the *Press Telegram* this morning?" Andre yelled into the phone. He was referring to a story telling about Burney having been struck by a hit-and-run driver. He was comatose and lay dying while his bereft uncle spent most of his days and nights sitting by his bedside.

"No, Harry, I haven't but I was just about to call you. I just got the first report in the mail."

"I knew that s.o.b. would kill again. Since he killed Zella, there are a couple other people that I am sure he killed."

"Yeah, Harry, I know about Juanita in '58 and Frank Stewart in '60. Maybe we can do something about it this time."

I was in a real hurry to get off the phone so I could contact the coroner to have Burney's remains brought down to be autopsied. Harry wanted to talk, though. He reminded me of all the hard work he had done on Zella's case, and wanted to make sure someone would follow through on Burney's death. I assured him that we would work on this case just as thoroughly as he had worked the Zella case. Finally, he hung up. I called the coroner's office and talked to Phil Schwartzberg and told him what we had. Schwartzberg said, "Has this got anything to do with the guy that killed his wife a few years ago?" "Yes, Phil, I think it just might be. The victim's uncle was the suspect back then."

"I'll send a crew right out, Whitey," he said, and was about to hang up when I said, "Phil, while you are at it, would you order a copy of the hospital report?" He said he would, and hung up.

The coroner's office picked up Burney's remains at the mortuary in Long Beach where arrangements had already been made by the uncle for cremation. It was a good thing it was Sunday; otherwise we would have had no *corpus delecti*. Burney was to be cremated the next day.

Doctor Kenneth Chapman performed the autopsy on Burney's remains September 5, 1961. Sergeant Bob Chapman and I were present throughout the post mortem examination. Ordinarily, watching a post-mortem examination didn't bother me too much. Somehow seeing the remains of this teenager in such a condition was revolting as hell. It's hard to imagine how anyone could be so heartless as to cause so much suffering as Burney Archerd went through.

The following is from my notes taken at the time of the autopsy:

> The external examination of the remains revealed surgical wounds with sutures on each side of the head over each ear, also on each side of the head near the crown. There was also noted a tracheotomy incision on the throat and an embalming incision just above the right clavicle. There were

also noted sutured incisions on the inside of each ankle. There appeared to be contused abrasions on the left buttocks, a large abrasion on the left shin area, contusions of the left ankle and the left knee and under the right thigh. There was a contused abrasion outside the left wrist and the left cheek. The above-mentioned abrasions were later determined to be frostbite from prolonged exposure by being encased in a hydrothermal low temperature blanket for the purpose of reducing body temperatures. There also appeared to be needle marks on the inner elbow of both arms. There was a "Y" incision, apparently started by another autopsy surgeon prior to victim's being removed to the coroner's mortuary; however, these were only superficial cuts.

Senior Deputy Trichler took identification pictures, and colored slides were taken of what appeared to be needle marks on both outer hip and thigh regions. Slides were also taken of these needle marks after they had been incised. This incision showed infection of the needle track and a white crystalline residue. Specimens of tissue around these incised needle marks were preserved by Doctor Chapman for future examination.

We talked with Lakewood Traffic Sergeant Glenn Schuck. He told us that Archerd and Gladys had come to Lakewood Station about two p.m. September 6 to thank him for his cooperation in the matter. Archerd gave Schuck a sketch of the intersection of Coldbrook Avenue and Rocket Street in Bellflower where the alleged hit-and-run occurred. He made this drawing, he said, at the direction of Burney.

At Long Beach Memorial Hospital we found that Burney had been admitted to the ER at four-twenty p.m. August 21. Doctor J. Sullivan examined him. X-rays of the head and hip were taken. The head x-rays were negative.

The right hip showed what appeared to be a slight fracture of the hip joint. Burney was awake and alert, fussing about not being allowed to smoke. The admitting history was that a truck had hit him; he sat on the curb for a while, and then hitchhiked home. He felt fine except that he had a headache and a sore hip. Nothing outstanding was noted about the preliminary examination except the dilation of the left eye. The uncle was told to get a Consent for Surgery slip signed, left about five p.m., returned at seven p.m. with the signed slip. Attending nurse noted eight a.m. August 22 that the left eye was dilated and did not react to light; five p.m. still dilated and was reacting to light. Burney's left pupil was less dilated at seven p.m. than it was at five p.m. He was restless, unhappy and threatened to walk out of the hospital. His blood pressure, respiration and pulse remained the same throughout the night. At eight a.m. the following morning his blood pressure and temperature were normal; his pulse was slightly below normal. He was drowsy and stuporous. At eight-thirty a.m. he turned over on his back and responded, at ten a.m. he was still hungry after eating breakfast. Blood pressure was the same and pulse was better. A notation on the chart read, "Uncle there at 6:00 p.m."

Burney was difficult to wake for dinner; once roused he visited with his uncle at seven p.m. Apparently, there was some improvement in his condition, at least until his uncle, William Dale Archerd, came to visit. After dinner, Burney had a Coke and some ice cream. In spite of this sugar intake his blood pressure dropped to sixty-eight, he perspired and could not be aroused by the time Archerd had left.

Doctor Ross Duggan was called by the intern and arrived at ten p.m. Archerd was notified that Burney was being prepared for surgery and he needed a consent form signed. Following surgery Burney was taken to I.C.U. where it was noted on his chart, "Uncle visiting throughout the day."

A spinal tap was taken and showed his spinal sugar was 11 milligrams percent. Normal spinal sugar is 40 to 70 mg percent. The constant presence of Burney's "loving" uncle and the low spinal sugar count did it for me. I was thoroughly convinced that Archerd had somehow injected Burney with a fatal dose of insulin. I was also certain he deliberately watched that poor kid die.

I made preparations to talk to all the doctors, nurses and anyone else who had come in contact with Burney and Uncle William. I had no idea where this investigation would take us, but I was surely ready to give it one hell of a try.

By now, Walt Thornton was working with me. Walt was an outstanding investigator, well respected among his peers. You have to have a portrait parle, or word picture, to get the full impact of his contribution to the Archerd investigation. Walt stands about six-feet-three-inches and weighs in at one hundred eighty-five. At that time he had reddish-brown hair combed into sort of a pompadour. When he became agitated a cowlick would fall down into his eyes, giving him the appearance of a mean s.o.b. His slender athletic build was usually covered by a baggy tweed suit, white shirt and trademark bow tie. Walt was a darn good athlete. He played on several departmental championship ball teams. I always thought he could have gone higher than lieutenant, the grade at which he retired. I think he liked having fun more than he cared about getting a promotion. After all, he had the best job in the department, that of a homicide investigator.

I got to know Walt really well during our investigation of the Archerd case. I had worked several "quickie" murder cases with him before we finally got started on this case, but I didn't find the true Walt Thornton until then.

Walt lived in the Whittier area and I lived in Bellflower. One morning it was Walt's turn to drive. He came by my house about seven-thirty and picked me up in his 1960 Ford

Falcon sedan. It was cold that January morning; Walt had the heater running full bore. I could feel the heat as I got in. I started to roll down the window. No handle. I should have suspected something was wrong right away when I saw the condition of his clothing and wild hair. There were also some greenish yellow stringers stretching between his lips when he talked. Big, dumb me really didn't get the full impact of his appearance for a couple of miles when we stopped at a traffic signal. Walt had "snuck" out a "silent" death-type stinker and wouldn't look at me. His shoulders were heaving with laughter. I couldn't get the car door open; there was no handle there. I screamed at him, "Walt, you rotten son-of-a-bitch! Let me out of this shit house!"

He only laughed louder. He thought that was the funniest thing he ever pulled. At that moment I would have beat the hell out of him, but there wasn't enough room in the little Falcon.

After wrapping up a case he had done a good job on, Walt loved to go down to Li Po's in Chinatown and celebrate by washing away memories with Uncle Wally Lee's cheap vodka backed up with some noodles. This combination had a devastating effect on Walt's digestive system; increasing the natural flatulence about tenfold.

He took pride in the development of his new persona. It seems that about three times a week he would come in late, walk through the secretaries' offices and drop one of his "silent death-bombs." This really pissed off all the secretaries. One morning when I was acting Lieutenant, he didn't come in until about ten o'clock. I was shorthanded and had everyone I could find out working new cases. If another case came in, I would have had to go myself and leave our office vacant except for the secretaries. Walt came in looking as if he had slept in his car; actually he had. His old tweed suit was baggier at the knees and elbows than I had ever seen it. The crotch of his pants was hanging down almost to his knees. His eyes looked like two piss holes in the snow; the cowlick was livelier than usual. He staggered over to my desk and rasped rather groggily, "Whitey, I'm sick as hell. I gotta go home."

I said, "Suffer, you s.o.b., I'm out of bodies. Get over to your desk and start answering phones!"

About noon a couple guys came in after wrapping up what they had been working on, so I told Walt to go on home. I had finally evened the score with him. As a matter of fact, that was about the time he acquired the handle of "Shorts." It seems that someone caught him in the restroom throwing away a pair of shorts with fresh skid marks on them.

It wasn't but a few days later that he pulled his post-Li Po tour through the secretaries' offices, pausing just long enough for all the girls to get the full benefit of it. As I saw him pause there I thought I could see the flatulence drift toward the noses of all our well-thought-of girls.

Marge Carbajal suddenly stopped typing, placed a Kleenex over her nose and ran into the Lieutenant's office screaming, "Lieutenant Walsh, I can't stand it any more. I want a transfer. NOW!"

The Sheriff had been looking for a good personal secretary, and Marge was good. She went to work for him the next day.

Margie and I were always good friends. Several years later, I would call her and say, "Margie, I have to see The Man." She would come right back and say, "Walt isn't with you, is he?"

Then she would laugh. It sure wasn't funny when it happened, though.

Incidents like this were part of the job. Diversion from seeing all those dead, degraded people of every ilk and description imaginable take many forms. Some men couldn't take it at all, and transferred out as soon as they could. Others couldn't be driven away with a shotgun. The job had its ill effects on everyone. I think divorce and alcoholism were at the top of the list. If alcoholism didn't cause a divorce, both spouses became alcoholics. Looking back on it, I don't see how I lasted almost fourteen years working homicides. I wouldn't change a thing, though. I didn't become an alcoholic, nor was I divorced. Midge must have seen some good in me and kept me straight for almost fifty-one years.

7
Burney

W alt and I talked to everyone that had been near Burney from the time he was admitted to the hospital until his death. That included three shifts per day every day he was in the hospital. There were several nurses, doctors and interns, candy stripers and VolunTeens. We also studied Burney's hospital chart until we were as familiar with it as the medical personnel were.

Burney had told Ken Trevethick, a VolunTeen, that he was hit by a truck while riding his go-cart. He told others that he had been walking when he was hit by a truck. There was not enough variation in his story to positively state that Burney had fabricated the accident. The fact was that he had some injury prior to being admitted to the hospital. The only thing that really indicated an injury was revealed by the x-ray of his hip which showed a small fracture of the right hip joint, and of course, dilation of the left eye. The x-ray of the skull revealed no fracture.

We talked to Doctor John K. Ross-Duggan, the neurosurgeon. He stated that he examined Burney on

August 22, 1961, and found a mild tenderness in the right parieto-occipital scalp but no contusions, abrasions or lacerations on Burney's body or extremities. There were no external injuries to the right hip, but tenderness to the right buttocks was noted whenever the right hip was moved. Doctor Ross-Duggan stated that this could have been a several days old trauma, but there was a chip in the right hip socket.

A spinal tap was done August 21; two red cells were observed which is within normal limits. Blood count normal. Another tap made three days later disclosed a normal count of cells. Doctor Ross-Duggan performed a bilateral anterior temporal and posterior parietal burr holes and a ventricular-ography.

I asked, "Doctor, what about his drowsiness while in the hospital?"

He replied, "Perfectly consistent with a brain injury."

"Well, what about his low spinal and blood sugars? Is that consistent with a head injury?"

He replied, "No, as a matter of fact, one would expect an increase in blood sugar and urine sugar. Our findings were the opposite."

I told him, "Doctor, we have reason to believe Burney was given a lethal injection of insulin. Having said this, now do you have an opinion as to Burney's cause of death?"

"I would say that his condition could have been caused by an injection of insulin, at least a fifty-fifty chance." Shifting in his chair, he continued rather irately, "I'll tell you this though; no one on this hospital staff is guilty of that!"

"I'm not saying that at all, Doctor. We have reason to believe the boy's uncle deliberately murdered him. He had every opportunity, as he was in and out of Burney's room several times a day. In fact, he was in Burney's room shortly before he became comatose. We believe he set that kid up and watched him die."

"What on earth could anyone gain by killing that fifteen-year-old boy?" he said, with disbelief.

"Well, Doctor, there are many reasons one person might have for killing another person. We believe that in this case his reasons might be about the same as the ones he had in the other deaths we suspect he caused. We will just have to find out what that reason was," I said, as we prepared to leave.

"Fellows, I will do anything I can to help you in this case," he said as he stood and shook hands with us.

"Oh, by the way, did Archerd say why Burney's grandmother didn't come down to sign the consent slip?" I asked. His reply was, "He said she was too feeble to come down."

Walt said, "Whitey, let's go canvass the neighborhood and see what we can find out."

We headed for the Carmelitos housing project, a low rent government housing facility. This county island was surrounded by the city of Long Beach, and had been a source of all kinds of trouble, long before I worked it, when it was part of the Norwalk Station patrol area.

We talked with Robert and Wynda Whitsett at their home, 789 Via Carmelitos, which was next door to Jenny May Archerd, Burney's grandmother. Mrs. Whitsett told us that she saw Mister Archerd arrive at his mother's residence about one p.m. August 21, and that Burney came home about an hour later. Burney rolled up her garden hose for her. She noticed that he was wearing clean Levis and a blue sport shirt. She saw no dirt in his hair or on his clothes. She went on to say that Jenny May had told her that Mister Archerd had gotten a job for Burney delivering blueprints. She didn't know how he was to deliver them.

On September 7, Walt and I interrogated William Dale Archerd and his wife of three years, Gladys Theresa Archerd. They had responded to my request that they come to Lakewood Sheriff's Station for an interview. Mister

Archerd came dressed in a neatly pressed suit with tie and freshly shined shoes. He stood about five feet eleven and weighed one hundred sixty-five to one hundred seventy pounds. His silver hair was thinning; his eyes were pale blue. His talk was slow and measured and rather low in tone. At first glance, the impression he gave was that of a banker or a successful business man.

While Walt was questioning him, I would be taking notes and vice versa. I'm sure that Archerd knew that we were taping our conversation, but he acted as if he didn't care; he had his story down pat, and it never varied. Without the information we already had about him, we would have been inclined to believe him. Freely and without hesitation, he answered all our questions.

We then called in our stenographic reporter, Mia Miller, to record our interrogation of Mister Archerd.

"Archerd stated that he was using the alias of James L. Arden in his business and occupation as a salesman employed by the Visan Nutritional Laboratories, and had been employed by this firm for approximately three months as an outside salesman concentrating in Southeast Los Angeles County and Orange County areas. Mister Archerd stated in substance that he had been caring for his mother, Mrs. Jenny M. Archerd, of 791 Via Carmelitos, Long Beach, who was in ill health. She had been caring for Burney since the death of his father, Everett Burney Archerd MW-52, from an apparent heart attack while at his place of Employment at the Richfield Oil Company Dominguez Station on 1-22-60. At this time, Everett Archerd's estate was left to victim, who was then legally placed under the guardianship of William D. Archerd in Department 4 of the Superior Court on 3-28-60, Case #427040. Mister Archerd further stated that at approximately three-thirty p.m. 8-21-61, while he was at an unknown location in the La Habra-Fullerton area, he made a phone call to his mother, who at that time advised him that the victim had just arrived home and had been involved in some type of accident. Mister Archerd stated that he then responded to the Via Carmelitos address and upon his arrival at approximately four p.m. he observed abrasions on the left and right palms of victim's hands, blood on one of his elbows, a red mark on his right hip and that victim also had dirt in his hair and that his head was tender. Mister Archerd stated that victim appeared to be rational and talked coherently, stating that he had been hit by a red truck while crossing the street at the intersection of Coldbrook and Rocket. Mister Archerd stated that he attempted to contact Doctor Harry Ison, who had treated his mother, Mrs. Jenny Archerd, on a previous occasion, but that Doctor Ison's office was closed and that he therefore transported victim to the Long Beach Memorial Hospital. Mister Archerd stated substantially the facts contained in the first report submitted by him to the Lakewood deputies. Mister Archerd further stated in response to questioning that to the best of his recollection victim was wearing blue jeans and a sport shirt at the time of the accident and that victim had a five hundred dollar life insurance policy that had been taken out at the Inglewood Office of the Prudential Insurance Company when the victim was five years old. He stated that he had retained an attorney to represent him in a legal action against the registered owner of the vehicle involved in this incident. He further stated that a Mister Delaney was a private investigator retained by his attorney and was presently actively investigating the case. He stated that he had talked with an insurance adjustor representing Parkwood Chevrolet, a Mister Ralph J. Simpson."

Following the interrogation of our suspect, Mister W. D. Archerd, we showed him Burney's receipt for his driver's license learner's permit. This permit had been given to us by Sergeant Glenn Schuck, the Lakewood traffic accident investigator, who received it from Archerd during his initial investigation of the alleged hit-and-run where Burney was alleged to have been hit by a "red turck."

Archerd said, "Yes, that is what Burney gave me on the way to the hospital."

"Is all that writing Burney's?" I asked. There was obviously writing on the receipt that could have been written by two different people.

"No, the writing in pencil is Burney's and the writing in ink is mine."

"This is all Burney's writing that appears to be a license number 'P97166', 'red tr', and in longhand, 't-u-r-c-k'?

He answered, "Yes."

"And the rest of the writing is yours," Walt continued.

Archerd said, "It is. As you noticed, I misspelled Cold-brook the same as he did because I left out the 'd'."

"Where were you when you and Burney were examining this piece of paper with the drawing and writing on it?" Walt asked.

"We were in the emergency room. Burney was on the table. That was before the resident came in to examine him."

Sergeant Schuck had told us that he had already located the truck after having traced it through a couple different owners. The current owner was Parkwood Chevrolet in Lakewood. The truck was sitting on their used car lot at the corner of South Street and Bellflower Boulevard, four blocks east of

Bellflower and a block north of South Street. You could actually see the car lot from the alleged hit-and-run location.

It is interesting to note that Archerd bought his 1959 Chevrolet convertible from Parkwood Chevrolet; he also co-signed for Burney's dad to buy a 1959 Chevrolet station wagon. More about that, later.

Walt and I went to the car lot, and sure enough, there sat a red pickup truck, license number P97166. We talked to Bob Letchworth, the car lot manager, and he told us that as far as he knew, that truck hadn't been off the lot for about six weeks. We looked the truck over as well as we could. To us it didn't look as if it had been moved for some time. We noted that it was parked in such a position that the license was visible from the street and could have been read by anyone driving by.

We had Marty Klein from our crime lab examine the truck. He looked it over minutely and could find no evidence that anyone or anything had been hit by that truck. Marty started the truck and drove it around the block. The engine was noisy, the gear box even noisier, and the chains that secured the tailgate rattled loudly. In his opinion, anyone with normal hearing could hear that truck coming at least half a block away.

Just to make sure, we talked to every salesman that worked at the car lot. They all swore that the truck hadn't been off that lot in several weeks.

When we finished talking with Archerd, we talked with his wife, Gladys, for a while. She was a neatly dressed, fifty-ish lady of average size and blue-gray hair. She was eager to talk with us and told us generally the same things Archerd had told us. Gladys went a little farther and described Burney's condition in more detail than Archerd had.

I asked her, "Mrs. Archerd, when you last saw Burney alive, how did he appear to you?"

Her reply was, "Well, when we first got there, he was asleep and completely wet with sweat. We had trouble rousing him and when we did, he said he wanted to go home, and wanted a cigarette. He kept dozing off, and we thought it best if we let him sleep. Dale put a dollar in the night stand for him that Grandma had sent along. I bent over to kiss him good-bye, but he was so sweaty, I could hardly stand to touch him. His blankets were soaking wet. We checked out at the nurses' station and were on our way out when I looked back and his feet were moving. That's the last time I saw him alive." She gave a sigh of relief as if to say, "There, I got that over with."

Gladys wasn't really a lot of help except for her description of Burney sweating profusely, and his feet moving. We believe that Burney could have been starting to have grand mal seizures, which go along with an overdose of insulin. We thought that with Archerd's background of assisting doctors at Camarillo State Mental Hospital in administering insulin shock therapy to schizophrenic patients, he could have put a stop to Burney's steady decline if he wanted to. Instead, he watched that kid go through the symptoms of insulin overdose and rapidly go downhill.

We knew it is best not to become emotionally involved in an investigation, but our involvement was irreversible. As we continued to canvass the neighborhood, we found some of Burney's friends. One was a young lady who volunteered in the juvenile ward at Long Beach Memorial, "M.J." Keown. She was a seventeen-year-old neighbor who worked at the Dairy Queen near Burney's house. Burney and his buddies all hung out there. M.J. went down to see Burney about three-thirty p.m. August 23rd. She bought him a 'Coke and talked with him a while.

Walt asked her, "What did he tell you happened to him?"

Her answer was, "Out looking for a car or motorcycle and a truck hit him, spun him around. He sat on the curb, dazed. The driver got out and asked him if he was hurt. He told the driver he didn't know. You should talk to his best friend, Jim Miller. He just lives across the street from Burney. Oh! Burney also said he wanted to talk to the cops himself."

Jim Miller didn't have much to say, except that Burney's grandma said that Burney had been hit by a truck and was in the emergency hospital. This she told him between noon and two in the afternoon of August 21.

Another acquaintance, Raymond Almes, said that he saw Burney between noon and one p.m. August 21, walking east on Via Carmelitos. Burney stopped and they talked a while, had a cigarette, then the uncle drove up in a white '59 Chevrolet Impala. Burney got in the car and they drove east.

"Did Burney tell you anything else that day?" I asked him.

"Yeah, he told me that he didn't like his uncle, as he was always hitting him."

Raymond also said that he was present one day when Archerd grabbed Burney by the shirt and said, "Never raise your fist to me, or I'll let you have it." A half hour later, he saw Burney with a bloody lip.

Walt asked Raymond, "Did Burney tell you anything about getting a job?"

"Yeah, he said his uncle got him a job delivering blueprints."

Walt followed up with another question. "Did he say how he was going to deliver those blueprints?"

"He said he was going to get him a car, said he had five thousand dollars in the bank from his father's death."

BINGO! Now we are getting somewhere. Walt's eyes shot up and darted my way. I knew what he was thinking. We both were thinking the same thing. We remembered that Archerd had told us that Burney's dad died on the job at the Richfield Oil Company. There had to be some workman's compensation payoff and maybe some other compensation.

We could hardly wait to get to Lakewood Station, so we could ask our Industrial Relations unit to check if any settlements were made as a result of Burney's father's death.

We still had a few more people we needed to talk to before we could leave the area. One was Bucky Styber. We asked Bucky the same questions we had asked Raymond Almes.

His answer was, "He told me his uncle was getting him a job delivering blueprints and that he would get him a "'57 Box Chevy," meaning four-on-the-floor.

"Bucky, how did Burney get along with his uncle?" I asked.

"Not too well, I think. He told me that if his grandma ever died, he hoped he would die too, because he didn't want to live with his uncle."

"Did Burney ever tell you anything about having money?"

"Yeah, Burney always had money in his pocket; said he had five thousand dollars in the bank from his father's death."

It was getting late and neither of us had had dinner at home with our families in several days. Even so, we headed for Lakewood Station where we called Lou Kronague in Industrial Relations and asked him to check on any compensation to Burney's father's heirs as a result of his dying on the job.

"I'll have the info for you by ten a.m. tomorrow," Lou said, positively. Lou was a six-foot-three-inch, two hundred-fifty pound man, not too heavy around the middle. He was a pipe-smoking sort of guy that could charm a person out of his socks. At ten the next morning Lou was on the phone, just as he had promised.

"Whitey, you must call Pat Doherty at Orange Coast Adjusters in Santa Ana. He says Liberty Mutual paid seven thousand dollars to Jenny May Archerd as trustee for Burney Kirk Archerd, and one thousand dollars attorney fees to the law firm of Rose, Cline, and Marias."

He gave us the industrial accident file number as well as the Liberty Mutual file number. "There may be another policy under Operating Engineers. I'll check that out and let you know."

Walt and I walked a little straighter after that good news. It was the first stroke of good luck since Zella's death. The insurance policies, along with the fact that Archerd had visited Burney in the hospital at least three times a day, gave us an extra boost to keep charging.

We had to locate where the check was cashed or deposited. We called Pat Doherty who promptly traced it down for us. He put us in touch with Clarence Pester of the U.S. National Bank in north Long Beach. The bank was a short walk from Jenny May's apartment. Mister Pester referred us to Mister G.H. Galloway, operations manager for the bank. Mister Galloway furnished us with signature cards signed by William Dale Archerd and Jenny May Archerd as trustees for Burney Kirk Archerd. The account was opened August 1, 1960, and closed August 28, 1961. The initial amount was six thousand dollars. The first withdrawal, five hundred dollars, was made December 15, 1960 by Jenny May. An additional one thousand dollars was deposited to Jenny May's 10 Plan (Christmas account). The next withdrawal was made December 18 by Archerd in the amount of one thousand one hundred twenty-five dollars. He made all the remaining withdrawals March 17 for three hundred seventy-five dollars and one thousand dollars; June 6 for two thousand dollars, and August 28, for one thousand seventy-four dollars and thirty-four cents, closing the account.

There was also a savings account for Burney Kirk
Archerd (Minor) with William D. Archerd, Guardian. This
was the mortuary benefit from the Operating Engineers
Union. The original account balance was one thousand
twenty-five dollars. All withdrawals were made by Archerd.
The last withdrawal was nine hundred eighty-one dollars
and forty-two cents, closing the account September 30,
1961. Following the money trail, we had found our motive.

Jenny May was found dead in bed by Archerd and his
cousin, Mrs. Evelyn Manes, August 24, 1961. She was pronounced dead by Doctor Ison, and cremated at Sunny Side
Mausoleum two days later. Doctor Ison signed the death
certificate; there was no autopsy. Cause of death, apparent
heart attack. Another setback!

Walt and I found Evelyn Manes at her home in Long
Beach. She said that Jenny May called her about five-thirty
p.m. August 21. "What did she call about?" I asked.

"She said Burney was in the hospital after being hit by
a truck. Said she didn't know where or how. Dale came
home, took Burney to the hospital. Dale and Gladys came
by my house about eight-thirty p.m. on August 23. First
time I had seen Dale in some time, maybe a year or a year
and a half. Dale and Gladys debated whether or not to go
by Jenny May's and tell her that Burney might have to be
operated on. But they finally decided not to, as Jenny May
would be in bed."

"Had you talked to Dale since that night?" I asked.

"Yes, he called me when he got home. Said the hospital
called and wanted him to come down and sign a consent
slip," she said. "Dale picked me up on the 24th. We went
to Jenny May's to tell her that Burney had been operated
on. He opened the door with his key and after knocking,
yelled 'anyone home?' I went in Jenny May's bedroom and
the bed hadn't been slept in. Dale went into the kitchen.
I found Jenny May in the other bedroom lying face down

catty-corner across the bed, fully clothed except for shoes. There was a piece of paper on the pillow with a phone number on it. I think Jenny May had been crying because I found two damp hankies on the floor near the chair. Doctor Ison said she had been dead about eight hours."

Mrs. Manes seemed genuinely upset about the deaths of Jenny May and Burney. We thanked her for her cooperation and left. As we pulled away from her house, I said to Walt, "You know, we have Archerd spending lots of time at the hospital with Burney. He sure as hell had the opportunity to jab Burney with a needle and could have done it without being noticed. I know seven thousand dollars isn't a great deal of money, but I don't think that's the only reason he killed that kid. There was a great deal of animosity between Burney and Archerd. That aggravation and the money combined could have caused him to kill the kid."

"Whitey, what do you make of Jenny May's death? Do you think he could have killed her, also?"

"Yeah, Walt, I think he is capable of just about anything. Try this on for size: just say that Jenny May found out about Archerd going south with Burney's money and confronted him with it. He could have juiced her up before he went to the hospital. That's about right, time wise. He couldn't afford to be the one that found her dead so he took his cousin, who he hadn't seen in a year and a half, along and he let her find Jenny May."

"I think you hit the nail on the head, Whitey, but we'll never be able to prove he killed his mother. She was cremated two days later, and we didn't know about either death until ten days later. That s.o.b. sure was moving in a hurry."

"We can't worry about that now, so let's just concentrate on trying to prove he killed Burney. We have to finish canvassing the neighborhood," I said, as we headed for the Carmelitos housing projects.

We followed up on what Ken Trevethick told us about Burney saying that he wasn't going to fix up his go-cart that he had wrecked, as he was going to get two hundred dollars for a car. We located a go-cart shop on East Market Street just outside the housing project. A Mister James D. Harris was the owner of Karts & Parts. We showed him Archerd's mug shot and he said, "That's the guy that brought this wrecked go-cart Enduro and wanted to sell it. He didn't like the price I offered him, so he left, saying 'I guess I'll just give it to some kid in the neighborhood.'"

Walt asked him, "When did he come in?"

"Around the first of the month," Harris answered.

Walt followed up with, "What kind of condition was it in?"

"Pretty well beat up. The frame was bent and the paint was scraped down to the metal. It sure wasn't worth what he wanted for it."

We then stopped by Lindberg Junior High and talked with Burney's teacher. She told us she had attended Burney's funeral and that Burney was in her class last school term. She thought he was a nice young man but a poor student.

We showed her the driver's permit that Archerd had given us and asked her if that was Burney's writing.

She replied, "I don't remember his writing being that good. But he could at least spell 'truck!'"

We continued to try to locate anyone in the Carmelitos housing project to see if they knew anything about Burney's death. In this search, we found Jane Ferrell, an acquaintance of Archerd, Burney and Jenny May. Jane came to Lakewood Station at our request and gave us a stenographic statement. She told us that she lived at 801 Via Carmelitos with her three children. Her apartment was directly across the back parking lot from Jenny May's home. She knew

Jenny May and Burney quite well and saw them regularly several times a day.

I asked her, "Do you know William Dale Archerd?" and showed her a mug shot of him.

"Yes, that's him," she answered.

"Do you know how he and his mother got along?"

"Yes, I think they got along well together. I know she took phone calls for him and would receive mail for him."

"How did Dale and Burney get along?"

"Well, I know that Jenny May used Dale as a weapon over Burney's head to get him to do things she wanted him to do. Outside of that, I don't know what their relationships were between each other," she said.

Then I asked her, "How well do you know Dale?"

"I thought I knew him pretty well. Well enough to go to Vegas with him and Stella and John Lawrence," Jane responded.

I asked her, "Who is Stella?"

"She's my next door neighbor. We talk a lot and sit with each other's kids from time to time. Her name is Stella Morin."

"Tell us about the trip to Vegas."

She went into great detail as to how Dale had planned a combination business and pleasure trip. The story was that John Lawrence had some property up around Reno that was supposed to have oil on it. He was to meet someone in Las Vegas who wanted to lease the land for oil drilling. Archerd was also supposed to meet someone there to consummate some sort of business deal of his own.

"Do you remember when it was that you all went on this trip?" I asked.

"I know exactly when it was. March 5, 1960. I have it marked on my calendar," she replied.

"How long were you there?" I asked.

"We just stayed over night and came back the next afternoon," she replied.

"Where did you stay in Las Vegas?"

"I don't remember the motel, but it was right across the street from The Pancake House. Our rooms were side by side."

"Who did you share a room with?"

"With John Lawrence. Stella stayed with Dale."

John Lawrence was an ex-con who had done time with Archerd in San Quentin and Chino. Archerd and Lawrence escaped from Chino and enjoyed a few days of freedom before being caught and sent back to Chino.

I then showed her a mug shot that she readily identified as Lawrence. She went on to describe her relationship with him as a friend. She had dated him several times before the Vegas trip, but hadn't heard from him since. She described Archerd and Lawrence as good friends in that they had partnerships in business dealing. She thought the deals might have been on the shady side, but couldn't be sure.

"What would you say the relationship between Archerd and Stella was?" I asked.

"I would say that they were sweethearts," was her quick reply.

"Do you know if Stella ever took any other trips to Las Vegas with Archerd?"

"I don't rightly know, but I do know that Archerd and Frank Stewart, Gladys' ex-husband flew to Vegas on a 'business trip' and that Stella drove his car up there to meet them."

Walt and I did a double- take, gulped a couple times and quickly got ourselves under control. This was the first time we had heard of anyone else being involved in the Frank Stewart case. Ain't life beautiful!

"Tell us more about Stella," I quickly asked.

"She's married to a sailor, Phillip Morin, who's at sea a great deal of time, so Stella keeps company with Dale while Phil is away."

We quickly wrapped up our interrogation of Jane Ferrell, and then reread Sergeant Dick Humphreys' notes on the Frank Stewart case. Nowhere could we find any mention of Stella Morin. Naturally, we zeroed in on her and did a thorough background check. We found out that she had worked as a telephone operator for Pacific Telephone. We obtained a copy of her application for employment, handwriting exemplar and a photograph.

We called Paul Fasnact of the Long Beach office of Naval Investigation. He gave us a rundown on Stella's husband, as well as some information on Stella. He told us that she was living with her mother in Miami.

Then we did some rechecking of Humphreys' reports and found out that Archerd had taken out a sixty-two thousand five hundred dollar flight insurance policy on Frank Stewart, making Gladys the beneficiary; and a policy for eighteen thousand dollars, making Jenny May Archerd the beneficiary. The policies covered the insured from portal to portal or terminal to terminal in this case.

With this information, we decided that maybe our old adversary may have been involved in other accident scams. We checked with the Los Angeles Index Bureau and found that Archerd had been the victim of several slip-and-fall accidents on construction sites while he was employed as a folding door salesman. He was the beneficiary of several workmen's comp claims that paid him for his injuries, plus money loss from his "disability." There was a startling claim that this time listed Archerd as the victim of a hit-and-run accident while he was on the job. We also found that he had filed a bodily injury claim in the amount of fifty thousand dollars against the owner of the car that struck him!

✠ ✠ ✠

8
Phony Hit-and-Run

We spent the next day or two running down all the information we could gather regarding this accident. Archerd had filed a hit-and-run complaint with the California Highway Patrol; we quickly obtained a copy. The investigator of the accident, Patrolman Ron Hiles, told us that he had talked to Archerd October 10, 1960 at Huntington Memorial; that Archerd's statements were made freely and voluntarily. Archerd told him that he had parked his car at the curb on Boston Street and Lake Avenue in Altadena, got out and started across the street, noticed a car coming toward him. He stopped, the car stopped, and the driver motioned for him to go ahead. As Archerd started across the street, the car started forward and hit him, knocking him to the pavement. While he was lying down, he got out a business card and wrote the license number down.

The driver got out, helped him up and into his car, then left saying, "I'm going to get some help," then drove off. Archerd said, "I gave chase until I became dizzy and stopped, went into a drugstore for help. The next thing I remembered, I was in the hospital."

Actually, Archerd went into a barber shop operated by the father of Chief Vic Riseau of our department!

Archerd was admitted to the hospital, complaining of severe headaches. He was in the hospital for several days and released, as not having any serious intracranial damage. He came back to the hospital November 8, complaining that his headaches were getting worse. Doctor Benjamin Crue examined him and said, "He surprised us all, meaning the neurosurgeons that had seen Archerd several times, by having a very large fixed dilated left pupil." – Shades of Burney Kirk Archerd.

We checked with the owner of the car, a Mister Joseph Crossley. He told us, "Yes, I owned a 1957 Plymouth Fury. I had it advertised in the *Pasadena Star News* for sale. I got a phone call from a Mister Pierce. He wanted his wife to come by and pick up the car so they could have their mechanic check it out. If it checked out, they would buy it. This lady came to the door and said she was Mrs. Pierce, and that her husband had called previously. 'If it's okay with you, I would like to try it out and let our mechanic check it out.' I showed her how to operate the push button type gear shift and she drove off, saying she'd be back in about an hour."

I showed him the pictures we got from the telephone company, and asked, "Is this her?" He replied, "I can't be sure, but it sure as hell looks like her."

By this time, Walt and I were really getting itchy. Adrenalin was pumping furiously; we couldn't do things fast enough. It was getting late in the afternoon, so we decided to unwind a little. We stopped at our favorite watering hole, Li Po's, down in Chinatown. Finally, after several vodka tonics and some of Uncle Harry Lee's noodles, our wheels stopped spinning and we got our minds back on track. I

went on home just a little shit-faced and left Walt holding
down one of the bar stools.

Walt was bright-eyed and bushy tailed the next morning;
I came in a little worse for wear. I hoped that I could come
alive a little bit as we had a command performance before
the Chief at ten a.m. After several cups of coffee and a few
trips to the head, things started coming into focus. I was
ready to see the Chief.

Chief of Detectives Floyd Rosenberg, Captain Al Etzel,
Lieutenant George Walsh, Walt Thornton and I gathered
in the Chief's conference room for show time. The Chief
said, "Whitey, I hear you and Walt have been a little bit busy.
Why don't you start off and lay out the picture for us?"

I ran on for about an hour, laying out the whole investigation from Zella on through Burney. We hadn't yet done
any work on the Jones case, but we were about to get around
to it. I filled them in on our latest discovery and explained
what we had planned for the future as far as our investigation went. I ended up by telling them that if things worked
out right, I thought we could possibly file complaints in the
Zella and Burney cases, using Frank Stewart and Juanita
Plum Archerd cases as similar acts. Naturally, we couldn't
file those cases; they happened in Las Vegas, out of our
jurisdiction.

I told them of our plans to develop more information
on the Frank Stewart case as well as Archerd's own hit-and-
run. I explained that we needed to talk to Stella Morin in
person. A talk with her might lead to other information
about Archerd's escapades.

Most of what I told them, they already knew. Walt and
I were very diligent in submitting a short memo every few
days as information developed. Captain Etzel didn't dis-
appoint me by asking questions until he came to one that
neither Walt nor I could answer. That was, "What about the

Jones case?" We had no answer, simply because we hadn't had time to even think about it.

In general, everyone was pleased with our progress. We got the routine "atta boy" slaps on the back and "go get 'ums." The chief said, "Fellows, develop the flight insurance aspect and also that phony hit-and-run Archerd reported. And get on the Jones thing."

We walked out of that conference with big sighs of relief and the thought of, *Let us alone and we'll do the job.*

We went back to Associated Aviation Underwriters, the company that dispensed flight insurance to its customers via coin operated machines. At that time, you could buy flight insurance for 25 cents per six thousand dollars. We learned that Stewart's slip-and-fall claim had been investigated by Reno T. Wilkinson, a local Las Vegas claims adjuster. He was hired by the insurance company, whose offices were right here in Los Angeles. Actions had been filed in respect of the sixty-two thousand five hundred dollar policy.

As we talked further, I found out that their head man was the commanding General for the 452nd Bomb Wing Light, the organization which I was with in Japan and Korea in the 1950s. I doubt that my being a Staff Sergeant in the 452nd Air Police unit carried much weight with the General, but we were treated kindly and the flow of information was mutual. I think both parties came out with a winning hand as a result of this exchange.

When it came time for Walt and me to fly to Miami to talk to Stella, this insurance company came up with the funds for both of us.

A few days after our conference with the chief, captain and lieutenant, another conference was scheduled with Joe Carr, head of the Trials Division of the District Attorney's office. Present at this conference were Carr, Etzel, Walsh, Thornton and me. I ran the same scenario by Joe Carr that

I had with our chief. At the end of the presentation, Mister Carr said, "Whitey, I never did like circumstantial evidence cases. What we need is just a little more direct evidence and you just don't have enough right now. Keep at it and I'm sure we'll get there sooner or later. By the way, I want to see Zella's autopsy report." We walked out the door thoroughly disappointed and discouraged.

Walt turned to me and said, "God dammit! How many more people are gonna die before we nail that bastard?"

Back down in the captain's office, I said, "Pelon, we want to go to Florida and talk to Stella."

"Knock that Pelon shit off, Whitey! Dammit, you know how tight the county is with taxpayers' money. I don't think we stand a chance of them coming up with enough money for one of you, let alone both of you."

"Al," I started out a little more respectfully, "Do you think the county would come up with enough money if the insurance company would come up with air fare for both of us?"

"By golly, that's worth a try. Let me run it by the Chief. Maybe he can use some of his 'buy money' for lodging and meals." He bolted out the door and was back ten minutes later. "The chief says if they're willing to pay air fare, we can pay the rest. He said to tell you, don't overspend."

I called Mister Griffin at Associated Aviation Underwriters, and ran the idea past him. "Sounds like a deal to me. I'll have the tickets delivered to you." An hour later, a messenger appeared with two round trip tickets to Miami.

☆ ☆ ☆

9
Stella and Miami

I left a note on the captain's desk: *Al, we are leaving L.A. for Miami at one twenty-five p.m. tomorrow, 1/14/61, via National Airlines flight 30, arriving Miami nine-thirty p.m. The insurance company paid our five hundred forty-four dollar plane fare and a hundred forty dollars in expenses. We can be contacted through the Dade County Department of Public Safety. We will keep you advised at all times re our progress. In the event it is necessary to go to Portsmouth, Virginia, we will call. And if we need more money, we will call. Copies of reports necessary for complaint are on your desk should we need them. Joe Carr has been advised.*

The above reference to Portsmouth is because Phillip Morin, Stella's husband, was stationed there. We didn't want Stella to know that we were coming. We were afraid she would move to Virginia before we got to Miami. We had no reason to worry though, as we had been told by Jane Ferrell that there was a marital rift between Stella and Phillip.

I got a hold of Ed McClue, head of our extradition unit, to see if he had any connections in Miami. He said, "Yeah,

I know a fellow down there. He owes me a small favor. Let me give him a call."

He got on the phone for a few minutes, then turned to us and said, "This fellow is ex-NYPD. His name is Goldman. He moonlights as head of security at the Sands Hotel. Said he'd have someone meet you at the airport and book you into the hotel."

McClue was an expert in extradition laws. He could talk most of the fugitives in our jails into waiving extradition, so there would not be any problems getting the extraditee out of our jail and back to the jurisdiction where he may have committed his crime. McClue was legendary. In fact, he knew more chiefs of police and Sheriff's around the country than our own sheriff did; he had been helpful to me on more than one occasion.

Finally, we were on our way to Miami, just like some snow bird from Canada. The difference was ours was not a pleasure trip. Just like Goldman promised, there was our personal taxi waiting for us at the airport; a skunk-colored Dodge with a full Christmas tree on top in the form of blue and red lights. We were deposited at the Sands Hotel. When we checked in to our rooms, there was a fifth of Jim Beam and a full bucket of ice. Goldman showed up shortly and officially welcomed us to Miami.

"I'll pick you up at seven-thirty a.m., take you down and turn you over to the boys at Homicide. They can take it from there. Have a nice visit and I'll see you later this evening."

We had a little Jim on the rocks; then we decided to check out the bar downstairs. They had a piano player who was out of this world. He would play and sing anything you could name. We noticed that the clientele was mostly Italian couples from Chicago, in their mid-forties. They didn't pay a lot of attention to Walt and me; they just kept doing the twist and having a good time. It was fun listening to the random conversations. I think they made us as the fuzz and were testing us a bit. We had been in the business long enough not to bite, so we played it cool. We didn't stay late; six a.m. came mighty early.

It turned out we would have to wait until after five p.m. to talk to Stella. We found her working as a receptionist at a funeral home. I think she had been waiting for us a long time and was just a little bit relieved to finally see us. Jane Ferrell must have talked to Stella following our visit with her.

Stella agreed to accompany us to Miami Homicide if we would pick her up at five. She liked her job and didn't want to lose it. Stella was a little under weight, stood about five foot five inches and weighed maybe a hundred ten pounds. She had a full head of shoulder-length, shiny black hair and her eyes were almost black. Her complexion was clear and a little bit tanned, and she was dressed nicely in a plaid skirt and matching sweater. She didn't look like the ordinary shack job. She was cordial and willing to talk to us.

The commander of the Homicide Bureau assigned us a car and driver to use as needed. We picked Stella up promptly and took her down to the Public Safety building. We were allowed to use one of their interrogation rooms. We made sure she was comfortable, and then I said to her, "Stella, I think you know why we are here. We are here to find out what you know about the activities of William Dale Archerd, also known as James Lynn Arden. We know that you are acquainted with him and participated in some of the things he was involved in. We want you to answer our questions truthfully and help us as much as you can. Are you willing to do this?"

Her reply was, "I'll try."

I continued, "You know, Stella, we wouldn't have come all the way back here if we were on a fishing trip, so to speak. We have some pretty good information and believe you can fill in the blanks for us, okay?" She merely nodded and looked away rather resignedly.

We never gave a thought to the possibility of giving her immunity, even though she definitely was a co-conspirator in the hit-and-run incident involving Archerd. We weren't interested in prosecuting her on any charge. Our only thoughts were to get enough information to land William Dale Archerd.

At first, she tried to get us to believe that she and Archerd were just friends and that there was nothing else between them. That first session was one of sparring by both sides. Stella was trying to find out just how much we knew and if we intended prosecuting her. When it became apparent to her that we didn't want to charge her with anything, she became more cooperative, but not leveling with us all the way. We had been talking with her for a couple hours about how she met Archerd, and what part she had to play in the Frank Stewart matter.

She told us about the first trip she and Jane Ferrell had taken with Archerd and John Lawrence. Her story was almost word for word like Jane's. Finally, I said, "Stella, tell us in your own words about your trip to Las Vegas when Frank Stewart ended up in the hospital." This demand wasn't in as gentle a tone as I had used before.

Stella sat up straighter, locked her hands together and clasped them between her knees. She began a long dissertation about how she was involved in the case:

"Dale called me on the phone and asked me if I would like to go to Las Vegas. I said, fine. He said he was at the airport there; that he would be at my house as soon as he could get there, and that he would discuss it with me. He got to my house early afternoon around one-thirty or two. I saw him and Frank get out of his car and go into Jenny May's house. Shortly, he came to my house and said he wanted me to drive his car to Las Vegas; that he had some business to take care of; that he was flying in that night; that it was important that I get ready and get on the road. He wanted me to be there by ten or ten-thirty p.m. so that when he arrived, I could pick him up at the airport. He used my telephone, using a credit card, called Las Vegas, and made reservations at the Sal Sagev Hotel under the name of Mr. and Mrs. Don Nightingale.

"After he made the phone call, he said he had to fill the car with gas and wanted me to ride down with him. He went to the trunk of his car, took out a small package wrapped in brown paper, and told me he wanted me to take the package with me to Las Vegas. He told me not to let the package out of my sight. He then asked me if he could use my car to drive to the airport. I told him he could. He and Frank left in my car and I got ready and left Long beach for Las Vegas about four-thirty p.m."

I interrupted her. "Stella, did you ever and do you now know any Mr. and Mrs. Don Nightingale?"

"No, I never heard of them before."

"Did you have the package with you?" I asked.

She said, "I had it locked in the glove compartment of the car."

At this point, I think maybe she was having second thoughts about telling us any more about her trip. She became evasive in answering our questions, and it was obvious to Walt and me that she was holding some of the story back. She definitely did not want to talk any more.

I said to her rather sternly, "Stella, why in hell are you, a young, good looking married woman, playing around with this character, who is about twice your age?"

Her reply was, "Well, you know."

Walt was sitting reared back on two legs of his chair with his eyes closed, seemingly not paying any attention to our conversation. Suddenly, he sat forward and got right in her face. He said in a loud voice, "Fer Christ sakes, Stella! Was

he that good in bed that you would do almost anything for
him? What'd he do, go down on you?!"

"Well, yes," she replied, timidly.

From that point on, Stella did a complete turn around
and laid out all of her involvement with Archerd to us. She
got back to where we had left off, and then continued,
"I only made one stop on the way to eat and get gas. He
hadn't given me any money, so I had to use my own gasoline credit card. I didn't have any trouble finding the hotel.
I parked in the garage there, registered as Mr. and Mrs.
Don Nightingale, 803 Via Carmelitos, Long Beach, California, my home address, just like he told me. I waited in the
room for his phone call."

I broke in, "Where was the package he had you bring
with you?"

"I took it up to the room with me. I didn't open it."

I asked her to describe the package again. "It was about
the size of four king size cigarette packs, wrapped together
in brown paper."

"Did you receive a call from Archerd?"

"Yes, it was about midnight," she replied.

"This was on March 16, 1960?"

"Yes, he wanted me to come to the airport and pick him
up."

"What did you do with the package?"

"I took it with me in the car and drove to the airport.
When I arrived there, Dale and Frank Steward were waiting
for me. Dale was on one side of Frank and a colored porter
was on the other, supporting him and walking him toward
the car."

"Are you talking about McCarran Airport in Las Vegas?"
I asked.

"Yes, they put Frank in the passenger side of the car. I
scooted over in the middle and Dale drove. I told Dale I
had the package with me and he said, 'I don't need it now.

Frank slipped and fell in the restroom of the airport and hit his head. I'm going to take him to the hospital to be checked.'

"On the way there, he stopped at a pay phone. When he got back in the car, he seemed upset in that he couldn't locate this doctor. All this time, Frank was holding a hand-kerchief to his head. I asked Frank if he was hurt bad; he said he didn't think so."

"What hospital did Dale take Frank to?" I asked.

"He was taken to Southern Nevada Memorial Hospital in Las Vegas. Dale was gone twenty to thirty minutes, and when he got back in the car, he said they were going to keep Frank overnight for observation. Dale and I went back to the hotel. He took the package up to the room. He was awful jittery, said he needed a drink, and so he went to the whiskey store and came back with a bottle of Jim Beam. While we were having a few drinks he was still jittery and nervous. He told me that Frank hadn't really fallen at the airport; they were just pretending because they had taken out flight insurance, and that as long as it happened on air-port property, they could collect on the insurance."

"Did he tell you how Frank took the fall?" I asked.

"He said that Frank was so stupid that he couldn't even take the fall himself. So Dale had to take the fall; then Frank took his place on the floor."

"Did he have anything to say about the package?"

"Dale said the package contained medication that he was going to give Frank that would make it look like Frank had really hit and hurt his head. The medication was to make it appear like Frank had a heart attack. He might become nauseous and maybe lose consciousness for a short time, but he would eventually be as good as new.

"I woke up the next morning about ten. Dale was already dressed, said he had to go to the hospital and check on Frank, and give him the medication. Dale took the package into the bathroom. When he came back, he had a handkerchief in one hand and a syringe in the other."

"A hypodermic syringe?" I asked.

"Yes, he wrapped it up and put it into his coat pocket."

"What happened next?" I asked.

"We checked out of the hotel and drove to the hospital. He asked me to come inside with him. We went up to the second floor, and I sat down in the waiting room. "Dale walked down the hall to Frank's room. He was gone for about twenty minutes. I wanted to get up and run. I didn't know where to run to, as I didn't have any money, so I got up and went back to the car. Ten minutes later, Dale came back to the car and asked me why I had left. I said I felt better sitting in the car. I asked him if he gave Frank the medicine. He said 'No, I damned near got caught. I had to ditch the syringe.' He was really put out."

Stella continued, "We went and had breakfast and he said, 'We have to go back to the hospital, but first I have to get some more.' I thought it was medicine, or whatever it was he was going to give Frank, and that he would have to see this doctor to get it. I sat in the car while he went into the doctor's office. He came back and told me that the doctor was phoning the drugstore with a prescription for Dale to pick up. We drove to the drugstore; Dale picked up the prescription, and we drove back to the hospital. We parked; Dale took a syringe, needle and vial of medicine out of his pocket. He filled the syringe with the medicine, wrapped it up in a handkerchief, and put it in his pocket. I sat in the car while he went into the hospital. He was gone about twenty minutes. He came back and said, 'Everything is taken care of. Now we can be on our way home.' About a mile away from the hospital, he took the vial and threw it into the weeds as we drove toward home. As we drove along, he told me, 'I don't like people crossing me up. I know people all over the United States, and when someone does me dirty, I get them paid back.'"

"Stella, did you have any fear of him at that time?" I asked.

"Yeah, he scared hell out of me," she replied.

"Stella, do the vial and syringe have any special meaning to you?"

"Yes, my aunt was a diabetic and had to take insulin shots. I have injected her many times."

"Was there any resemblance between the vial that Archerd used to fill the syringe with, and the vial that you used when you injected your aunt?"

"Yes, the vials were exactly the same, as well as the syringe. I believe Dale injected Frank with insulin," she stated, emphatically.

"Did Archerd drop you off at home?"

"No, he drove to the Los Angeles airport where I picked up my car. He drove off and I headed for Long Beach. I got lost on the way, and it took me an hour and a half to find my way home."

"When was the next time you saw Archerd?" I asked.

She replied, "I believe it was March 23."

"What happened then?"

"He came to my house and said that Frank had died; said the injection had nothing to do with his death; that Frank had heart trouble and that the excitement of planning the insurance deal had been too much for him, and he had a heart attack and died. He told me that there would be insurance investigators, but that he really didn't believe they would bother me at all. He brought this package that was wrapped in brown paper towels, and unwrapped it. It was the syringe. He wanted me to keep it for him; he didn't want it found at his house or in his possession."

"What else did he say?" I asked.

"He said that if the insurance investigators came to my house, that I should tell them that a Don Nightingale, myself and two other women left for Las Vegas on the March 16 for a pleasure trip; that when he got his insurance money he was going to give me several thousand dollars, as he knew my husband and I were in debt."

"Stella, what did you believe was Dale's intent when he told you he was going to give Frank the medication?"

She answered, "Well, I surely didn't think he was going to kill Frank! I knew what he was doing wasn't right. I thought he was doing it just to collect the insurance money."

"Did Dale ever mention John Lawrence having anything to do with this scam?" I asked.

"Yes, he told me John was supposed to take the fall, but he had been missing since March 7, so he got Frank to do it instead. He also told me that he wanted to find Lawrence to make sure he wouldn't tell anyone about the insurance deal and try to collect for telling of the plan."

"When did Dale tell you this about Lawrence?"

"Right after the insurance investigator came by the second time."

"Did Dale ever tell you who the beneficiary was on that sixty-two thousand, five hundred dollar policy or on the eighteen-thousand dollar policy?"

"No, he did not, but he asked me if I could use an extra five thousand dollars."

"Did he offer you anything else?"

"Yes, he showed me a man's ring that had a solitary diamond in it. He said he would have the diamond reset in a ring for me."

"Did he tell you where he got the ring?"

"He said it was Frank's; that Frank owed him some money, and he was keeping it until he was paid."

"Did you ever accuse Dale of killing Stewart?"

"No. He told me more than once that the medication he gave Frank didn't have anything to do with his death. I never ever realized Frank's death was anything more than an insurance fraud. The reason being, I thought an autopsy should show that the medicine caused his death. Now, I believe Dale intended from the start to kill Frank for the insurance money."

It was getting late and Stella needed to be home with her family, so we told her, "Tomorrow, we want to talk to you about the fire that totaled your Taurus and your taking over the payments on Everett's '59 Chevrolet station wagon. Think about it. We'll see you at five p.m. tomorrow. Thank you for your cooperation."

We believed that she told us the truth to the best of her ability and that she was cooperating with us whole-heartedly.

10
More of Stella

The following morning at breakfast, checking over the menu, we noticed that the price of meals was about three times what they were at home. We did a quick calculation of how much money we had between us, and discovered we didn't have enough to last two more days. We figured that we would spend that evening learning all we could about Stella's car fire and how she and her husband became the owners of the station wagon. Then the following day, we would explore the alleged hit-and-run involving Archerd.

I got on the phone and called Etzel. "Al, Walt and I may be held hostage if you don't send us some money to pay our hotel bill."

His reply was, "Aw, bullshit! You guys are just padding the account. I know how that story goes."

"Al, the prices in this area are about three times of those at home, particularly this time of year. The hotel room goes for thirty-two dollars a night, breakfast five dollars, lunch seven dollars, dinner twelve-fifty. The only break we're getting is for the room. They're charging us twenty-four dollars a night," I told him.

He finally relented and wired us the money. He was just doing what he thought was necessary; besides, I knew his bark was worse than his bite. I knew, though, we had better bring back receipts for everything we had spent.

That evening, we decided to unwind a little. We went down to the piano bar and found it jumping. The same group of Italians from Chicago was there, singing along with the piano player. The men all wore dark suits with white shirts and ties. Their dark, thick hair was slicked down with something that made it shiny. All the males reminded me of Rudolph Valentino.

The ladies were in their finest gowns with lots of jewelry on their wrists and necks. The necklaces looked like diamonds that weren't trying too hard to hide the enormous cleavage that most of them were so proud of. I was reminded of Ralph Gannaway telling me about a time he was at an elegant party and all he could see was "tits and diamonds." The dance floor was always crowded with dark haired females with their beehive hairdos so stiff that they would break before they would bend.

After a few days stay at the Sands Hotel, the Chicago clientele relaxed a great deal and became friendlier. As I said before, I think they had us made for the heat. Finally, a couple of good looking ladies came over to our table, and said, "Come on, you guys, we know you're the heat, but don't let that keep you from having some fun."

One grabbed Walt by the hand, the other one grabbed mine, and led us out on the dance floor. The piano player was doing his best Chubby Checker routine, "*Come On, Baby, Let's Do the Twist.*" It was just what we needed: a little relaxation. I think we twisted with all those great gals. Their husbands kept our drinks filled. What a party!

The next afternoon, we felt more relaxed and more alert. We picked Stella up promptly at five o'clock, took her down to Dade County Homicide, and did our bit about Stella's car fire. Stella told us that she and her husband, Phillip, had bought a Ford Taurus from Foothill Motors in Pasadena. The salesman was none other than John Lawrence, the man that was to have originally taken the fall at the airport. She said the car was a lemon from the start, and that they had paid too much for it. The payments were more than they could handle. She had complained to Archerd about the bum deal and wished that she could run it off a cliff. Archerd said to her, "I can take care of the car for you."

"How will you do that?" she asked.

"Why don't you go to the movies this afternoon, and when you come out, everything will be taken care of," he told her.

She took Anita Garcia, her neighbor, with her to the movie. She parked the car in the last row, just as Archerd had told her to. When they came out of the movie, the car was gone. She called Long Beach police to report it stolen. They advised her that it hadn't been stolen; it had been burned. "I guess that's what he meant when he said it would be taken care of," Stella said.

I asked her, "Why did you and Archerd agree to have your car taken care of?"

"He wanted us to take over the payments on Bernie's father's '59 Chevy station wagon because he had signed for Everett when he bought the car and he, Archerd, couldn't make two car payments. Further, I wanted to get out from under the lemon I bought from John Lawrence."

"Stella, did Archerd give you any money so you could take over payments on the station wagon?"

"Yes, he had Jenny May write out a check for one hundred dollars, and I made one payment."

"What happened to the station wagon after you took possession of it?"

"Phil and I drove it to Florida, then to Portsmouth, Virginia, where it was repossessed."

"How much were the payments?"

"Ninety-six dollars and ninety cents."

"Did you ever make any other payments on the station wagon?"

"No," she answered, "we didn't have the money."

The next interrogation was about Stella's involvement in Archerd's alleged hit-and-run. She told us that Archerd had called her around noon October 19, 1960. He wanted her to meet him in Pasadena. She drove her car to a location he had given her. She thought it was a laundromat. Archerd was standing out front with a newspaper in his hand. He told her that he was going to make a call to a person who had a car for sale, and he wanted her to pick it up. Archerd called from a pay phone inside the laundromat and returned in five or ten minutes, saying, "I found just the right car."

Stella followed him to another location in Pasadena, where they parked, and she got into his car to drive to La Cañada. On the way, he said, "I want you to go to the door, tell the man that you are Mrs. Pierce; that your husband called regarding trying out the car. You want to take it to your mechanic to check it out."

Archerd let her out at a house and drove off; she went to the front door and knocked. When a man came to the door, she told him what Archerd had told her to say, and then promised the man she would have the car back shortly. He gave her the keys. As she drove down the street, Archerd drove off and she followed him to another location.

I asked her, "What were you wearing during this episode?"

"I had on a suit, hat and gloves," she replied. "I pulled up, Archerd got out of his car, got in the passenger side, and said, 'Let's drive it;' and told me where to go." Archerd explained that the reason he had gotten the car was because he wanted to get off work so he could take care of the Frank Stewart business."

"What was he going to do with the car?"

She replied, "He was going to pretend the car hit him; he was going to the hospital to be checked out, didn't expect to stay too long."

"What happened next?' I asked.

"He directed me to a semi-isolated place and stopped. Dale got out, bumped against the right side purposely, bent the antenna, got back in and we drove off. I never even got out of the car."

Archerd directed her to a grocery store parking lot where she parked the car. Archerd told her, "I'll wipe the fingerprints off everything I have touched. Since you have gloves on, there is nothing for me to wipe."

They both got in Archerd's car, he took her back to her car; she drove home.

"Did you hear from Archerd after that?"

"Yes, a few days later, he called me. He told me he was in the hospital and that he had been the victim of a hit-and-run accident, just as if it had really happened. He said he was feeling pretty good and would be out, soon."

"Did you ever see Archerd again?"

"Yes, I saw him on November 1, which was the day we left the Long Beach area for good. I have never seen him since."

When our interrogation was finished, we asked Stella if she minded going over what she had told us of the three incidents that she and Archerd were involved in. Her reply was, "I'd be happy to. There's no curfew on my time."

We called in a stenographic reporter, Bob Clark, and took a verbatim statement from her. These statements were witnessed by Detective Ron Lynch of Dade County Department of Public Safety. Since there were three separate incidents, we took three separate statements.

It had been a long day; my stomach was beginning to growl. I knew Walt was having hunger pangs, too. I said to Stella, "Would you like to go to dinner with us?"

She said, "I surely would; it's too late to eat at home, and it's been a long day."

The three of us found a nice, quiet restaurant and had a pleasant, leisurely meal. Stella promised that if she remembered anything that we might want to know about, she would write to us. We both left our business cards with her.

The statement reporter told us he would have Stella's statements typed up by noon. We wanted Stella to read them, make any corrections needed, and initial them. We had nothing to do until noon, so Ron Lynch said, "Why don't you take my car and tour the city? You have been at it pretty hard for several days."

We took him up on the offer. He handed us the keys to his brand new Thunderbird convertible; we were off like rich snow birds from New York. With the top down, we could see the clearest blue sky I have ever seen, accentuated with a few scattered cotton ball clouds. We felt good, knowing we had accomplished what we came to do. To make things right, we bought a couple Cuban cigars to smoke while we enjoyed the clean, fresh air.

Stella came to Homicide Bureau on her lunch hour, read all three transcripts, made a few corrections, and said, "I hope you convict that evil man! I'll be ready to testify when you need me."

We thanked her for her willingness to tell the whole truth, even if it did incriminate her. She would turn out to be an outstanding prosecution witness. Later that afternoon, we boarded the airliner and headed for home. We slept all the way to Los Angeles.

✫ ✫ ✫

11
Las Vegas

On our return to Los Angeles, Walt and I slept in a couple of hours and came in to work around ten a.m. We were greeted by hoots and other derisive kidding, such as, "Yeah, back from your winter vacation in Florida. How does it feel to come back to the snake pit and have to mingle with us lowly peons?"

We wasted no time bringing Walsh and Etzel up to date on the information that Stella had provided. After we had answered the required questions, we eventually ran into that ultimate question that we couldn't answer. I don't remember what the question was, but it didn't matter. Etzel was just being himself. He then said, "Get in there and get your reports up to date, then come in and see me again."

The next morning, we came in at the usual time and found that Etzel was already in and was reading the lengthy report. When he was finished, he stuck his head in the door of the squad room and waved Walt and me into his office. We pulled up a couple of chairs and waited while he called Walsh to join us. "Fellows, it looks to me like you still have lots of work to do on this case. What do you have in mind? I know you have some sort of agenda."

I beat Walt to the punch. "Al, we want to go to Las Vegas and look into the Stewart matter. We want to have as much information as there is to help us prove that Archerd is the murderer we know he is. We would like to get this done as soon as possible before those witnesses are lost to us."

"I knew you were going to say that and I've been thinking about it." Then he turned to Walsh. "George, can we afford to let them both go?"

Walsh replied, "You know we have four or five guys tied up in court and a couple off sick. Several more are working on cases that will keep them tied up for weeks. I don't see how we can spare both of them."

"I agree with you. Let's send Whitey. Walt has several cases that need some work."

When I picked up my airline ticket and expense money, I learned that Pat Shields, who was working Forgery-Bunko, was going to Las Vegas, too, so we flew over together on January 23, 1962. Our DC-6 headed out over the Pacific, banked right over Malibu, and then headed for Las Vegas. It had snowed overnight and the hills around Malibu and Gorman were covered with snow, as were the local mountains from Angeles Crest all the way to Las Vegas. I had never seen so much snow over southern California.

When we checked in at the Detective Bureau of the Clark County Sheriff's Department, Dick Newsome was standing there. He had just been promoted to agent-in-charge of Southern California, Nevada and Arizona for the National Auto Theft Bureau, and was making his initial rounds to meet all auto theft investigators in his area. I had worked with Newsome for four years when he was a lesser agent in the N.A.T.B. We shook hands and made small talk, then agreed to have dinner at the Stardust Hotel that evening. He was still the same five-foot-nine, one hundred fifty pound, youthful cigar smoker who wore size forty regular suits which he bought off the rack without alterations. Sergeant Bob Runkle of Clark County Sheriff's Department was assigned to work with me. I had been talking to him on the phone from time to time, and he was already familiar with the two deaths that occurred in their jurisdiction. Runkle was a seasoned law enforcement officer, and we worked well together.

The first place we stopped was Southern Nevada Memorial Hospital. Mister Whipple, the assistant hospital administrator, showed us Stewart's hospital records. He had been admitted at twelve-thirty a.m., March 17, 1960, accompanied by a man who said they were on a confidential business trip and that Mister Stewart had slipped on a banana peel in the men's room at McCarran Airport and struck his head.

Doctor Kenneth Turner wrote the admitting order, noting that there was a small laceration to the back of Stewart's head, and that his left eye was dilated larger than his right eye. At six a.m. both eyes were the same size. Doctor Ross Sutherland was called in an hour later. Stewart was conscious and able to give a history. He checked that patient again at four p.m. and noted that he was perspiring profusely and having third degree convulsions similar to grand mal seizures. At this point, Doctor Sutherland called Doctor Ver Brugghen for a consultation.

When I asked Mister Whipple for a copy of the hospital report, he replied, "Sure, you can have a copy if you have a subpoena *duces tecum.*" This referred to a writ ordering a person to produce certain documents. I had to settle for taking notes from the report.

I wanted to talk to Doctor Sutherland to follow up on finding the doctor that Archerd had stopped to see. Mister Whipple gave us his office address. It was exactly where

Stella said Archerd had stopped. We told the doctor that we wanted to see him about Frank Stewart. "I don't remember anyone by that name. Let me see if I can find a record of him. You know, I can't remember the names of all the patients I have treated or consulted on. I do a lot of work for the government out at the Atomic Energy test site, and for a few insurance companies."

He finally came up with Stewart's file. "I examined him back in March, 1960 for Reno Wilkerson, an adjuster for Associated Aviation Insurance Company. I was paid a hundred dollars for the examination. I have worked for Wilkerson before, and know him well."

"Do you remember any of the particulars about the case?"

"Yes, I remember I was puzzled that he died, because his injury was so minor. Besides, when I first saw him at seven a.m., he seemed to be okay. I later called in Doctor Ver Brugghen, and he was as mystified as I was."

I then showed Doctor Sutherland a picture of Archerd, but he did not remember ever seeing him. "We have information that he came here on March 17, 1960, and got a prescription for insulin," I told him.

"That's absolutely not true! Here in Nevada, all a person has to do is mention his doctor's name and sign a register to purchase insulin," he said, angrily. I thanked him for his help and resolved to talk more with him later.

The next thing I wanted to do was to locate the pharmacy where Stella said Archerd had filled the prescription for insulin and a syringe. We found the building exactly as she had described it, across the street from a dime store, right around the corner from the doctor's office. "Professional Drugs" was still painted in black, edged with gold leaf on the front window, along with a sign that said "For Rent." Sergeant Runkle promised to find out what happened to the business and report to me the next day.

It was getting late, about time to meet Dick Newsome for dinner. We headed back to the Stardust Hotel. Just as I walked into the room, the phone was ringing; Newsome was calling from the dining room. We had become good friends while working commercial auto theft cases together. We also got together with other members of N.A.T.B., our own auto theft investigators, and wives. We reminisced about some of our old cases as well as a couple of New Year's Eve parties. Newsome had a couple more days work in the Vegas area; we decided to have dinner together again.

The following morning, I contacted Reno T. Wilkinson. I learned right away that he was acquainted with Sergeant Runkle, and was up to date on the Frank Stewart matter. An independent insurance adjuster, Wilkinson had several steady clients in the Las Vegas area, including the Thunderbird Hotel. We had lunch there while he filled me in on Stewart.

"Mister Wilkinson, how well do you know Doctor Sutherland?" I asked.

"I guess I know him about as well as I know anybody, why?"

"Well, we have a witness that states that she was with our suspect when he went into the doctor's office and got a prescription for insulin and a syringe."

"I'll tell you this, if you think the doctor is involved with any skullduggery, you are badly mistaken. That doctor has more business than he can handle, and he is scrupulously honest. That is the reason I use him when I need an honest medical opinion. In fact, I paid him a hundred dollars to examine Stewart for my clients."

"Thank you very much, I needed a good endorsement right about now," I said.

Runkle got back to me shortly after lunch with information about the Professional Drugstore. The pharmacy was owned by a Mister Delbert Potter, who had closed the business in July, 1961. He was presently working as a pharmacist at Larnin's Drugstore. We talked with Mister Potter briefly, and arranged to meet him after work. All the remaining stock from his pharmacy was stored at his daughter's house.

We had some time to kill, so we went to the Sal Sagev Hotel, which is Las Vegas spelled backwards. We located a registration card in the name of Mr. and Mrs. Don Nightingale, just as Stella said we would. We took the original registration card, photocopied it, and left the photocopy for the hotel's files. I told Runkle that I would like to have pictures of the hotel, doctor's office and pharmacy. He got on the radio and, about twenty minutes later, a departmental photographer showed up to take the photographs I had requested.

I recruited Newsome and Shields to help us at Mister Potter's daughter's garage. It was piled high with boxes filled with various drugs and other sundries. I was sure happy to have the extra help. Mister Potter was a friendly little man, sixty-ish, balding, with blue eyes and a fringe of gray hair. I learned that he had earned his way through pharmaceutical school as a professional boxer. He claimed to be a challenger for the world lightweight championship.

"Mister Potter, what we are interested in is your log book listing the sales of insulin, hypodermic syringes and needles," I said.

He was apologetic. "Boy, oh boy, that's really going to be a problem. You know, when I closed my pharmacy down, I had to get out in a hurry. The log books are in packing boxes somewhere in here. The contents of each box are listed on the lid, but I don't know exactly where those log books are."

About four hours later, we had waded through most of the boxes and had found his log books. We photocopied the pages of sales reports that were dated around March 17, 1960. We didn't expect Archerd's name to appear, and it didn't. We hoped we could match his handwriting to one of the signatures. No such luck.

I went back to the hospital to review Stewart's records, and made notes of which nurses had attended him, as well as who came and went from his hospital room, including his roommate. I would have to talk to them all, eventually. Since Doctor Sutherland had called Doctor Adrian Ver Brugghen in for consultation, I knew I needed to talk to him. He was kind enough to see me between patients. Doctor Ver Brugghen was a rather solidly built person, and, as his name indicated, his manner and brusqueness suggested that he was of German extraction. He let you know where he stood without hesitation.

I told him that I wanted to know about Frank Stewart and his consultation with Doctor Sutherland. He clearly remembered Stewart and the situation, and asked why I was interested in the case.

"We think Mister Stewart was deliberately murdered," I said. He quickly did a double-take and tried hard to control his rapidly rising temper. "You don't think anyone from the hospital or medical staff had any part in this!"

"No, no, Doctor. We think the person he came to Las Vegas with and gave the admittance history killed him. We think this person injected Mister Stewart with a lethal dose of insulin after he was admitted," I quickly replied.

"Well, from what I remember of this man's physical condition, you are going to have one hell of a time proving it!" he stated emphatically.

"Doctor, let's get back to when you were called in to consult with Doctor Sutherland," I urged. "How did you find the patient, originally?"

"First, I read the admitting history and studied his chart. I noted that he had had a convulsive seizure about four p.m. I saw him at five-thirty p.m. after he had been given three grams of sodium amatol, which put an end to the

seizures. He was warm and perspiring, which is typical following convulsive seizures. He could not be aroused, but
he had bilateral Babinski signs. Because of his apparent
comatose condition, his loose neck and Babinski signs, I
felt I was seeing the aftereffects of a convulsive seizure."

In rechecking the patient's hospital report, I did not
see any report of a blood or spinal sugar test. I figured that
I had about all the information I could get in Las Vegas.
Shields was weary of following me around and was ready to
go home. So was I.

12
Gladys Revisited

Back in Los Angeles, Walt and I met with Walsh and Etzel; I brought everyone up to date on the results of my trip. We discussed what our next move would be. We knew we couldn't prosecute Archerd for killing Frank Stewart because the act occurred out of state. We also knew we couldn't even file murder charges against him on Zella and Burney. "What about Gladys," Walt asked. "She could be next on his list."

I think we all were worried about that, ever since we started the Burney investigation. No one said a word for a few minutes.

"Why don't we pick her up at work without letting her know we are coming, take her to East L.A. station and talk to her? Whether or not we get anything from her, we have to warn her that Archerd might consider her a threat and kill her," I said.

Etzel said, "Yeah, we might be held responsible if that were to happen!"

I took Bob Chapman with me to pick Gladys from her job at the Elks Club in Alhambra. On the way, we stopped by the crime lab and dropped off the hotel registration card from the Sal Sagev Hotel along with a handwriting exemplar that Walt and I had taken from Stella while we were in Florida. John Harris, our handwriting expert, took a cursory look at both samples. "Unofficially, I think these two samples were written by the same person. I'll have an official report for you in a day or two, naming all the points of comparison," he said.

I liked doing business with John. He never steered me wrong and was always pleasant to work with. His position was not that of a sworn law enforcement officer, but civilian in nature. He was soft-spoken, in his late fifties, balding, and wore a hearing aid. He was about five feet seven, and weighed roughly 150 pounds. He always wore a dark suit with a gray snap brim hat. His demeanor exuded competence – a perfect witness in the court room,.

The handwriting exemplars told us that Stella had been truthful concerning the statements she gave us in Florida. I felt that things were looking up for us and that we were on the right track in piecing together the actions of this compulsive sociopath killer.

I had talked to Al Stewart, the manager of the Alhambra Elks Club, and told him we were on our way to pick Gladys up for interrogation. Mister Stewart was a friend to many law enforcement officers in the area. I had been there once for lunch with an FBI agent when I worked auto theft. At that time, I recognized several people; one in particular was Mel Viney, Chief of Police of South Pasadena. Mel and I had worked patrol together at Norwalk Station in the late 40s.

Mister Stewart was true to his word. He had made arrangements for someone to take Gladys' place while she was gone, without her knowing that we were coming. She was not completely surprised to see us, however, and accompanied us to East Los Angeles Station without complaint.

Walt was waiting for us when we arrived. Chapman excused himself; he was working on other cases. We took Gladys into an eight by ten foot interrogation room, gave her a glass of water, and made her as comfortable as possible under the circumstances. I told her, "Gladys, we brought you here because we need more information that we feel might help with our investigation."

She replied, "I'll tell you anything I know that you think might help you."

"There is another reason we want to talk to you: your personal safety. We think your husband has killed at least five people, including at least two wives. We think you are in real danger and may be next on his list."

This shook her up quite a bit. She nervously wadded up a small handkerchief and rolled it around in her hands. "I don't think I'm in any danger. Dale loves me very much. He is so good to me," she said, obviously not completely convinced. Walt took over the questioning at this point, and went over what she had told us when we talked to her about Burney's death. Her story never changed; we felt she had been truthful at that time.

After we cleared up a few points regarding Burney's death, we zeroed in on the Stewart death. I asked her if she knew Frank Stewart. "Certainly! I was married to him for over twenty years and then divorced."

"Have you remained in contact with him since?" I asked.

"Yes, I would see him from time to time. We remained friends," she replied.

"When did you marry Mister Archerd?"

"I married him twice. The first time was October 4, 1958, under the name James L. Arden. I remarried him on May 22, 1959, under his real name, William Dale Archerd."

"Is there any other connection between Frank and Archerd?"

"Yes, Dale was gone from home for four days in August of 1961. He came home around midnight on August 17. I had just received a phone call from a hospital in Las Vegas, telling me that Frank had died."

"Did Archerd know anything about Frank's death?"

"He said that he had heard Frank was in the hospital in Las Vegas, and that he had gone there to check on him. He said that Frank was okay when he saw him at seven p.m."

"What did you think of Archerd having been gone for four days and being in Las Vegas with Frank?"

"Well, it got me to thinking on it a little, so I started paying particular attention to everything I heard and saw. I went through his pockets and found an airline ticket to Las Vegas in the name of Don Nightingale. I thought that was strange, because Don was in an Army hospital on those dates."

I started on a different tack and asked her if she knew how many times Archerd had been married.

"I think at least three times that I know of. I think I've met them all. There was Dorothea, Eleanor who was the mother of his twin sons, and Juanita."

"Gladys, there was another wife before Juanita. Her name was Zella. She died shortly after Archerd married her. Then he married Juanita, who died on their wedding night. We believe he injected them with lethal doses of insulin."

"Dorothea told me that if I wasn't careful, he would inject me with insulin, just like he did to Zella and Juanita. She said I was too nice a girl to be mixed up with the likes of him."

"Now, do you see why we are concerned for your safety?"

"I understand, but he wouldn't do that to me. He loves me," she whined.

"That's what Zella and Juanita thought too, Gladys," I reminded her.

I continued, "Let's get back to Burney's death. Tell us what the mood was in your house following Burney's and Jennie May's deaths."

"Dale was kind of hard to live with, and we weren't getting along too well. Around the last of September or the first of October 1961, he wanted to go to Hawaii to sort things out, so we bought him a ticket at the travel agency. His son, Bob, and I took him to the L.A. airport. He called that night and wanted to come home, so I wired him a ticket. I picked him up the next day."

"Did you ever see any medical tools such as syringes around the house?" I asked her.

"Yes, I saw a syringe, dilator, darning needle, a red tube and speculum. And there was a vial with a rubber cover, too. He kept that in the refrigerator. He said it was sterilized water. I think those tubes were abortion instruments," she said. Her voice trailed off, apparently realizing that she was married to a man that wasn't very nice. She told us that her three daughters by Stewart didn't like Archerd. They thought that he was a phony.

I then asked her if she knew of any insurance policies on Frank. "No, but I think my daughters collected a small payoff as a result of his fall at the airport in Las Vegas. I don't know how much it was."

We felt that we had learned as much as we were going to from Gladys, so we took her back to the Elks Club.

On the way back to the office, Walt asked, "Whitey, I wonder what that trip to Hawaii was all about."

"I don't know, Walt, but I'll bet he had another scam going, don't you?"

"Yes, that bastard doesn't do anything unless there is something in it for him. At least we put her on notice that she could be next. We might have saved her life. Right now, we can't prove a damn thing. I wish we could come up with some direct evidence. We need something to kick start us again."

By the time we got back to the office, it was getting pretty late. We sat down and started a To-Do list. First, we had to find out about John Lawrence, the guy that had gone to Las Vegas with Archerd, Stella, and Jane Farrell. We ran a record check on Lawrence; he was originally from Cincinnati, Ohio. We dictated a short letter to the Cincinnati Police Department, asking them to run a local check on him.

Next, we contacted Guy Walker of the State Board of Pharmacy to locate Dorothea Archerd Sheehan. A few days later, we heard from Mister Walker. He gave us Dorothea's home address and phone number.

At about the same time, we received word from the Cincinnati PD that a John Lawrence had died of natural causes in October, 1961. We didn't pursue that lead any further, mostly for economic reasons. To this day, I regret not following up on that lead. I remember that Stella had told us that Lawrence was originally supposed to take the fall instead of Stewart. Archerd had told her he was worried about Lawrence ratting on him to the insurance company. He told her that he "took care of" anyone who crossed him. We wanted to keep our options open, though, in case we needed something else to add to our already bulging case file.

United Airlines agent John Clark checked his passenger lists for William Dale Archerd and James Lynn Arden. A J. Arden had flown from LAX on Flight 95T at five p.m. September 29, 1961 to Honolulu, returning the next day on Flight 94.

✼ ✼ ✼

13
Hit-and-Run Follow-up

Based on the information from Gladys and the mention of Dorothea's name in Andre's earlier reports, I called her and told her I wanted to talk to her about her ex-husband.

She said, "I'll be happy to talk to you, but not in front of my husband. He works rotating shifts."

I made arrangements to see her the following day, as her husband would be working the day shift. She told me that she was aware of Jennie May's and Burney's deaths, but suspected nothing. "I can't imagine he would kill his own mother and nephew!" she said, incredulously.

But I had to postpone our meeting. The workload was about to bog the whole bureau down; I had to begin working other cases again. Dorothea readily agreed to get together later.

Meanwhile, things were beginning to happen on the hit-and-run incident that allegedly put Archerd in the hospital. He had filed a fifty-thousand dollar injury claim against Mister Crossley and his insurance company. Naturally, investigators for the insurance company were interested in the information we got from Stella. We agreed to supply them with a copy of Stella's statement about her part in staging the alleged accident.

Walsh, Thornton and I went to Carr's office and brought him up to date on our entire investigation. Carr still felt that all we had was circumstantial evidence of several crimes with no direct evidence. He was right, and we knew it, but we felt we had to keep this case in front of him at any cost.

One morning, I got a call from attorneys Bob Ruther and Charles Morris, who were handling the case for Mister Crossley's insurance company. They wanted to get together with Walt, Carr and me. I didn't know what good that would do for their case, but we set up the meeting, anyway. It was still the same old story: "Get me some direct evidence."

A month later, Ruther called. "Whitey, I just got a call from Archerd's attorney. The pre-trial hearing for the Crossley matter has been set for November 15, 1962, and they want a deposition from Stella. The attorney will want to talk to Stella before the deposition."

"That's okay, just call me prior to her making that deposition," I told him.

A few days later, Ruther called back. "I just had a call from Archerd's attorney, and he wanted to know about the Stewart case. I don't know how he found out about that case, I sure as hell didn't tell him! If I find out anything, I'll let you know. By the way, at the pre-trial hearing in Florida, our attorney questioned Stella, using her statement taken by you early on. Their attorney demanded a copy and we had to give it to him." The pre-trial hearing was continued until March, 1963.

Eventually, Stella gave her deposition and was questioned by Archerd's attorney. As promised, we received our copy from Mister Ruther, attorney for the insurance company. It was almost exactly like the one she had given to us in Florida. Now Archerd would know that Stella had told us everything she knew. With this in mind, we called his attorney and told him that Stella's life was in jeopardy.

His reply was, "Her statement to you is full of holes. She makes a lousy witness. I'd like to get together with you and discuss it." It would be a cold day in hell before we would sit down with him and discuss our case.

The pre-trial hearing was held and a date set for trial. There were several continuances and other delays. Finally, on August 20, 1963, in Department Two of the Los Angeles County Superior Court, the Crossley case was dismissed with prejudice, thus ending any possibility that Archerd would collect the fifty thousand dollars he had worked so hard on. We hoped that was an omen that things would start falling into place concerning the rest of our investigation.

14
Archerd's Flight to Honolulu and Other Scams

In December, 1962, F.B.I. Agent Francis Galloway came into our office and asked for me.

"Sergeant White, I understand you are working on a case involving a Mister William D. Archerd, a.k.a. James Lynn Arden."

"Yes, we have been working on several cases involving him since about 1947. Why are you interested in him?"

"It's kind of a long story, but I'll make it as short as I can. On the twelfth of this month, as a result of the enlargement and remodeling of Honolulu Airport, they were cleaning out the storage that held lockers used by passengers to store items while they waited in the airport. In locker number 120, they found a brown leather briefcase. It contained a metal tackle box which enclosed sixteen sticks of dynamite, a two foot fuse with a dynamite cap attached, some galvanized wire, a box of ninety-nine Number Six dynamite caps, a quantity of 20-penny nails and two-inch finishing nails. According to airport records, the briefcase was deposited in that locker between noon September 30, and noon October 1, 1961. Gold initials W.D.A. were on the locking cap. A baggage tag from the Alexander-Young Hotel in Honolulu was attached. Records from the hotel reflect that James Lynn Arden of 1110 East Emerson, Monterey Park, California, registered at nine fifty-five p.m. September 29, and departed the next day. We know that he traveled from LAX to Honolulu on United Airlines Flight 95. The one-way ticket was purchased from a travel agency in Arcadia in the name of William Archerd. That name had been crossed out, and the name, James Arden, added." Walt looked wide-eyed and shrugged. He didn't say a word; he didn't have to. We both knew we were about to find out what Archerd was doing in Hawaii.

Galloway continued, "Our handwriting examiner determined that the handwriting on the hotel registration card was William Dale Archerd's. We also learned that a flight insurance policy in the name of James Lynn Arden, maximum coverage of seventy-five thousand dollars, was issued September 29, 1961."

Later, F.B.I. agents came by with the briefcase in question and wanted me to go with them to the Elks Club to see if Gladys could identify it as Archerd's. At first, Gladys had said it was the briefcase he always carried; she later denied it. Still later, Galloway said he had talked to Archerd. Archerd admitted that he went to Hawaii in September, 1961, because he and Gladys had had an argument. He was afraid it would become violent. He said he got in a poker game at the hotel and won twenty thousand dollars. He went to a dime store, bought a box and string, wrapped the money up, put it in his briefcase, and mailed it home. The money never arrived. He said he complained to the post office. The briefcase looked like his, but he couldn't be sure. Galloway said that Archerd agreed to take a polygraph, appeared on the stated date, but then refused on advice of his attorney.

Galloway wanted to talk to Dorothea about the briefcase; I wanted to ask her about the Jones case. Galloway showed her the briefcase. She said, "It looks like his. I remember it having a strap across the top with W.D.A. in gold embossed on it. These initials have been scratched off."

Galloway said, "Our lab says that the initials seemed to be W.D.A., but it was hard to tell. They had been scratched pretty deep."

Dorothea wasn't much help to Galloway, but since I had been trying to set a time to talk to her, I asked when she was married to Archerd.

"I was married to him from 1948 to 1956, when he had our marriage annulled and he married Zella. I told Zella she was too nice a woman to be married to the likes of him." Dorothea wanted to talk, so Galloway and I sat and listened. We occasionally interjected a question to keep her talking.

I also told her a little about the Frank Stewart case. "Oh!" she exclaimed. "That reminds me. While we were living in San Francisco, we were having financial troubles. Dale came home all excited one day, and said he was going to pack a bag, get an airline ticket, buy some insurance making his twin sons beneficiaries, and another policy making me and my son beneficiaries. Then he would build a device with gasoline, take it aboard the plane, and blow it up. That would solve all our financial problems."

She went on, "I read a detective story once where the murder was committed by insulin injection. I discussed this with Dale and he told me that was the way to commit the perfect crime, as insulin is a natural body hormone."

Galloway had no more questions; I asked her what she knew about the Jones matter. "You mean Bob Jones, the one that ran into the tree up in Ice House Canyon near Baldy?"

"Yes. Are you sure his name is Robert Jones? I can't find anyone by that name that died as a result of a traffic accident."

"That's as close as I can come to it. All I know is that his wife works at the library in Fontana. Dale had him brought to Kaiser Hospital in Fontana where Jones died. Dale told me that Jones had molested a babysitter and was about to go to trial. He wanted me to buy some insulin which he would give to Jones to give the appearance of a head injury, just enough to keep Jones in the hospital while Dale got the girl's family out of town. That way, he could avoid prosecution."

"Ted Nissen told me that you might fill us in on some of Archerd's activities," I told her.

"Yes, I talk to Ted once or twice a year. I told him I thought Dale was injecting people with insulin. You know he was Dale's parole officer?"

Galloway was getting a little nervous and wanted to end the interrogation, so I arranged to come back later to talk some more to Dorothea about the Jones matter.

A few days later, Walt and I had a few minutes to discuss our case. I brought him up to date on the briefcase and Dorothea's cooperation. Walt chuckled a bit, and said, "Now we know why he went to Hawaii. The s.o.b. didn't have the guts to blow himself up. I'll bet he had someone else in mind to carry the dynamite and explode it aboard the plane. Like I said, he never does anything unless there's something in it for him."

At about the same time, a couple of LAPD detectives from Forgery-Bunko came in the office. Allen Makshanoff and Jack Stiff were seasoned investigators; they didn't pussyfoot around. No small talk, strictly business. I guess they were just as overloaded as we were, with the brass breathing down their necks. Stiff said, "I hear you guys are interested in a dude by the name of Archerd."

"Yeah, that s.o.b. has us running around in circles. What's your interest in him?" I asked.

"Well, we have this Adam Henry in custody for forgery. Seems he cashed two one thousand dollar checks allegedly written by an eighty-three-year-old widow up in La Cañada. Says he was given the checks by a James Lynn Arden. They were to split fifty-fifty. Says this Arden sold our victim some hearing aids and while he was sweet talking her, he also sold her an old electric golf cart that had seen better days, for three hundred dollars. The victim went to another room to get her checkbook, wrote him a check for the hearing aids and another for the golf cart. Arden asked for a glass of water. While she was out of the room, he took two blank checks from the back of her checkbook."

"That sounds like our boy, all right. He always conspires with someone else and lets them take the fall." I gave them a brief rundown on our cases involving Archerd.

"Well, I see you have your hands full with your investigation, and won't be any help to us. Good luck. I don't know if our suspect could be of any use to you. We've got our case made on him, so if you are so inclined, have at him!" was his reply. I took their suspect's name and mug shot for future reference. It wasn't long before their suspect appeared on our scope.

✤ ✤ ✤

15
Other Investigations

It became harder for Walt and me to get together. We were back to the same old grind of changing shifts and investigating new cases. We had to take our turns at the four to twelve and twelve to eight shifts. Investigations included suicides, accidental deaths, drug overdose deaths, extortions, abortions, and anything else that the chief needed. The chief knew that he could count on the Homicide Bureau to do a complete investigation, no matter what the assignment was.

I even investigated a case or two of gonorrhea at one of our county jail facilities. It seems that an inordinate amount of venereal disease was showing up with inmates that had been in jail too long to have contacted it on the outside. The jail physician wanted something done before the whole facility became infected.

We drove to the Mira Loma minimum security facility in Antelope Valley and checked in with Jim Gregg, the duty sergeant. I had worked with him at Norwalk station back in the 50s. Cal Bublitz was my partner in this "crime of the

century." Gregg greeted us with, "Whitey, I sure am glad to
see you. I've been taking the heat for this dastardly deed.
Hell, there's nothing I could do about it. I've talked to all
the so-called victims and they won't tell me shit. Anyway,
I've set up a place for you to conduct your interrogations.
You know, this facility was originally an airfield where the
Canadian Air Force trained their pilots. The interrogation room is right up there in the old control tower." He
pointed to the tallest structure.

Gregg had all of the infected inmates isolated; he
brought them in one at a time. He was right; after the
fourth one we talked to, no one would admit to anything. I
think it was number five that we really zeroed in on. He was
a smooth skinned, roly-poly guy, about five foot nine, and
two hundred twenty pounds of sweetness. I started out by
asking him, "Francis, how long have you been in this jail?"

"Well, let me see, I thinks I been in here 'bout five
munts."

"How old are you, Francis?"

"I's thirty-two years old."

"Have you ever been in jail before?"

"Yessuh, I's been in jail 'bout fifteen years of mah life."

"Now, Francis, I want you to be completely honest with
me. Are you a homosexual?"

"Well, I been known to participate in what you might
call homosexual activities."

Jim Gregg was sitting in a straight-backed chair, leaning
against the wall. His hat was pulled down over his eyes. If
I hadn't known better, I would have sworn he was asleep.
With Francis' last statement, I heard a snort, followed by
some serious giggling. The chair was just about to slip out
from under him when I asked my next question.

"Do you have any problems getting along with other
inmates?"

"Nosuh, sergeant. I knows how to do time!"

"What do you mean by that?"

"Wellsuh, I gets me a good cell mate and takes good care of him. I buys him gee-gaws and looks after him."

"Do you mean sexually?"

"Yessuh, I sure does!"

Bublitz, who hadn't said a word until now, said, "For Christ sakes, Francis, *does* you have to take care of the whole damned compound?"

Gregg couldn't hold it any longer; his chair slipped from under him and he laid on the floor in convulsive laughter.

Francis and the rest of the infected inmates were bundled up and sent back to isolation in the main jail, where they recuperated from the dreaded illness. Chalk up another successful investigation.

We were no closer to having enough evidence on Archerd than Harry Andre was back in 1956; not even close to finding the 'smoking needle of death.' Stops had been placed on Archerd's name and aliases with the CII (Division of Criminal Identification and Investigation), Los Angeles Police Department., F.B.I., and local police agencies. There was nothing left to do but follow up on the Jones and Plum cases. Those cases were unusable at this point; there was no direct evidence, and they were outside our jurisdiction. We resolved to work on them as time permitted. What a laugh! About all we could do was to stay abreast of our current cases. We were really spread thin. It was uncommon in those days for anyone to have a steady partner. With only sixteen men in the bureau, someone was off sick, on vacation, or in court.

I don't know how it came about that I worked more cases with Roy Collins than anyone else. One cold, cloudy December day, the county road department was cleaning debris from culverts along Malibu Canyon Road. A couple miles south of Ventura Boulevard, they were forking tumbleweeds from the culvert when they discovered an eight-month-old, blonde-haired, blue eyed baby girl, wrapped in an old comforter. The comforter was made of wool squares sewn together. There were yarn ties looped through the center of each square. I remember one just like it that my mother made. She had it spread on the bed that I shared with my two brothers, Sam and Blythe. This little girl was laying there so peacefully with not a visible mark on her body. She looked as if she was sleeping.

I had been in the barrel while the rest of our crew was at lunch at the LAPD Academy. I called the lieutenant who sent Roy Collins out to help me. While I was waiting, the road crew did all they could to help me by keeping traffic moving. I walked up and down each side of the road, looking for anything that might be unusual. Actually, I had to keep moving so that I wouldn't lose it and bawl like a baby. I didn't want those men to see the tears that were building up. The baby was a perfect image of my daughter, Janet, when she was that age. The hardest part about my job was seeing children abused and mutilated.

It didn't take a brain surgeon to realize the only physical evidence was the baby and the comforter. About this time, the hippie generation was in full bloom in the Malibu hills. Roy and I knew them all by their first names before we wrapped up this case. I think we talked with everyone within a five mile radius, with no luck. After we became acquainted with the hippie families, we were convinced that the baby was not one of theirs. But we knew she was loved by someone, possibly the person that put her in the culvert. She had been placed there carefully, her face shone as if it was freshly scrubbed. Her clothes, including her diaper, were clean. Tumbleweeds had been piled over the mouth of the culvert to protect her from animals.

The autopsy determined that there was a *contra coup* type injury to her head and bruises around her ankles. In his report, the pathologist stated, "It seems that someone took this baby by the ankles and swung her head into a wall."

Roy and I had copies of her footprints sent to every county Bureau of Vital Statistics in the state. Photos of the comforter and artist's drawing of our victim were circulated to all the news media in town. The pictures were shown for several weeks on television and in newspapers, to no avail.

About two years later, Roy took a call from the Salt Lake City Police Department. "You fellows find an eight-month old baby girl in a culvert in your area about two years ago?"

As the detective talked, Roy motioned excitedly for me to pick up the extension. I picked it up just in time to hear, "We have this lady here in our hospital. She has both forearms in a cast. Her common law husband beat her with a tire pump. She tells us that a couple years ago, she and her husband and baby were in Los Angeles, looking for work. They weren't having any luck and were desperate. The husband came back to their motel room drunk; the baby hadn't had anything to eat all day and was crying. That animal grabbed her by the ankles and hit her head against the wall."

Roy asked, "Did she tell you where they were from?"

"Yes, they came from rural Virginia. The baby was delivered by a midwife. No record of her birth anywhere."

We didn't waste any time flying to Salt Lake City. We brought that animal back, convicted him and had him on his way to San Quentin faster than any trial I can remember. Sometimes, you get just plain lucky.

16
Back to Reality

I poured myself into my work, but every time there was a quiet moment, I would wonder what scam Archerd was pulling now, who was he setting up for a kill – Gladys, or some unsuspecting co-conspirator. These quiet moments were fewer and farther between, though. The population of Los Angeles County was exploding with a marked increase in crime. Finally, we got two additional men, but it didn't help much.

One thing I hated to do was work abortion cases. Wahlke loved to work abortions. I was stuck with him on a case involving a quack of a doctor who had done time in Q *(San Quentin)* for abortion and was back at it again. The doctor flew his 'patients' in from all over the country. Wahlke received a tip from a young lady who was a student at one of our large universities. She knew of someone that the doctor had performed an abortion on. She took Wahlke around to several locations and pointed out residences of victims. Wahlke always drove his TR4 roadster with the top down. He wore a pork pie hat and, despite his chunky frame, always looked like he had just stepped out of *Esquire* magazine. He was a fan of the big band era and would sing or whistle those old tunes; while driving one of his victims around, they would play "Name That Tune." It wasn't long before he had them so relaxed that they would tell him anything he wanted to know.

He worked up information that a flight was coming in from Kansas City with two or three patients for the doctor. He knew who the transporter was, but not where the abortions were to take place. Three teams were hastily organized to tail our subjects. We had some primitive walkie-talkies; luckily, we were always within a quarter mile of each other and able to make contact. We would alternate riding our subject's tail. We finally followed the car to a home in the middle of an avocado grove in the hills of Hacienda Heights. The transporter did not have a key to the house and had to sit and wait for the doctor. This gave us time to get into position to observe who was coming and going.

We found a resident who proved to be one of my son's professors at Long Beach State University. When we told him what we had in mind, he readily agreed to let us observe from his patio. We were only about fifty feet from the house, but we could only see the driveway to the garage because of the avocado trees.

The professor said, "You know, I knew there was something going on over there. I know the owners are honorable people. They're away on a trip. They must have rented the house while they were gone. Strange cars come and go all hours of the night."

Shortly, a car pulled into the garage. We knew it had to be the doctor when his patients exited the other car and entered the house. After about five minutes, we all moved toward the house. That was my first experience with an avocado grove; leaves a foot thick and dry, to say nothing of spider webs. It sounded like a herd of elephants was running through the grove. Apparently no one heard us, for as we kicked in the kitchen door, the first patient was in the stirrups and the doctor was about to commence his D & C. As a result of that fiasco, the doctor was seeing patients in San Quentin again. No abortions, though.

About the red TR4. It had a rear view mirror on each of the front fenders. The mirrors had to be adjusted manually; they couldn't be reached from the cockpit. Several of us delighted in moving the mirrors every time we passed Wahlke's roadster in the parking lot. Pissed off? Oh, you bet! He would come into the Bureau red-faced and so hot, one could imagine smoke and flame erupting from his nostrils and ears. This prank soon got old, though, and we had to select another target to harass.

I worked one homicide with Wahlke. A fellow walking along a rural road just over the Orange County line kicked a small cardboard box which felt heavy on his foot. He took a closer look. Inside the box was a human head. He quickly dropped the box and called the Orange County Sheriff's Department. For some reason or other, it was decided that whoever belonged to the head had been killed in our jurisdiction. Wahlke and I were the only ones around, so we were assigned to investigate this case.

We picked up the head at the O.C.S.D. and delivered it to our coroner's office. Our crime lab took the necessary hair and tissue samples, cleaned up the head, styled the hair in what was thought to be the style worn by women of the approximate age at that time. Cecilia Kienast, the first lady detective to be assigned to the Homicide Bureau, checked her missing persons reports. She found two or three possibles. We quickly eliminated a couple of them and decided that one in particular had to be our victim. We had the picture of the head and a picture of our missing person. Wahlke and I spent considerable time comparing the two. I told him that it had to be her; the hair, color of

the eyes, and the age were the same. Jim didn't say a word
for some time. Finally, he passed the pictures around to
six or seven guys that happened to be around during the
change of shift. Each one took a long look, made their
comparisons, and all agreed. "It has to be her."

Wahlke said, "Nah, that's not her." There was a chorus
of, "Bullshit, Wahlke, that's gotta be her!"

His reply was, "Five bucks says it's not."

I threw down my five bucks. Jim said, "Anyone else want
some of this?" Wahlke was well known for his love of gam-
bling; he would bet on anything. Everyone knew he lost
more than he won. All eight guys threw down their money.

"Is everyone down," Wahlke asked as he peeled off two
twenties, then said, "Now I'll prove to you that this missing
lady does not belong to this head. Just look at the ear lobes
on the head. They are almost non-existent and grow to her
neck. The lobes on the missing lady's ears are pronounced
and appear to be floppy."

Everyone grabbed for the pictures at once and yelled,
"Jim, you rotten bastard, you set us up!" Jim did his vil-
lage idiot giggle, shuffled the bills, neatly folded them, and
stuck them in his pocket.

We discovered that the box the head was found in originally contained a one gallon thermos jug from Sears. We
took the box over to the Sears store on Soto Street and
showed it to their head of security. He said, "Give me a
couple days and I may have an answer for you."

We were hardly back to the office when he called. "Fellows, I got lucky. This thermos was a mail order. Here is the
name and address of the person ordering it."

We copied the name and address and were out the door
like a shot. At that location, we found the husband of our
victim. We asked if he minded us coming in. He held the
door open for us, and said, "Please come in. What can I do
for you?"

"We'd like to talk to your wife, if you don't mind," Wahlke said.

"She's on a trip and won't be back for a couple weeks," he replied.

We asked for and received permission to search the house. We found a hair brush with several hairs in it. While Wahlke continued to look around, I called Cliff Cromp, our criminalist, and told him what we wanted. He and an assistant came out with the necessary tools and removed the trap from the bath tub. The contents were recovered and later analyzed. While Cromp and his assistant were at work, Wahlke and I continued questioning the husband. He stuck to the story that his wife had left the day before on a trip.

Cromp told us, "Unofficially, I would say she was dismembered in the bath tub. There is bloody water and what appear to be bone fragments in the trap."

Knowing that Cromp would never make such a statement if he wasn't sure of it, we placed the husband under arrest and put out an all-points bulletin. Several days later, we were notified that a leg was found in the Big Bear area, and a torso in Ventura County. The body parts were eventually identified as that of our victim. We never found the rest of her; her husband wasn't talking. Slam dunk conviction.

Fred "Sam" Savage and I worked a couple of cases. One which I'll never forget was that of a beautiful little black girl about seven years old, found floating just off the Santa Monica coastline. She was fully dressed in a neat, clean, skillfully made print dress, white underpants and knit undershirt. Her hair was plaited in neat pigtails with red ribbons tied at the ends. Her shoes were patent leather with straps across the instep; white socks trimmed in red matched the print dress and hair ribbons. Someone obviously loved this little girl, for it took lots of love to have dressed her so neatly and carefully. There were no marks of trauma on any part of her body. The only marks of any kind were on one cheek, and appeared to be post-mortem, caused by crab bites. The cause of death was determined to be drowning; her lungs were full of sea water. She hadn't been in the water for many hours, probably just long enough for post-mortem gases to raise her slender body to the surface.

Both Savage and I had trouble keeping from losing it. Can't you just see two big, hard-nosed detectives sobbing? We thought surely someone would report her missing in a day or two, but that didn't happen. We had photographed, fingerprinted and footprinted her, then had a bulletin prepared with as much information as we had. These bulletins were sent to every police agency in California, and every elementary school district within a hundred mile radius. Her picture and story were printed in every publication we could think of. We made personal appearances at several grammar schools.

Everyone in the Homicide Bureau offered their ideas and gave us their encouragement. Someone had to know of her disappearance, but not one call came in from anyone, anywhere. To this day, I think of that little girl and wonder who she was, and how she came to be lost without someone missing her. I guess I'll never know.

We had a Chief of Detectives one time that was not the ordinary run-of-the-mill chief. I think he thought he had psychic powers. Let's just say he was different.

Walt Thornton and I had a case in the Lennox area where a slightly overweight, buxom lady in her early twenties was raped and murdered in her home. There was no forced entry, indicating that it was someone she knew or at least let into the house voluntarily. She was found lying on her back, completely nude with forty-nine stab wounds on her torso. There were also some small puncture type wounds in her kidney area which were indicative of her being forced at knife point to obey someone's commands. There were also defense wounds on her hands and fore-arms.

We had only been working the case about two days and were making no progress. We were through with the scene and gave the landlord the okay to clean up the mess, so he could re-rent the apartment. We came in late in the after-noon, worn to a frazzle, as we hadn't slept or showered for thirty-six hours. Norm Hamilton was the lieutenant at that time. He met us at the door and told us the chief wanted to see the crime scene. He thought he might be of some help to us. The chief wanted to go to the scene at eight o'clock the next morning. I told Hamilton, "Hell, Norm, we have already had the house cleaned up. There's not even any furniture in it."

Hamilton said, "Golly, fellows, why did you do that?" We just turned our backs and walked away. We didn't think it was necessary to answer.

Hamilton went to see the chief and was back in five min-utes. "Chief said that's okay, he thinks he can get the feel of it, anyway."

I looked at Walt, he looked at me and said, " Kee-rist!"

Walt and I were there when Hamilton and the chief arrived. We all walked in together. The chief put his hand over his brow, closed his eyes, walked around the room a couple of times and said, "Fellows, your suspect works the night shift at Douglas Aircraft."

Hamilton and the chief walked out. Walt said, "Whitey, the only way we're going to keep that asshole off our backs is to solve this case in a hurry."

We had it solved the next day. As usual, our instincts were correct. The suspect was the "best friend" of our victim's husband and had admired her cleavage for some time. He knew the husband was going to be away, went to the location, she let him in, he propositioned her, she refused. The rest is history.

I have to admit that the chief wasn't far from wrong, though. The suspect did work the night shift in a machine shop, although not at Douglas. Psychic powers – maybe?

That chief didn't last long, thank God. I heard that he joined Richard Nixon's presidential campaign. As far as I remember, this was the only other case I ever worked with Walt Thornton.

These cases were not all, by any means, that I was involved in from 1963 to December 1966, when I started the Mary Brinker Post Arden Archerd case. Archerd did come to my attention during 1965, however, when he was arrested by Pomona Police Department for driving under the influence. This notification came from Leon Epps at CII, who flagged the Pomona Police Department report as a result of the stops Mister Epps placed on Archerd's name. I made a notification in my notebook with the intention of following up on that information in my first free moment. What is it they say about good intentions? I surely supplied one huge paving block to that road to hell! The next entry in my notebook was when I learned of Mary's death.

✲ ✲ ✲

17
William Edward Jones

Marty Deiro was my new partner. His mind was not cluttered with a lot of irrelevant facts; he could look at things from a fresh perspective. The District Attorney's office had assigned a first rate prosecutor, Ray Daniels, to help us in our investigation and hopefully prosecute that evil bastard. We were about to try and prove beyond the shadow of a doubt the murders of William Edward Jones in 1947, Zella Winders Archerd in 1956, Juanita Plum Archerd in 1958, Frank Stewart in 1960, Burney Kirk Archerd in 1961, and Mary Brinker Post Arden Archerd in 1966. I knew this was going to be one hell of a challenge that would require a lot of hard work and a great deal of luck.

A few days after Daniels was assigned to work with us, he was rear-ended in his new Buick. As a result, he spent a couple weeks recuperating from his injuries at the French Hospital in Chinatown. Marty and I would stop by every few days and brief him on what we had been doing. We told him that we had been successful in locating Dorothea and that we would wait until he was released to talk to her.

Daniels was eager to get out and get going. I could tell that he was champing at the bit; he hated to be held back by his injuries.

We had located several other witnesses in the Jones matter, including two of his sisters. One sister was still working at the Kaiser Hospital as a nurse; another was a housewife living in Riverside. We had been relying on Dorothea's earlier statement that Jones' name was Robert. As soon as we learned that his true name was William Edward Jones, the cards started falling into place. We also did considerable work on the Zella Archerd case. We located her daughter and son, and told them that we would call on them as soon as Daniels was available to be with us.

The Office of Naval Investigation located Stella for us. She still lived in Florida. We already had her signed statement from 1962. We sent her a copy and asked her to read it again and call us if she found that she was mistaken. She called and told me that she stood by her statement; it was exactly as she remembered it. "Just give me enough notice, and I'll be there to testify to everything I have told you," she said.

We were following the money trail for each victim. We had insurance company representatives and bank officials all lined up, so we could lay out what Archerd gained, or hoped to gain, from the death of each victim. We researched the medical records of each victim and located most of the doctors and nurses, as well as hospital records of each victim.

When Daniels was discharged from the hospital, we were waiting for him with more information than most men could process in several weeks. Daniels was an extraordinary man and a fine attorney. When our first meeting was over, he took copies of our reports and notes home with him. At seven-thirty the next morning, Marty and I were in the coffee room, sipping on cups of stale coffee so strong that it could have curled my hair (if I had any) when Daniels walked in, poured a cup of coffee, took one sip and spit it in the trash. He said, "How the hell can you drink such stuff? It tastes like lye!" About then, Baby Jane, our super-secretary, walked in, washed the coffee urn and made fresh coffee.

When we had started on our second cup of coffee, Daniels said, "Well, fellows, let's get this show on the road. We're going to take one case at a time and talk to all the witnesses you've located. From this point on, I don't want you taking notes. Your notes are discoverable and mine are not. I'll do the note taking. First, let's start with Dorothea. She can give us a head start on Archerd's background, as she was married to him at the time he worked at Kaiser Hospitals in Oakland and Fontana."

I called Dorothea. She agreed to see us at ten that morning, providing we would be through talking with her before three. She didn't want her husband around while we were there. We were concerned about scaring her to death when three suits, two of us as big as the side of a house and one five feet seven in his elevators, walked in on her.

I had talked to her a couple years before. She remembered me, so we really didn't have to worry. This was our first co-interview by the three of us. I took the lead and introduced Daniels and Marty. Then I went into our spiel about the case and what we suspected. Right off the bat she said, "Look fellows, I know this guy Archerd better than any of you. Whatever you say to me or ask me will not shock me. I will be as honest with you as I can, and tell you what you want to know."

I let Daniels take over, as he would be the one who would question her on the witness stand. A couple hours later we walked away, satisfied that she had told us all she knew about Archerd.

Dorothea told us that she first met Archerd in 1946 when they both worked at Kaiser Hospital in Fontana. She was employed as a special nurse; Archerd was working in an industrial management trainee program. He told her that he had been employed as a first aid attendant at Kaiser and had previously worked at Camarillo State Hospital. He was a nurse working with doctors in treating mentally ill persons with insulin shock therapy. He had also worked as a nurse at Cedars of Lebanon Hospital.

Dorothea and Archerd were married August 27, 1949. At that time, she was interested in writing novels. She talked to Archerd about the use of insulin and that this would be a good way to kill someone in her story. He agreed and showed an interest. However, a short time later, she read a detective story where a murder was committed by the use of insulin. Since someone else had used this method, she decided not to write such a story.

Daniels asked her, "Did you know William Edward Jones?"

"Yes, but I thought his name was Robert. Dale and I met them socially, but were never close. Dale told me that Jones had driven a babysitter home one evening and had raped her. The girl's family was really upset. He wanted to get Jones out of circulation for a while until he could get the babysitter and her family out of town. He wanted me to buy him a vial of insulin. I bought the insulin at a pharmacy and gave it to him when he and Jones came over that evening."

Daniels asked, "Did you buy any syringes at the time you bought the insulin?"

"No, he already had syringes; he used to give his wife, Eleanor, and himself vitamin B-1 injections."

"Did you know at that time that Archerd intended to kill Jones?"

"The thought never entered my mind. I just thought he was trying to help Jones out."

"Did you know how Jones was admitted to Kaiser Hospital?"

"I heard a few days later that he was found passed out in his car that ended up against a tree up near Mount Baldy. The next thing I heard was a call from Dale. He wanted to know if I was available to act as a special nurse for the Jones family. I told him I would."

"When did you receive this call from Archerd?"

"Saturday evening, just before I went to bed. A short time later, I got a call from the hospital asking me if I was available. I said I was; I was told to report at seven o'clock Sunday morning."

"Who was present when you arrived at Jones' hospital room?"

"The Jones family. They were there up to and including the time Jones died."

Daniels took Dorothea through Jones' hospital chart. She pointed out that he had been admitted at one a.m., October 11, 1947, and that convulsions started at three a.m. the following morning. The patient was breathing irregularly and perspiring profusely at nine a.m. that morning. The patient was given aspirin, codeine and Demerol at five a.m. and glucose continually until he died at eleven a.m.

"When was the next time you saw Dale Archerd?"

"A few days later. I asked him what happened, if he had given Jones too much insulin. He simply said that Jones was no damned good, that he had raped quite a few babysitters and that he was better off out of the way."

At that point, Daniels was slowing down a bit, as if trying to line up the facts. So I started asking Dorothea a few questions.

"Did you initiate the annulment of your marriage to Archerd?"

"No, that lousy bastard did! I found out that his marriage to Eleanor was still in effect, as no divorce had been

filed. Our marriage was annulled May 14, 1954. I agreed
to the annulment because I wanted to correct the situation
and re-marry him. The next thing I knew, he had married
Zella the day after the annulment!"

Dorothea could barely contain her anger. Her eyes
were wide and her speech louder and sharper the more she
talked. I let her cool down a bit, then asked her, "Did you
ever meet Zella?"

"Hell, yes, I met her! I told her what a rotten son of
a bitch she had married. I told her she would never be
happy, married to him."

"When did you learn of Zella's death?"

"I think it was a day following her death, the latter part
of July, 1956. He came around and told me about the 'robbery' in their home and about their being injected in the
buttocks during the robbery. I asked him if insulin had
been used and he kicked me in the ankle under the table,
and looked around to see if anyone overheard our conversation. He just kept coming around. We were making
plans to remarry."

"Did you know Juanita Plum?"

"Yes, she lived on Prospect Street in Monrovia. She
lived next door to the Bemmers. Dale and I both knew
the Bemmers. Dale started putting moves on Juanita.
The next thing I know, he is living with her. Shortly after,
there was a fire there. On the night of the fire, Dale
came by my place at one a.m. and stayed about half an
hour. I found out later that he was supposed to be in Las
Vegas at that time. Someone told me that while he was in
Las Vegas, he went out for a drink, took a plane back to
L.A., visited me, and when he left, took his clothes over
to Kathleen McConnell's, an old girlfriend's place, then
flew back to Vegas."

"Do you know of any other dealings Archerd had with
Juanita?"

"I know she gave him some money to start up a business. I think it was a phony business that Dale could write checks on, but I can't be sure of this. Oh, he told me that Juanita came to him and asked for a piece of jewelry that he had taken from her. He refused. I asked him, don't you have any pity for your victims? He said no, they asked for it."

That was a pretty good story and deserved a lot of checking out. We headed back to the Hall of Justice to review what we had learned and to lay out the steps we were to take during the course of this investigation. We knew we had to talk to the attending physician at the time of Jones' death, as well as members of his family who were present at the hospital when he died.

The three of us were together on an average of eighteen hours a day. Our singular motivation was to gather enough evidence to prove beyond a shadow of a doubt that Archerd had killed our six victims by injecting them with a lethal dose of insulin. From the first week of April, 1967, until the last week of March, 1968, we were inseparable. We got to know each other's strengths and weaknesses as well as we knew our own. We shared our most personal problems and at times, dealt out advice as well as criticism. None of us resented the criticism; we took it in the same spirit as the well-meant advice.

At times, we would get into some heated discussions and there would be brief flares of temper. These discussions usually resulted in complete agreement between us. We never ended a day without complete harmony.

With the information that Marty had developed from checking Archerd's employment records at the Kaiser Steel Mill and the hospital, we were able to locate several persons that knew him well, including business people around the community of Fontana.

Wilnora Harrison was a registered nurse employed by Kaiser Hospital. She was also Jones' aunt. We talked to her at home, showed her a picture of Archerd, and she readily identified him as Dale Archerd. She said she knew him as someone that held a responsible job around the hospital. She also said that Archerd and her nephew were close friends.

Daniels started the interrogation with, "Mrs. Harrison, when was it that you first saw your nephew at the hospital?"

"It was about eleven-thirty a.m. on Saturday, October 11, 1947."

"What was his condition when you first saw him?" Daniels asked.

"He was breathing very heavily, perspiring profusely, and very much in shock. His body movements were very jerky. He was also unconscious, and I felt like he was terminal," she said as she wiped away a tear.

"Who was there when you first saw him?"

"Well, there was Dale. He was in and out all evening long. I saw Dale give my nephew an I.V. I asked the floor nurse to get an order from the doctor for something to relieve his convulsions. She brought it in a syringe with a needle and said the doctor would be up in a bit and give it to him. Archerd said, 'Tell the doctor not to bother. I'll give it.' Dale injected it into the vein. This was about one or two o'clock, Sunday morning." She went on to describe the convulsions that Jones was having.

Mrs. Harrison was relieved about seven-thirty a.m. Sunday morning by a young nurse that Archerd had brought in. She did not remember her name.

I asked Mrs. Harrison if there was anyone else in the room during the time she was with her nephew.

"Yes, my sister, Leila Thompson, who is also a registered nurse, was with me most of the time. The rest of the family was in and out throughout the night."

"Had you heard anything about Jones being accused of molesting a twelve-year-old babysitter?"

"Yes, as a matter of fact, all the family members raised money to give to her family to get them out of town. I don't know how much was raised, but I contributed five hundred dollars. My sister, Jones' mother, sold two lots in Fontana and gave all that money, but I don't know how much. Also, Mrs. Thompson gave around five hundred. Two of Jones' sisters also contributed. Thelma, Mrs. Glenn, put up around five thousand. I really don't know how much we collected totally."

Then Daniels asked, "Mrs. Harrison, who ended up with this money after it was collected?"

"All the money was given to Dale. He was supposed to give it to the babysitter's family."

Daniels again. "Mrs. Harrison, was Mister Jones a diabetic?"

"No sir, no one in our family was a diabetic, as far as I know. He was a perfectly healthy, normal person."

"Thank you, Mrs. Harrison, you have been most helpful."

Thelma Glenn, one of William Jones' sisters, told us that Archerd and Jones were friends. About a week or two before Jones died, she was at his home along with several other people: Jones, his wife, Agnes, her aunt, Leila Thompson, who was Wilnora Harrison's sister, Archerd, and a man she didn't know. This man was in the living room. The purpose of the meeting was to gather as much money as they could to get the family of the twelve-year-old babysitter out of town in order to subvert Jones' prosecution for rape of the babysitter.

Daniels asked her, "Mrs. Glenn, how much money did you contribute?"

"I think about five hundred, maybe a thousand. No more than that."

"Who did you give this money to?"

"Dale Archerd was standing there by the kitchen sink, and he took all the money."

"Did you ever find out who the man in the living room was?"

"Archerd told me he was the father of the babysitter."

"Did Archerd tell you what he was going to do with the money?"

"He said he was going to see that them 'Okies' were going to leave the state; that he would follow them and see to it that they did just that."

"Do you know how much money was collected by the family to pay off the sitter's family?"

"Not exactly, but I think it was in the neighborhood of ten thousand dollars."

I finally got a question in, as Daniels was catching up on his notes. "Mrs. Glenn, what was the status of Mister Jones' health?"

"As far as I know, he was as healthy as a horse. I've never known him to be sick."

"Had he ever been hospitalized before this incident?"

"Yes, he had a car accident a few years ago, and hurt his legs pretty badly. He spent some time in the Santa Fe Hospital in Los Angeles."

"As far as you know, was he a diabetic?"

"No, there has never been a diabetic in our family."

Daniels resumed the interrogation. "Did Mister Jones ever complain of any of the following symptoms, or have you ever observed these symptoms: faintness, profuse sweating, weakness, extreme hunger, rapid pulse or heartbeat, inward trembling, headache, visual disturbance, mental confusion, disorientation, coma or convulsions?"

"No, never," she answered.

The next person we wanted to talk to was Doctor Alvin Sanborn, who was director of the Permanente Medical Group and Kaiser Hospital in Fontana. We made an appointment to see him at nine a.m. the following day. He was waiting for us with Jones' hospital record on his desk. Doctor Sanborn was a quiet spoken man, about fifty, six feet tall, slender build. There was an unmistakable air of confidence about him. I sensed that he was eager to help us, and would cooperate with us all the way. I was right.

Daniels surprised the doctor with his direct in-depth approach. He went over every line of Jones' hospital record, from admission, until Jones died. Near the end of the interrogation, Daniels asked, "Doctor, now that we have reviewed the entire hospital records, and what we have told you of our suspicions, do you now have an opinion as to the cause of death?"

"Mister Daniels, at this point, I would have to say he died from hypoglycemia, caused by an injection of insulin."

My opinion of Ray Daniels soared to a new level. Not only was he a great prosecutor, but his medical knowledge was extensive. I think Doctor Sanborn was likewise impressed.

We spent several days at Kaiser Hospital, with nurses, lab technicians, and anyone else we could find who was willing to talk to us about Archerd or Jones. Daniels inspected records of every lab test of any of Jones' body fluids, and spent hours having lab technicians explain to him the process of testing such fluids. He recorded the chain of possession of each sample tested to insure that no other patient's fluid was tested by mistake, and that said fluid was, in fact, Jones'.

While Daniels and I pursued the case from the medical angle, Marty was out gathering more information on the alleged rape. He found the original report at the San Bernardino County Sheriff's Department and obtained the rape victim's true name and address at that time.

Marty also found Sam Knox, one of Archerd's golfing buddies. Knox ran a used car lot on Merrill Avenue in

Fontana. We talked to Knox the next day at his business. He told us that he had sold a used Buick to a man named Keafer. He was told by a friend that Jones was involved with a babysitter incident, and that the girl was Keafer's daughter. Knox was somewhat reluctant to talk to us about his used car deals. A little gentle persuasion assisted him in a dramatic recall of events. Knox produced a report of sale, dated September 23, 1947, for a 1934 Buick, California license 75E910. He stated that Jones and Archerd paid $308.50 for the car. Archerd took the car to Keafer, but returned it shortly, saying that Keafer wanted a better car. Knox refused. Archerd took the car back to Keafer. The family left that day for Indiana, and never returned. It's amazing what some people can remember with a little gentle persuasion!

When we got back to the Hall of Justice late that afternoon, we sat down and reviewed what we had learned about the Jones case. Since it wasn't in our jurisdiction, we had done very little work on it. Now that we had found that Jones' symptoms were the same as our other victims, we knew that we had to investigate the case as if it was ours. Marty Deiro had done a good job running down leads while Daniels and I were otherwise occupied. The following is an example of Marty's orderly mind, taken from his notes:

Sequence of Events:

9/10/47 10:30 p.m. Alleged babysitter incident.

9/12/47 3:30 p.m. Jones arrested.

9/13/47 Jones arraigned in Fontana Justice Court. Released $5,000 bail.

Between 9/19/47 and 9/23/47 Jones and Archerd together at Sam Knox's used car lot. Archerd took two cars for Mrs. Keafer to look at. She didn't like either car.

9/23/47 Jones paid $308.50 cash for a 1934 Buick sedan. Archerd took the Buick out to Mister Keafer. Archerd and Mister Keafer signed papers for the car. The Keafer family left California and never came back. Archerd followed them to Yuma, Arizona, gave them $300 and sent them on their way.

10/3/47 Mrs. Glenn brought money to Jones' house, gave money to Archerd. He said the man in the living room was babysitter's father. The father wanted more money and said he would leave town. Archerd said he would follow them and make sure they did.

10/6/47 San Bernardino Sheriff's deputy went to serve subpoenas to Mr. and Mrs. Keafer to appear at preliminary hearing re the alleged rape, which was set for 10/8/47. The Keafer family was gone.

10/7/47 Day before preliminary hearing. Archerd told Mrs. Engleman that suddenly the family was coming back to town, that he would meet them at the state line and shoot them if they continued on. Jones' mother said, "No." Archerd got more money from Jones' family to pay them off.

10/10/47 Jones stopped by mother's house but wouldn't come in for breakfast. That same day, Archerd called Dorothea, and told her to go buy him some insulin. Near supper time, Jones and Archerd went over to Dorothea's, where she gave him the insulin.

Jones told his wife, Agnes, he was going to Camp Baldy to make arrangements for the two of them to spend the week-end. He never returned.

10/11/47 12:40 a.m. Jones admitted to Kaiser Hospital. Agnes and Archerd at hospital after 1:00 a.m. Jones family at hospital all day Saturday and Sunday.

10/12/47 Dorothea on duty 7:00 a.m.

Jones died 11:00 a.m. Archerd and Jones family present.

After we had checked and rechecked this chronology, Daniels said, "Whitey, we need to talk to the babysitter's family. We need to verify the facts surrounding the Keafer family and their leaving town. Do you think we can find them?"

"Ray, if they haven't disappeared off this planet, we'll find them. And, by the way, who do you think the man in the living room really was?"

It took a week or so to make arrangements for me to fly to Cincinnati. The county, as usual, had money problems, and the powers that be didn't look too kindly towards financing air fare, meals, and accommodations on a mere investigation. Since there was no superior court case to charge the expense to, I had to wait until an extradition came up in the proximity of my destination. The closest any fugitive that warranted being brought back for trial was waiting in jail at Kankakee, Illinois.

Finally, the extradition papers were ready for me at the district attorney extradition section, along with a county credit card and airline tickets, from Elwin Holt, the lady in charge. I had known her for several years; I had gone after fugitives before and was familiar with the procedures. I still got the usual admonition; "Whitey, take good care of that credit card and use it only for car rental and gas. We are flying you to Cincinnati and from there to Chicago. You'll have to drive down to Kankakee and pick up your prisoner."

I could tell right off that this wasn't going to be a pleasure trip. I flew into the Cincinnati airport at Covington, Kentucky, rented a car, drove on a ferry across the Ohio River into Indiana, and got into Lawrenceburg a couple hours before dark. Sheriff Carl Gillis welcomed me with a big smile and a firm handshake. He was about forty-five years old, roughly six feet tall, with a full head of hair which was starting to gray at the temples.

Traditionally, counties in the Midwest are considerably smaller than here in California. Things move at a much slower pace, and people have time for one another. Sheriff Gillis was definitely a people person, and he genuinely loved to talk. He introduced me to his wife, who was head dispatcher, matron, chief cook and bottle washer. She was busy and had little time to talk.

Earlier, I had informed the sheriff, by phone, of the purpose of my visit. He had the necessary information ready for me. "It's a little late to go out to the Keafer place; we go to dinner about six. Why don't we wait until first thing tomorrow? This is our usual evening to have dinner with the resident state trooper. I want you to meet him, anyhow."

What could I say but, "I'm ready when you are. But I need a place to sleep tonight. Where's the closest motel?"

"It's about twenty miles out, but I wouldn't recommend it. You can sleep in jail tonight. Don't worry, our apartment is on the top floor, and we have an extra bedroom and bath."

This was a new, up-to-date facility. The sheriff's office was on the first floor, the jail on the second and third floors.

We had dinner at a local restaurant. The state trooper proved to be a congenial fellow, about thirty. It didn't take long to find out that my two new acquaintances were dedicated professional law enforcement people. The conversation was relaxed and lively. Eventually, we ended up talking sports. I found out in a hurry that we were right in the center of the basketball belt of the country. "Baasket Bawl" was the only thing of importance in their world. Poor Mrs. Gillis was almost bored to tears!

The next morning, the sheriff took me out to meet my witnesses. We found that the mother and father had passed away; the only other person who could possibly remember what went on back in 'Californy' was our rape victim's sister, Rose Turpin, who lived in Cincinnati. I hoped she would be sharper than anyone in the family we had talked to so far. She wasn't.

Rose's apartment was on Race Street in downtown Cincinnati. The building was a two-story, red brick structure, probably built around the turn of the last century. The mortar was crumbling and several bricks were missing from the walls. The only entrance was from a small rear courtyard. Her apartment was on the second floor. I started up the stairs, not knowing if my weight would cause them to collapse. I hugged the wall as I went up, and then carefully picked my way across the porch.

I finally made it to the apartment door, where I was met by Rose, a five foot two inch, one hundred eighty pound hulk of flesh which was absolutely the worst picture of a human being imaginable. There were eight people living in that two room apartment. There was one forty-watt bulb hanging from the ceiling by a cord about three-quarters of an inch thick. Most of it was grease soaked fuzz from years of frying food in the cramped quarters.

After meeting Rose and her family, it took a few minutes to gather my thoughts. My mind had wandered a bit, and I was thinking, *What in hell have I got into here?*

I asked Rose, "Do you know why I'm here?"

"No, sir, I don't."

"You are Carrie Keafer's sister, aren't you?"

"Yes, I am, is she in some kind of trouble?"

"No. Do you know where we could find her?"

"Yes, she's out in Chino, California. Why do you need to talk to her?"

"Do you remember the time Carrie was molested back in 1947?"

"I sure do, that's when the family moved back to Indiana."

Rose went on to tell me that she knew William Edward Jones as her insurance agent. She knew Sam Knox, as she bought all her cars from him at his car lot in Fontana. She said that Jones' mother came by the day after he was arrested and offered Mrs. Keafer three hundred dollars to drop the charges on Jones. Mrs. Keafer refused. Three or four days later, a short, heavy-set man came and offered her a thousand dollars. Finally, an agreement was made September 23, 1947, when Archerd delivered a 1934 Buick sedan. The Keafer family, except for Rose, left California that same day and never returned. About two weeks later, a police officer came out to serve a subpoena for the preliminary hearing, set for October 8.

Another sister of Carrie's, Verna Keafer Asten, who was sixteen at that time, did make the trip to Indiana. She was present when a man and woman came over and talked to her parents about dropping the charges on Jones, and their leaving the state. Eventually, all ten of the family left in a car that was given to them. A man traveling alone in another car followed them all the way to Yuma, Arizona. This man bought them breakfast and gave her mother three hundred dollars. Mr. and Mrs. Keafer died after moving back to Indiana.

Marty and I spent many hours trying to locate and identify the short, heavy set man that appeared at Jones' house where Archerd collected all the money, and the man that appeared at the Keafer house and offered them a thousand dollars to leave the state. That man is still a mystery.

I took an extra day and drove up the Ohio River to Ashland, Kentucky, for a short visit with Midge's mother, brother and sister-in-law. If I hadn't, my name would have been mud around our house. A couple days later, I picked up my fugitive in Kankakee, drove to O'Hare airport, and caught my plane home.

My prisoner was a congenial sort, who wanted someone to talk to. He was a native of the area and proud to point out places of interest. Not having had too much sleep since I had restarted trying to nail Archerd, I wasn't much interested in any detailed conversation. I did, however, note that the terrain was very flat with a black gumbo appearing soil. Great dirt for growing hybrid De Kalb corn.

We landed at LAX around midnight and were met by a deputy from our Lennox station. Our fugitive was booked and sent to the county jail. I got in my car, hoping I could make it home without nodding off. That was the longest forty-five minute drive I can remember.

Midge was still awake when I got home, and naturally had to hear all about my trip. I managed to give her the highlights before I dozed off. I wanted to know what was new at home since I had been away, but it had to wait.

18
Zella

The following day Marty, Daniels and I met in our fifth floor closet we used as an office and discussed where we were in the Jones case. We had just received a six-page, single-spaced typewritten letter from Jones' sister, Mary Englemann, from Crawfordsville, Oregon. She stated in detail all she could remember of the facts following Jones' arrest, his 'accident,' hospitalization, and death. Her story verified those of her sister and aunts. She was sure in her mind that Archerd had caused Jones' death, and as a result, the deaths of Jones' mother, father and wife. We all felt that she would be a good witness, should we need her in the future.

Daniels said, "I think we have gone as far as we can at present on the Jones case. Let's set it aside for a while and concentrate on Zella's death."

I got the Zella Archerd murder book and handed it to him. "Harry Andre did a very thorough investigation of Zella's death and documented it in a professional manner.

Why don't you take this home with you tonight? Tomorrow we can decide where to start."

The next morning, he stopped by the coffee room at seven-thirty a.m. Marty and I were on our second cup of coffee. "The coffee's fresh, Ray, I just made it," Marty said.

Daniels didn't say a thing until he had finished about half a cup, then suddenly said, "Whitey, the first thing I want to do is interview Harry Andre."

"God damn, Whitey, you're psychic! You said that would be the first thing he wanted to do," Marty said with a chuckle.

We finished our coffee, and then we headed out to East Los Angeles Sheriff's Station, where Harry was presently assigned as lieutenant in charge of the Juvenile Bureau. I knew Harry would be there by the time we arrived. He always wanted to be a step ahead of the crew when they came in. He had just finished scanning reports that had come in overnight.

Andre said, "I'll let my J.G. make the assignments; let's go into the interrogation room where it will be quiet."

We spent a couple hours in that cramped room. Again, I was surprised at how much Daniels had assimilated from the murder book. He took Andre step by step from the first call from Covina Police Department through the entire investigation. It was, and still is, the policy of the Los Angeles Sheriff's Department to assist other jurisdictions with homicide investigations. Covina Chief of Police Allen Sills asked for our help. Andre and Claude Everley were assigned. Since there was a robbery reported, Sergeant Larry Picano from our Robbery Detail also assisted. Sergeant Art Gillette from the Narcotics Bureau was also assigned because the victims of said robbery were injected with some kind of drug.

Archerd had told Andre and Everley that their home had been invaded by some robbers who allegedly injected both Archerd and Zella in the buttocks. Neither the four L.A.S.D. investigators nor the Covina Police Department believed for an instant that there was any robbery. The "robbers" allegedly took around six hundred dollars from Archerd, put a pillow over his and Zella's head, tied them up and left. Zella became comatose, and never regained consciousness.

Archerd hired Velma Rosenau to care for Zella while he was at work. Archerd helped Velma change the bed sheets, as Zella had voided. When she first saw Zella, Archerd showed Velma two needle puncture marks on Zella's right buttocks, while he was telling Velma about the robbery. While at the house, Velma saw a syringe with a needle attached in the bathroom medicine cabinet. Sergeant Gillette searched the bathroom and found a 20-gauge hypodermic needle in a drawer of a cabinet by the sink. He *did not* find a syringe with attached needle in the medicine cabinet. About a week later, Covina police officer, Richard Hughes, found a vial marked NPH U80 insulin in a vacant lot about one hundred and fifty feet from the Archerd residence.

Archerd called Doctor George Chambers to come and examine Zella. Chambers arrived in the evening and Archerd told him the robbery story: Zella was conscious and able to talk; she didn't seem too upset about what had happened. The doctor gave her a grain and a half of seconal as a precautionary measure. He never gave her an injection.

Andre gave Daniels a rundown on his entire investigation. Daniels had already been clued in on all the work Harry had done, but wanted to get it from the horse's mouth, so to speak. He knew that we only had one shot at convicting Archerd and didn't want anything left undone. At this point, Daniels was up to speed on our whole investigation and was just as dedicated as Andre, Marty and I were.

Harry was aware of Juanita's death in Las Vegas in 1958, as well as Frank Stewart's death in 1961. He had told the

Las Vegas authorities that he suspected Archerd had murdered both of them.

It was amazing how easy it had been to locate witnesses after twenty years. Darlene Lopez, Zella's daughter, still lived in South Gate and was surprised when I called her to make an appointment to see her. The three of us drove down and spent a couple hours with her. She was a pretty lady, about thirty years old. She kept her middle class home neat and clean; pride of ownership was evident everywhere.

It was obvious that reliving the suspicious death of her mother twenty years ago was painful for her. She shed a few tears, then quickly calmed herself. "I know that evil man killed my mother as sure as I am sitting here," she asserted.

We didn't want to make it any more painful for her; we got right down to business. I showed her his picture. "Do you know William Dale Archerd?"

"Yes, I know him. I think I first met him at my mother's home here in South Gate in November 1955."

"Do you know how your mother met Mister Archerd?"

"She'd just sold her home that was awarded her from my parents' divorce. She had purchased a new house and was in the process of remodeling it. She had bought some folding doors from May Company, and after they were installed, she found something wrong and complained. The manufacturer, Modern Folding Doors, sent Mister Archerd out to make adjustments. This was in October 1955. She was quite impressed by him. She was led to believe that he had an important position with the company, and was quite well off financially. He continued to come and see her. Shortly, they talked of marriage. She believed everything he told her."

She paused briefly, wiped away another tear, and continued, "You know, she even bought him a new station wagon because the old panel truck he was driving was falling apart.

They took several trips to San Diego on business. He would drop her off downtown while he "took care of business," then he would pick her up late in the afternoon. She felt sorry for him because his 'first' marriage didn't work out, and it was so hard to take care of his and his ex-wife's sixteen-year-old twin boys. He told her he had some property in escrow that would net him seventy-three thousand dollars, and that he had had some trouble with his housekeeper and wasn't able to get his hands on any money."

Darlene excused herself to get a drink of water, then returned and continued where she had left off. "Since they were talking of marriage, he talked her into selling her house and moving into his. With his money tied up and her house was not out of escrow, she borrowed six hundred dollars from the bank for their honeymoon. They drove up to Reno on May 14, took a motel room, where she stayed while he went to make wedding arrangements. He was gone for quite some time. When he came back, he said, 'Let's go on down to Las Vegas, I don't like this town.'"

This was the same day Archerd had his marriage to Dorothea annulled. The next day, May 15, he and Zella were married in Las Vegas!

"Mother was so impressed with his medical background. She said she felt much better just knowing she had an almost-doctor in the house. She showed me needle marks on her upper arm where Dale was giving her iron shots."

At this point, Daniels asked her, "When was the last time you saw Archerd before your mother's death?"

"The early afternoon of July 25, he came to my apartment. He said he and Mother had been out to dinner early in the evening the night before. They got home about nine p.m. He put on some records. Mother went to the bathroom to change, when two men came out of the second bedroom. One had a gun. They put Mother and Dale in separate bedrooms. They put a pillow slip over Mother's head, tied her hands and gave her two injections. He told me he was injected, too, but freed himself, then freed Mother and called the police. He said they were tied up for about fifteen minutes and robbed of about six hundred dollars. He said Mother was all right, just a little upset. He had hired a registered nurse to stay with her while he was gone that day."

"Did you go over to see your mother?"

"No, my two-month-old baby was sick. I called my brother, Bob, and he agreed to go, but his gas tank was empty and he was short of cash. Dale went over to Bob's and gave him money to buy gas. Bob told me later he thought it was strange that when Archerd opened his wallet, it was full of bills. How could that be, when just the night before, he had been robbed of all his money?"

"What was your mother's health like just before she died?"

"She was in good condition, a touch of arthritis, but nothing serious."

"Do you know if she was a diabetic?"

"I know she was not! No one in our family has ever suffered from diabetes."

"Has she ever been in a coma, had high blood pressure, suffered from any blackouts or had periods of extreme hunger, or profuse sweating?"

"No, I'm telling you she was in near-perfect health!" as if to imply "Dammit, didn't you hear me the first time?"

Later, we would talk to Darlene several times to ask a few new questions or to clarify some of the things she told us.

As we headed back to the Hall of Justice, I said to Daniels and Marty, "That rotten bastard played her like a fine fiddle!"

Daniels said, "He sure knows how to pick his victims. But let's get on with this show. I want to talk to Doctor Chambers, then Velma Rosenau, Darlene's brother, Bob,

the realtor that sold Zella's property, and the bank peo-
ple who banked her money from the sale of the property.
Marty, why don't you start on that while Whitey and I find
Doctor Chambers?"

19
Happy Camp

Doctor Chambers was living in a little logging town called Happy Camp, which is about seventy miles southwest of Medford, Oregon, just barely in California. Daniels and I flew to Medford via PSA, Pacific Southwest Airlines, chartered a brand new Cessna 172, and flew down to Happy Camp. The weather was cold, cloudy and windy when we left LAX. By the time we landed in Medford, it was spitting rain. During the flight, we reviewed our case so far and were satisfied we were going in the right direction. As we then reclined our seats, Daniels said, "Whitey, you know what would be nice is if we could find a small county where I could be District Attorney and you could be Sheriff. We'd have it made."

"Yeah, Ray, that would be nice. No traffic, very little crime, and very low pay. Low pay with peace and quiet and no hassles has its points, though."

We had called Doctor Chambers from Medford and told him we would be down in about an hour. The Cessna got airborne before it really started raining. About twenty miles out and five thousand feet up, it turned to snow with five hundred foot down drafts occurring at irregular intervals. I had assumed the seat up front with the pilot, and Daniels sat in back. Those down drafts were so abrupt and violent that we lost everything in our pockets. I looked back and saw Daniels' briefcase floating above his head. His face was in a barf bag, which he missed about half the time. Our pilot didn't seem to mind the rough weather. He surely could handle that little plane.

There really wasn't much room in the cabin. I had to sit with my knees almost touching my chest. I wasn't too concerned about our safety until my chin met my knees at the bottom of a severe down draft. Finally, there was a fortunate break in the clouds, and I could see a small landing strip running along the Klamath River. The pilot eased it in, slide-slipping, and brought it to a stop at the very end of the short runway.

Doctor Chambers was leaning against a 1956 Ford Victoria with a ton or more of mud under the fenders. He was wearing a hunting cap with ear flaps, and a king size Mackinaw. His lace-up boots were kind of the worse for wear, but they were still capable of holding all that red mud without losing a single clod.

I climbed into the back seat; obviously, everything except human beings had been hauled in it. There were log chains, come-alongs, axes and other tools lying on the floor boards. We drove over to his office across the river and were met by an emergency case. A young boy had been accidentally shot in the shoulder by his buddy. Luckily, the .22 caliber bullet wound was a "through and through," and not life threatening.

Doctor Chambers told us to come in so he could talk to us while he worked on his patient. Besides, he had a waiting room full of patients with snotty noses, sore throats, and belly aches. Ray took notes all the time the doctor was talking and had enough information to enable him to examine the doctor in front of the Grand Jury.

We walked down the decomposed granite street that was covered with about a quarter inch of yellow-brown slurry, and stopped at the only restaurant in town. We ordered steak sandwiches and jumbo fries. We were oddities, the only two guys in the café wearing suits and street shoes. The old loggers were curious, but too polite to ask questions.

I asked the bartender where a good motel was and he said, "Don't have no motel, but that hotel across the street is the best in town. It's the only one."

Daniels poked me and said, "I'm not spending the night in this town! I'm calling our charter and have him pick us up ASAP!" There was never another word about being a district attorney in a small county!

The charter plane showed up with enough light to take off back to Medford where we caught a flight to San Francisco. That was the roughest commercial flight I have ever been on. With layovers and bad weather all the way to LAX, I got home about three a.m., feeling like I had been rid hard and put in the barn wet.

The next morning the three of us got together and exchanged information as to our activities. Daniels and I ran what we had learned from Doctor Chambers by Marty. He was surprised when we told him that the doctor remembered seeing only two puncture wounds on Zella's buttocks. "That s.o.b. gave her a couple more shots between the doctor's visits. No wonder she was comatose when he came back to see her," Marty said, excitedly.

"And another thing, Velma Roseneau wasn't a registered nurse. She was a caregiver from an employment agency. However, she had worked as an Licensed Vocational Nurse in years past," Daniels told him.

We passed on more of our talk with Doctor Chambers; Marty laid out what he had accomplished while we were gone. He had located Zella's real estate agent, Don Sawyer, and through him, learned that the total pay off to Zella from the sale of her property was slightly in excess of ten thousand dollars. The selling price was fourteen thousand five-hundred dollars. Three thousand five hundred sixty dollars and six cents $3,560.06 was paid to the lien holder, the Bank of America in South Gate, plus his seven-hundred-twenty-five-dollar commission for selling the property.

Archerd had called Mister Sawyer several times, wanting to know when the escrow was closing. Sawyer got the impression that Archerd wanted to use the money for a business deal somewhere in San Diego County. He also identified a picture of Archerd as the man he was talking about.

The escrow company, Crocker Citizens National Bank in South Gate, issued a check in the amount of $10,237.45 to Zella Winders July 13, 1956. This check was deposited the same day in Zella and Archerd's joint account at United California Bank in Covina. On that same date, there was a check written in the amount of five thousand dollars, deposited in the Bank of America in Covina, to the account of "W. Dale Archerd, 4910 N. Citrus, Covina." This was the address of Dorothea, Archerd's previous wife. Archerd's B of A account was closed August 7, 1956, with a check written in the amount of $5,014.71.

Of course, Daniels wanted to talk to everyone involved with the sale of Zella's property and the banking of the final check. He secured subpoenas *duces tecum* for all the paper work involved in each transaction. I knew what his intentions were; he was gathering all the evidence he could, to show that Archerd methodically set out to take all Zella's money, even if he had to kill her.

We had already established his *modus operandi* in the Jones case. That is, setting Jones up as the victim of a traffic accident, getting him hospitalized at Kaiser, where Archerd worked, and finally killing him with an injection or injections of insulin.

We still had to talk to all the pathologists and toxicologists who examined Zella, and made arrangements to do that as quickly as possible. Doctor Newbar, who was retired and was suffering from a serious heart problem, was found in Glendale. After talking with him for a few minutes, he said, "Fellows, I certainly do remember this case, but I'm not up to talking about it. Why don't you talk to Doctor Jerald Ridge? He's the pathologist in Ventura County. He assisted me in the post-mortem examination." We really wanted to have Doctor Newbar on our side; he was one of the best pathologists in California. As it worked out, though, Doctor Ridge proved to be a major asset to our case.

We gathered up the coroner's protocol and toxicology reports and headed for Ventura. Doctor Ridge made us welcome; after he perused the coroner's reports, he said, "Yes, I remember that case. I was so sorry that we couldn't have been more help to Sergeant Andre back in 1956, but there just wasn't the know-how available to us. We had to go by what we saw at the time. We couldn't say that Mrs. Archerd died from anything not covered in the protocol."

Daniels was satisfied that Doctor Ridge was a competent autopsy surgeon. He started quizzing the doctor on the steps taken during the examination. "Doctor Ridge, did you make microscopic slides of any tissue?"

"Yes, as indicated here, we took slides of the usual body organs, paying particular attention to the brain, liver and pancreas."

Daniels then formulated a series of hypothetical questions based on what was in the coroner's protocol and what Doctor Ridge now knew about Zella's death. Marty and I knew that Daniels was prepping himself, as well as our medical witness. We also knew that Daniels felt he had another eminently qualified witness to use at the expected grand jury hearing. Daniels really had the bit in his mouth and was headed for the home stretch!

20
Camarillo State Hospital

At our regular seven-thirty a.m. coffee klatch the next morning, Daniels said, "We are at the point where we need to know all we can about Archerd's background. Let's make arrangements to go to Camarillo State Hospital. We might strike it rich."

Marty got up and returned ten minutes later with the keys to a new green "undercover" Plymouth sedan. Before this investigation was over, we would have driven over twenty thousand miles in that car. Undercover means the car wasn't skunk colored, but it had the usual spotlights and fifteen inch radio antenna on it. We didn't fool anybody.

Marty said, "Let's go!" but Daniels thought we should call first.

I said, "Ray, I have found that in situations just like this, it's always better to hit 'em cold turkey. That way, if there is anything to hide, they wouldn't be prone to hold anything back. In this case, I'm sure they have nothing to hide, though."

"Well, if you say so, let's go."

Marty became our official wheel man. He liked to drive, anyway. Ray rode in the back seat with his three-ring binders, making notes and running different scenarios by us. Daniels had never been on the investigative side of a criminal case, and Marty and I thought we could teach him a thing or two. We soon found out that we had more to learn from him than he could learn from us.

At Camarillo State Hospital, we really did strike gold. The whole staff was eager to do anything they could for us. We started with the director of personnel, who furnished us with Archerd's personnel records, then steered us in the direction of where the Insulin Shock Wards were from 1939 through 1941. Camarillo State Hospital is now the campus of California State University Channel Islands, which opened for enrollment in the fall of 2002. The Spanish Revival architecture has been preserved, making it one of the most beautiful campuses of all the Cal State universities.

While at the hospital, we were able to identify some of the personnel that worked on the ward. We were lucky to find two trainees that worked with Archerd on the insulin shock ward: Leo Bradley Miller, who lived in San Francisco, and Evelyn Lucille Briggs, who lived in Three Rivers, California. The doctor in charge was Doctor Grace Thomas, an eminently qualified psychiatrist and expert in the treatment of mentally ill patients. She was a pioneer in the field of treating schizophrenics using insulin shock therapy. Her resume read like it came from Who's Who in Medicine and Who's Who of American Women. Actually, we had her resume from the National Directory of Medical Specialists.

Doctor Thomas was possibly in her late sixties. She had trouble walking, so it was necessary for her to use a cane. We talked with her at her home in Sonora, California, where she was director of Tuolumne County Mental Health Services.

Daniels started right in, showing her a picture of Archerd. "Doctor, do you know this man?"

"He surely looks familiar, but I can't say that I know him."

Daniels then filled her in as to the purpose of our visit. He started with Archerd's employment at Camarillo and gave her a rundown on all of our victims. He told her that we believed that Archerd learned about the effects of an overdose of insulin while he was an attendant in the insulin shock ward and that he had killed at least six people by injecting them with an overdose of insulin.

"Well, it's certainly possible to kill someone with an overdose of insulin. At Camarillo and all the other places I have worked, we were extremely careful when treating a mental patient with insulin. Anyone who is familiar with this type of therapy knows when to administer glucose to stop or reverse any action caused by an injection of insulin. The recovery is dramatic. Let me see that picture again. I think I can remember him as one of the attendants that worked on the ward. Seems as if he had been around hospitals a lot before coming to Camarillo, but I don't remember him, or any attendant, giving insulin to anybody. That was always done by a medical doctor. We did, however, require all our attendants to attend a class in the proper methods to use during treatment. The main thrust of this class was how to recognize symptoms of overdose and what steps to take to revive the patient."

Daniels continued, "Doctor, we would like you to review the medical history of each of our victims and review each patient's hospital record from the time they were admitted until their death. We are about ready to go to the grand jury with this case. We will need you a couple days before the hearing, so you can interview the family members. We'll pay you expert witness fees and your expenses while you are testifying. Are you agreeable to do that for us?"

"Oh, yes, I'll be happy to help you any way I can."

"We will give you plenty of notice so you can make any arrangements needed. By the way, do you have a preference for a hotel?"

"If you don't mind, I would love to stay at the Mayflower Hotel. It holds many precious memories for me," she answered.

"We'll see to that, Doctor," Daniels said, nodding to Marty, who made a note. Marty was just handed a new job: booking agent for all our out of town witnesses.

We left Sonora and headed for San Francisco. Daniels ensconced himself in the back seat with his three-ring binder and busied himself recording his conversation with Doctor Thomas. I heard him close his notebook, just as he said, "Whitey, do you realize what a jewel of a witness we just found? What a lovely lady and so qualified!"

"Yes, Ray, I think she will be one of our most important witnesses and she is such a lovely person. I wish all our witnesses were as well qualified and personable as she is."

Marty injected himself into the conversation with, "Yeah, I don't mind seeing that this nice lady has everything she needs. However, I think I'll have to have some help with the new assignment you gave me, Ray."

"Marty, you can handle it. When we get back, we'll make out a tentative witness list and then decide how much help you'll need. I have faith in you, Marty."

Marty's reply was a big Italian snort with the appropriate hand gesture.

We were headed for Bradley Miller's place on Noe Street. There was no one home, so we tried his neighbor. She said, "He won't be home 'til about 5:30; he works for the electric company. I saw him down the street working on a power pole a little while ago. He may still be there."

We drove about three blocks down Noe Street, and there was a power truck parked near a pole. We parked and I walked over. I said to a man seated behind the wheel, "Are you Bradley Miller?"

"Who wants to know?" was the reply.

I identified myself and said, "He's in no trouble. I just need to talk to him a bit."

"Then I guess you've found him. I'm Leo Bradley Miller, what can I do for you?"

"We need to talk to you about the years you spent at the Camarillo State Hospital as an attendant."

"That goes back a spell. I hope I can be of some help."

"We just came by your place. Would it be possible for you to take time and go back to your house so we can talk?"

No problem at all; I'll just let my partner finish up. No one will miss me."

He got in the car and we drove back to his house. Noe Street runs along the top of a ridge. The houses are very close together and are built right up to the sidewalk. Mister Miller lived alone, but his house was as neat as if he paid a full time maid; everything in its place.

After he made us welcome, he offered us a cold drink which we politely refused. It was my turn to make the opening spiel. "Mister Miller, do you know William Dale Archerd?" as I showed him a picture.

"Sure, I know him real well. I used to baby sit for his twins some when he and Eleanor wanted to go out. That was when we both worked at the hospital in Camarillo. I haven't seen Dale in several years. I still hear from Eleanor on my birthday and at Christmas. They've been divorced a long time. Why are you interested in him?"

"Well, we believe he has killed at least six people with injections of insulin. I understand you worked with him on the ward where schizophrenics were treated with insulin shock treatments."

He stepped back and almost stumbled off the curb. "I was sure afraid it would be something like that, but murdering six people – my God, what a horrible way to die."

He finally composed himself, then stated, "Yes, that's true. I worked at that hospital from 1937 to 1941. Archerd came to work there in 1939."

"Did you receive any special training while working on the shock treatment ward?"

"Yes, we all did. We took a course of instruction from Miss Silvia, a registered nurse."

"Did you take notes during this training?"

"Yes, we all did. I still have mine."

Bingo! You could almost hear our eyeballs click as the three of us looked from one to the others.

"Would it be possible for us to see those notes?"

"Sure, but it may take a while, they're downstairs," he answered.

He led the way down several flights of stairs. If you walked to the back of the house on the first floor and looked down, there was a drop of at least fifty feet to the ground. After reaching the lowest point, Mister Miller stopped and said, "Those notes should be right about here."

I looked where he was pointing. Packing boxes were stacked on a slant in piles about four feet high, and were all labeled with their contents by year. He started shuffling boxes. The three of us pitched in. Five dusty hours later, he shouted, "Here it is!" He opened the box and came up with several pages of neatly handwritten notes that told all about the process of treating mental patients with insulin shock therapy. The notes were as clear as the day he had written them.

"Was Archerd present at all the classes you attended?" I asked.

"Every one of them. He took notes the same as everyone."

"Then, as a result of this training, all of you in that class were qualified to assist the doctors in administering insulin shock therapy?"

"That's correct. We all knew the proper dosage to give and what to do to bring the patient back to normal."

Mister Miller loaned us his notes so we could make copies for our files. He told us he would be willing to testify and would be available most any time. We thanked him for his cooperation, and then headed for Three Rivers, California, where we would talk to another classmate of Archerd's.

Evelyn Lucille Briggs was an attendant at Camarillo State Hospital at the same time Archerd and Miller were. She took the same training and worked in the insulin shock wards. She identified Archerd as one of the persons with whom she carpooled and worked. Her last name at that time was Sammann.

Daniels asked Mrs. Briggs if she knew Doctor Grace Thomas.

"Yes, Doctor Thomas was in charge of the insulin shock ward."

"Did you ever see Mister Archerd giving insulin injections?"

"I can see a syringe in his hand, but I'm not sure he actually gave an injection."

"Who was the instructor of the classes?"

"Mary Silvia, an RN from the Department of Institutions."

Mrs. Briggs' statement was very similar to that of Bradley Miller. We were happy that we had two almost identical statements, plus that of Doctor Thomas. I told Marty, "Let's get this automobile headed south. My daughter's getting married in a few days and I want to help Midge get things set up."

Daniels said, "I've got to get home, too. I have a lot of medical research to do on this case and I want to do it while it's fresh in my mind. I can't believe we have accomplished so much on this trip. We have just talked to three of the most important witnesses in this whole investigation. There's no doubt in my mind that that he had the means and the opportunity to kill those six people, if not several others. Oh! By the way, let's call Doctor Arquilla when we get back and see how he is coming along."

The next thing I heard was Daniels shuffling his three-ring binder again. Marty kicked it up to about 80; six hours later we were back at the Hall of Justice. There was a note on my desk from Captain Etzel, "See me." That had to wait until the next day. Although I didn't do any of the driving on that trip, I was worn to a frazzle. I was averaging about four hours sleep a night, eating fast food on the run, and missing my family terribly. It must have been two a.m. when I finally pulled into my driveway. It was probably a good thing I didn't have a garage door opener. Otherwise, I might have spent the night in the car. Just getting out in the night air and raising the garage door woke me enough to drive in and make it to bed. I don't think Midge woke up, but I'm not sure. Some nights she deliberately feigned sleep, so I wouldn't have to talk.

Six o'clock came mighty early. Midge was shaking me, trying to wake me, and was about to give up when one eye popped open. "We need to talk before you go to work. I need some help with the wedding. Janet is about to wear herself out and me, too. Can't you take a little time off to give us a hand?"

I mumbled my way to the shower and felt some better afterwards. At breakfast, she said, "I want you to go down to Lakewood Gardens Community Center and make sure there are plenty of chairs and tables to accommodate all our guests at the reception."

I called in late that morning and left word for Captain Etzel that I would be in around ten a.m., as I had some personal business to take care of. I went down to the Lakewood Gardens Community Center. Their custodian assured me that accommodating our wedding party was no problem at all. I called Midge at her job and told her everything was taken care of, and not to worry.

She said, "Please get home at a decent hour so we can have a meal with the whole family. There won't be many more occasions for the four of us to dine together as a family." I heard her trying to stifle a sob.

"I'll do my best, Honey. I don't know what's in store for me; I have a command performance with Etzel as soon as I get to the office. I don't know what he has in mind."

I felt like I was letting her down big time by not being free to help her with planning what was to her the biggest event in her life. I walked into the captain's office, just as he returned from talking to the chief. "Whitey, I haven't heard from you in some time and the boss wants to know what's going on. I want you to bring us up to date as to where you stand in the investigation and what we can expect in the near future."

Then he started his normal ritual of asking questions, some of which surprised me. I was impressed by what he already knew. He kept asking questions until he found one I couldn't answer; then he was satisfied.

"Al, Ray and I have an appointment this afternoon with Doctor Arquilla. He has finished his tests on the brain tissue we gave him, and he wants to tell us about it."

"Good, but get that memo in as soon as possible, by nine a.m. tomorrow, for sure."

Daniels, Marty and I found our way through the maze at the U.C.L.A. Medical Center to Doctor Arquilla's office. He was glad to see us and said, "There's good news, fellows: I have examined the brain slides of Zella, Burney, and Mary, and was able to find severe brain damage in each case.

After reviewing their medical history, I am of the opinion that the brain damage was caused by hypoglycemia. Further, that the only source of this damage could have been from an injection or injections of insulin."

Daniels said, "Doctor, that's good news. Do you have any information yet from your radioimmunoassay of Mary's brain?"

"No, that will take a while. That assay is no simple test. All the control samples have to be just right. I'll let you know as soon as I have the test results."

Daniels and the doctor talked in medical terms so far above my head that Marty and I had trouble following along. We had our own conversation.

Marty said, "I knew all along that my *paisano* would come through!"

"Yeah, Marty, that Italian friend of yours is going to be our most important witness. I'm sure glad he is being so thorough. He knows he'll be making medico-legal history when he testifies in this case."

That afternoon, I sat down and dictated the following memo to our super-secretary, Jane Sawai:

"During the week of 5-15-67, brain slides from Victims 2, 5 and 6, were supplied to Doctor Arquilla from the UCLA Medical Center, and on 5-26-67, Doctor Arquilla advised Mister Daniels and Lt. White that he was able to detect brain damage from the slides, and after reviewing the pertinent medical history of each victim, it was his opinion that this brain damage was caused by hypoglycemia. Further, that this hypoglycemia caused such great damage to the brain tissue that the only source of this damage could have been from an injection of insulin.

On 5-28-67, Lt. White, Deputy Deiro, and Mister Daniels of the District Attorney's Office, contacted Doctor Grace Thomas at her home in Sonora. Doctor Thomas was the doctor in charge of the Insulin Shock Ward, Camarillo State Hospital, during the time our suspect was employed there, and it was hoped that she might recognize his photograph or remember him as having worked under her. She was unable to say definitely that she recalled the suspect; however, there was something familiar about him. Doctor Thomas was supplied with medical histories and hospital records of Victims 1, 4, 5 and 6, and was asked to review these records, as an expert in insulin shock therapy, to determine whether or not these victims died as a result of an injection of insulin.

On 5-29-67, the above-named investigators interviewed Mister Bradley Miller at his home in San Francisco, and as a result of this interview learned that Mister Miller was an attendant at the Camarillo State Hospital during the time our suspect was employed there. He had personal knowledge of the suspect working on the Insulin Shock Ward and had had many conversations with the suspect about vital signs of insulin shock as they appeared on patients being treated.

Currently, an effort is being made to determine how many witnesses will be available during the last week of June or the first two weeks of July, so a date for a Grand Jury hearing may be set."

I made it home by the skin of my teeth, just as Midge was putting supper on the table.

✻ ✻ ✻

21
Janet's Wedding

The wedding went off without a hitch. Janet was beautiful; all the bridesmaids were gorgeous in gowns that my mother had made. Mom was an expert seamstress, and had made all of Janet's formals, from Rainbow Girls right up through high school proms. I've got to say that I was one proud poppa, as I walked Janet down the aisle at Bellflower Presbyterian church. The church was packed; Janet and her new husband, Lonnie Lovingier, were very popular in school and had many friends. With all my relatives living close by, I think the rest of the crowd was outnumbered.

Lonnie looked like an ad in *Esquire* magazine, all decked out in his new tuxedo. He was a little pale around the gills, though. I don't know who was the most nervous, him or me. After all, I was giving away my Janet, my only daughter. Our son, Van, did his thing, seeing that everyone was seated properly. Damn! He was one good looking guy.

Midge wasn't one to cry easily, but as we walked by her on our way to the altar, I could see copious tears running down her cheeks. She was losing a daughter that she very much loved. As I sat down beside her, she said, "Daddy, isn't she beautiful?" I gulped some sort of an answer, for I, too, was about to lose it.

I think that was about the most beautiful wedding I ever attended. Jo Gannaway, her birth buddy, sang, "O Promise Me" with an emotional quiver in her beautiful soprano voice. She was about as close to being Jan's sister as could be, since Midge and Jo's mother, Evalynn, were pregnant at the same time.

All the guests showed up at the Lakewood Community Center for the reception. Midge had had a lot of help from her PTA friends. She bought hams and turkeys and her friends volunteered to cook them. Bonny Priddy, a cook at Mokler school cafeteria where both Jan and Van had attended, prepared the vegetables and desserts. What a great meal!

After the newlyweds finally left on their honeymoon, several of our closest friends came by our house where I poured the first round. After that, Ralph Gannaway tended bar. I took my Jack Daniels and water and sat in my recliner. I leaned back, and that's the last I remember; I didn't even finish my drink. The next thing I knew, Midge was shaking me, "Wake up and go to bed. Everyone has gone home." I barely remember crawling into bed. I didn't know how tired I really was. It turned out to be the longest night's sleep I'd had for the past year, and would be the longest for the next year.

✵ ✵ ✵

22
Las Vegas Again

The next morning, Daniels, Marty and I headed for Las Vegas. Marty, as usual, was at the wheel, and we were in Las Vegas before noon. As we cruised down the strip, a couple of punks in a souped-up Chevy pulled alongside, revved the engine a couple times and yelled over to Marty, "What are you f—n' San Francisco cops doin' over here in Vegas?"

"Lookin' for assholes like you, dip shit!" Marty replied.

They couldn't get away from us fast enough. They laid down about fifty yards of rubber and were gone. That's the last we saw of them.

Daniels said, "I think we need another undercover car, maybe a Buick or Chrysler."

"Hey, Ray, it wasn't the car they made, it was Marty's Dago face. He looks like a San Francisco cop," I told him.

"Yeah! Up yours, White!" He followed by the universal finger signal.

I was glad that Marty was a good natured fellow; I didn't want the ex-Pacific Fleet heavyweight champ pissed at me.

I had already laid out the places and people to see, as I had been there before. Daniels wanted to talk to our witnesses himself. He wanted to know what each witness was going to say when answering questions from the witness stand. He carried that big three-ring binder everywhere we went.

Our first stop was at the Stardust Hotel, where we had made reservations. (We got a better cut on the room rate there). We went to the Southern Nevada Memorial Hospital where Daniels wanted to see the layout and talk to as many people as we could locate regarding the deaths of Juanita Archerd and Frank Stewart. This included the admitting doctors, as well as nurses and patients that were there during their stay.

Doctor Ralph LaCana told us that he was on duty March 12, 1958, and had worked in that capacity for five years. He did not remember Juanita being admitted on that date, but identified his signature as it appeared on the hospital record which we showed him. The remaining handwriting appeared to be that of a nurse, A. Cullen. Daniels asked the doctor to examine the record, and then asked him, "On the record then, were you given any history concerning Juanita Archerd's illness?"

"Yes, that woman was brought in by her husband. She had been drinking."

"Was there any statement made by the husband as to the patient's condition?"

"The husband had said that the patient suddenly stopped breathing and became cyanosed before she came to the hospital. That was apparent."

"If there had been any history given you of this woman having taken an overdose of barbiturates, would it have been recorded?"

"Yes, if there was such a history, we would have hospitalized her, washed her stomach and kept her there for twenty-four hours for observation."

"All of this would have been reflected in your records?"

"Very definitely."

"Doctor, if a person is perspiring profusely, comatose and twenty-four hours later following the onset of a coma, wherein these symptoms are first observed, would this indicate an overdose of barbiturates?"

"No, sir, it could be an indication of an insuloma, or too much insulin."

Doctor LaCana was a straight-from-the-shoulder sort of person, and that made it easy to complete his interrogation in short order.

While we were on the subject of Juanita's death, we went to the Monie Marie Motel on Las Vegas Boulevard. We talked to Marie Allen, one of the owners. She was aware of what we wanted to talk about. Since I had called her earlier, she had the registration cards available.

I showed Mrs. Allen a picture of Archerd. "Yes, that's him. I remember him coming to our motel twice."

"Is there a particular reason you remember him?"

"Yes, the first time was in May of 1957. Mr. and Mrs. Archerd checked into room Number 2 and they stayed two or three days. He was gone for some time. Mrs. Archerd came into the office to answer a phone call. The call was to the effect that their house was burning down. Sometime later, Mister Archerd returned to the motel and told me that their house was afire. He was just down there and now he had to go back."

"Any other reason you can remember him?"

"Well, they came back almost a year later. He came in and asked me if I remembered him, and I said, 'I do, but can't remember your name.' When he signed the registration card, I recognized him as the same man whose house burned down about a year earlier. What made him even more memorable was that they wanted the same room as they had the last time. He said they were there to renew their wedding vows. Mrs. Archerd got sick and went to the hospital, then came back to the motel and died."

"What date did they check in the second time?"

"March 10, 1958."

"When was the next time you saw him?"

"About seven-thirty a.m., March 12. He came to the office and told me that his wife was very ill. He asked me to call an ambulance."

"Did the ambulance take her to the hospital?"

"Yes, but about two hours later, they both returned to the motel."

"Did you talk to them on their return?"

"I talked to him; he said his wife was better, so they released her."

"Anything happen after that?"

"He came in a couple hours later and said his wife was extremely ill and he was worried about her. He wanted me to call a doctor. I called Doctor Cherry. He came out and examined her. Doctor Cherry said she appeared to have had drugs of some kind, but was coming out of it."

"Did Archerd say anything at that time?"

"I heard him tell Doctor Cherry that she was a pill taker."

Mrs. Allen went on to say that Doctor Cherry said Juanita was coming out of it and to keep her on her feet, give her coffee and milk of magnesia. She noticed that Juanita was really helpless, that her face was swollen with beads of perspiration on her face and forehead. After Doctor Cherry left, the Archerds pulled their drapes closed. Sometime early afternoon, Archerd came to the office and told her that he thought his wife was dying. He called Juanita's daughter, Joan Swann, and told her that her mother was seriously ill. She called the ambulance again and Mrs. Archerd was taken away. She never saw Juanita again.

On the way back to the Stardust Hotel, I asked Daniels, "Who are we going to believe, Doctor LaCana, or Doctor Cherry? They each have a different diagnosis."

"Before we make up our minds, let's talk to Doctor Cherry. He is also the one who signed the death certificate."

Marty chimed in, "I don't have to wait, and I already have an opinion."

Daniels replied, "I think I know what your opinion is, Marty, and I tend to agree with you, but let's hold off for a while. You know Doctor Cherry is the one who autopsied Frank Stewart."

After dinner at the hotel we returned to our rooms. Daniels came in with his 'mobile brains,' the ever present big three-ring binder, which was never far out of reach. We orally critiqued what we had done that day and started planning our next move for the following day.

We knew who we were going to contact and what they could tell us. Daniels wanted to meet these people so we would know them better, thus making our interrogations more palatable for possible uncooperative witnesses. That proved not to be a problem; most of our witnesses were happy to cooperate. Some Nevada doctors may have been a little reluctant because the nature of this investigation might conflict with their competence.

Marty and Daniels headed out to see some highly touted lounge shows. They must have seen several; it was way past two a.m. when they wandered in, not too quietly. On the other hand, I played a few slots, a little black jack, and a few games of eight-spot, watched a high stakes crap game or two, then hit the sack around midnight. It had been a long day.

Daniels, Marty and I contacted Doctor Cherry at his office. He remembered both the Frank Stewart and Juanita

Archerd deaths. Doctor Cherry was on the down side of sixty – maybe a little older. He had almost a full head of iron gray hair, wore glasses, and smelled of expensive cigar smoke. He wasn't very happy being confronted by two, two hundred-thirty pound cops and one dapper Irish deputy district attorney. He settled down somewhat when he finally realized Marty and I were really a couple of pussycats.

He wasn't bothered by Daniels until Daniels started throwing medical terms at him. As soon as he understood that he wasn't going to be able to kiss us off, he quietly condescended to answer questions.

Daniels didn't waste any time after he had Doctor Cherry's attention. He asked him, "When did you first see Mrs. Archerd?"

"I think it was the morning of March 12, 1958."

"Was that at the Monie Marie Motel in Las Vegas?"

"Yes."

"Was there anyone else in the room?"

"Her husband; and I'm quite sure the lady that runs the motel was also in the room."

"Do you remember what he looked like?"

"No, I doubt it."

"Did the husband make any statement to you before you examined Mrs. Archerd?"

"He said she had been drinking and had taken an overdose of sleeping pills."

"What was her condition at that time?"

"She was semi-conscious and could not talk coherently."

"What time was that, Doctor?"

"Between nine a.m. and ten a.m."

"How long did you stay?"

"I think about ten minutes. I told him to get her up and walk her around, give her some coffee, be careful, don't let her get any more sleeping pills."

"When was the next time you saw Mrs. Archerd?"

"At the Southern Nevada Memorial Hospital."

"Let me show you a copy of the hospital records showing the admission date, diagnosis and treatment, her signs and symptoms, et cetera. Do you recognize any of your handwriting on that record?"

"Yes, this is my chart. She did come into the hospital March 12, 1958, at seven-thirty a.m."

"Who was the doctor that examined her?"

"That was Doctor LaCana."

"That was before you saw her at the Monie Marie Motel between nine and ten a.m.?"

"Yes, she was first admitted to the emergency room."

"Was she admitted to a regular hospital room in the early afternoon?"

"Yes, she was admitted at four-thirty p.m. on March 12, 1958."

"When did you first see her?"

"It was around five p.m. She was unconscious, her pupils were contracted, pulse and respiration poor, and she was cyanotic."

"Would you explain 'cyanotic,' please?"

"Well, she wasn't getting enough oxygen. She had a bluish tinge to her nails and skin."

"What treatment did you administer?"

"First, I gave her an SS enema, inserted a catheter to her bladder, then I gave her picrotoxin, which is a drug used to combat any of the barbiturates or any of those sleeping capsules."

"Any other medication?"

"She had several doses of picrotoxin; then on the thirteenth, I gave her a thousand ccs of five percent glucose intravenously. Later, she went into convulsions and I gave her Nembutal to try to control the convulsions."

"Was there a reason you gave her a thousand ccs of five percent glucose I.V.?"

"Yes, the cold perspiration she had is not exactly the result of an overdose of barbiturates. It shows that the patient is in some sort of shock."

Marty and I knew where Daniels was going with his line of questioning; we had heard him rehearse the long hypothetical question all the way to Las Vegas. He was able to get Doctor Cherry to say that he didn't think Juanita died of an overdose of barbiturates, as the symptoms were exactly opposite, but were an indication of hypoglycemic shock, due to an excess of insulin.

Daniels showed the doctor a copy of his autopsy report, which was, by the way, the shortest one I have ever seen. A complete autopsy report is normally several pages of detailed description of the condition of all the vital organs of the human body. Included is the toxicological lab report, citing an exact amount of toxic chemicals or drugs in the system of the deceased.

I knew Daniels was trying to get as much information from Doctor Cherry as he could, without putting him on the spot. It was apparent that the doctor wasn't used to being nailed down on every little detail concerning the death of a possible murder victim. He was fidgeting a little when Daniels switched tactics and started questioning him about the Frank Stewart case.

Daniels let the doctor peruse the hospital record and autopsy report, which laid out the slip-and-fall at McCarran Airport; Stewart's admission to the hospital at one a.m. March 17, 1960; his symptoms and treatment up through his death at ten thirty-five that evening.

After reviewing the reports, Doctor Cherry stated that, in his opinion, Stewart did not hit his head at all, especially in a fall to a tile floor. Any contact would have caused an injury that would have been noticed when the scalp was reflected. No such injury was noted. He found that Stewart had severe arteriosclerosis and that one of his cerebral arteries had ruptured, causing hemorrhage and death.

By considering the anatomic findings at autopsy, with the pertinent history of alcoholism, arteriosclerosis, prior C.V.A.'s, plus convulsions observed by Doctor Ross Sutherland between four and four-thirty p.m. on the seventeenth, he was of the opinion that Stewart's death was consistent with insulin shock. He believed that Stewart was injected with insulin after he was admitted to the hospital; probably around noon or shortly thereafter. Doctor Cherry was also of the opinion that the insulin injection caused the blood pressure to rise, the convulsions caused a rupture of the carotid artery, and death.

The interrogation lasted over two hours. Marty and I sat back and listened to a master interrogator wring good solid answers from a reluctant witness. Doctor Cherry was sweating profusely and had gone through several good Havana cigars. His collar was open, and his tie hung loosely around his neck.

On the way to lunch, I said to Daniels, "Ray, I think you were getting sort of perverse pleasure in raking that doctor over the coals!"

"No, Whitey, just doing what I do." That was accompanied by a sly grin and a short giggle.

Marty's contribution was, "Your ass, Daniels! You enjoyed the hell out of it, didn't you?"

"Yeah, but I didn't want to humiliate him too bad, just enough to let him know not to mess with me. We are going to need him. By the time we go to court, he is going to remember everything about both cases. I've got it all down in my mobile brains."

We spent the rest of that day locating and talking to nurses and lab technicians. It had been a very profitable day, so far.

Doctor Ross Southerland was in his late sixties or early seventies, about five foot seven, with thinning gray hair. He operated a clinic on Las Vegas Boulevard. I had talked to him in 1962, and had formed an opinion that he was probably on the questionable side. I made it known to Daniels and Marty. We talked to him in his office for about an hour. The doctor told us that he had examined Frank Stewart March 17, 1960, and found him completely conscious, complaining of only a light headache. This examination was at the request of Reno T. Wilkerson, an investigator who did work for several insurance companies in the Las Vegas area. For this examination, he was paid a hundred dollars. Doctor Southerland went on to say that at four p.m. on the seventeenth, he was in surgery at Southern Nevada Memorial Hospital near Room 206 where Stewart was located. He was called to Stewart's room, as he was suffering from sudden convulsions. He found him completely unconscious, in definite convulsions, with rigidity of both upper and lower extremities. He gave Stewart fifty mg of Thorazine and 3 g of sodium amatol, intravenously. This calmed the patient down; he was sleeping peacefully about an hour later. He called Doctor Adrian Ver Bruggen in consultation; he examined Stewart and ordered Dilantin. During the night, the patient suddenly expired.

Our next move was to talk to Doctor Ver Bruggen I had contacted him in 1962, without access to hospital records. At that time, he did not believe that Stewart fell and struck his head. I told him then that we thought he had been given an injection of insulin. The doctor's statement at that time was, "You are going to have one hell of a time proving it!"

This time, we had a copy of Stewart's hospital records. Doctor Ver Bruggen reviewed the hospital record and his consultation report. He mentioned that Stewart had positive bilateral Babinski's. His opinion was that Stewart had just had a convulsion. The doctor was aware of Stewart's arteriosclerosis; he stated that if insulin was injected into a person, their blood sugar would drop, adrenalin would increase as a compensatory mechanism, and blood pressure would rise, and would most probably rupture one of the victim's cerebral arteries. If all the above facts were true, then Stewart's death was most likely caused by an injection of insulin.

Of the three doctors in Las Vegas who had been involved in the Juanita and Stewart cases, in my opinion Doctor Ver Bruggen was by far the most competent. As we were walking back to our car, I said to Daniels and Marty, "If you want to get away with murder, do it in Las Vegas. Their medical examiner system is for the birds. I wouldn't like to work homicide anywhere you don't have confidence in the coroner's medical examiners."

"Amen to that," Daniels said, as he settled down in the back seat and started making notes in his three-ring binder.

As we drove away, I said, "Ray, we have just about completed our work here. All we have left is to check the Sal Sagev Hotel and get a copy of the registration card of Mr. and Mrs. Don Nightingale."

"Yeah, let's do that in the morning right after we talk to Stewart's hospital roommate and the security guard at McCarran Airport. I'm bushed and want to hit the sack early tonight."

The next morning, we located Frank Burns at his home. He said that he had entered the hospital March 13, 1960, and was released at nine a.m., March 17, 1960. He identified a picture of Stewart as the person that was admitted around midnight on the seventeenth. He saw Stewart around seven-thirty or eight a.m. He asked Stewart what his problem was, but didn't remember what he said. The new patient was conscious and talked coherently. Burns was then shown a picture of Archerd. He readily identified him as the man in the room sitting next to Mister Stewart's bed. When Burns was discharged at nine a.m., Archerd was still sitting next to Stewart's bed.

At the Sal Sagev Hotel, we talked to William Hayden, the night clerk. He couldn't locate the original registration card that Stella Morin had signed March 16, 1960. I showed him a Photostat that I had copied when I was trying to authenticate Stella's statements that Thornton and I took in Miami in January, 1962. In that statement, Stella had told us that on instructions from Archerd, she registered as Mr. and Mrs. Don Nightingale. Hayden readily identified his handwriting on the photocopy, although he could not remember either Stella or Archerd.

The photocopy put Archerd in that hotel. The Southern Nevada Memorial Hospital records, George Burns' statement that a man was still sitting by Stewart's bed when Burns checked out of the hospital, and Stella's statement that she and Archerd were in the hospital at that same time left no doubt that Archerd was there.

There was one more person we needed to talk to, Wallace Brewer, who was employed as a security officer at McCarran Airport. We found him at home on Charleston Boulevard. Brewer told us that he had worked as a security officer for five years, and had been in law enforcement work for forty-five years. On March 16, 1960, at about eleven forty-five p.m., he was having coffee in the dining room at the airport. He was approached by Archerd, who told him that a man had fallen in the men's room. Brewer and Archerd found an apparently dazed Stewart sitting on the floor leaning against the west wall. They helped Stewart to his feet. Brewer believed that Stewart could have managed to walk by himself, since he couldn't see any obvious injuries. However, Stewart complained of a headache and sore back. Brewer offered to call an ambulance, but Stewart declined, saying that he thought he would be all right; that Mr. and Mrs. Nightingale were going to meet them and take them to a hotel.

Stewart said that he came to Las Vegas with a hundred fifty dollars to gamble with and that he had reservations at the Sal Sagev Hotel. About midnight, Brewer helped Archerd walk Stewart out to the curb, where Archerd said Mrs. Nightingale was waiting for them. Brewer went back into the men's room and found a blackened banana peel that had been squashed. Archerd had said earlier that Stewart had slipped on a banana peel and fell, striking his head on the cement floor.

After checking again at the hotel, we could find no record of Frank Stewart having a reservation there. A truer statement would be that Archerd, in his own mind, had reservations for Stewart in the emergency room.

We had pictures taken of all the places Stella had told us about; the Southern Nevada Memorial Hospital, the location where the drugstore had been, and Doctor Sutherland's office. So far, Stella's statement had been completely verified.

We went back to the Stardust, retired to our rooms, refreshed ourselves with a little Jack Daniels and branch water, and reviewed our day's work, while Daniels brought his mobile brain up to date. We each had a few bucks left and set out to bring that casino to its knees. Good thing we had a county credit card, or we would have had to call home for more money. I think we had just about enough left for breakfast before heading out for the old Hall of Justice.

It sure was good to get home and sleep in my own bed. Midge was happy that I was home, too. We talked for a couple hours, as she brought me up to date with all the family happenings, including her job. She wasn't happy at work. One of the bosses kept hitting on her, the same one she suspected of doctoring the books. I told her it was all right if she wanted to quit, she didn't have to take anything from that creep.

I was just about asleep when she shook me and said, "You know, this is Van's last year in college and you haven't seen many of his ball games for the past two years. Don't you think you should try to find time to catch at least one more?"

"Is the season about over? I've lost track of so many things, lately. I'll do my best to see his next one."

I don't remember which game it was, but I think it was against Loyola Marymount. He started at second base, ended up pitching the last six innings, allowed no runs, but gave up six hits. I think that was the only college game he ever pitched in. Van hit over .400 that year. I still think he could have played pro ball with the best of them.

23
Grand Jury

At seven-thirty a.m. the next day, the three of us sat sipping fresh coffee that Marty had brewed, when Daniels said, "Fellows, we have a date set aside for the Grand Jury, but we have lots to do before then. We know how we are going to present it and who will testify to what. Getting them here at the proper time will pose quite a problem. Let's go down the list of victims, and try to get our witnesses before the Grand Jury in the proper order. I know that's going to be a problem. We are going to subpoena around one hundred fifty witnesses from all over the country and beyond. Some of them won't be available in the right sequence, and will have to testify out of order. That can't be helped. By the way, Whitey, how are you coming with the packages for our medical experts?"

"We are still working on it, Ray. We have copies of the medical history, autopsy reports, and any other information on Zella, Burney and Mary. We will be ready when you are. You know we still have to talk to Doctor Tranquada, so

I have set up a time. He wants to meet us for lunch at Carl's Café on Figueroa near the Coliseum.

Doctor Robert Tranquada was an expert on diabetes, its causes and treatment. He and Doctor Arquilla had collaborated on several articles pertaining to diabetes and its treatment, the use of insulin in treating diabetes, as well as the study of hypoglycemia and its causes. His qualifications in this field of medicine are unsurpassed. He is known worldwide for his expertise in diabetes research.

The following morning, Marty and I had all the medical records and autopsy reports of all six victims bound into a book about an inch thick. We had prepared copies for our medical experts, doctors Arquilla, Thomas, and Tranquada. It was a good thing that our tiny office was right next to the district attorney's copy and collating machines. I think by the time this case was completed, we had copied enough documents to make a stack four feet high.

We took a copy of each victim's medical history and any other documents which we felt would help our experts decide the probable cause of each victim's death. Doctor Tranquada met us at the maitre d' station and introduced himself. I guess Doctor Arquilla had described Daniels and me pretty well. After all, who could miss a six foot, two hundred thirty pound, slightly balding, white headed man with a red mark on his nose, and a five foot seven Irishman in suits, walking in together?

Doctor Tranquada was thirty-five to forty years old, about five-foot ten, and one hundred sixty-five pounds, soaking wet. He was wearing a neat blazer with contrasting slacks, and a black and red tie. His hair was cropped rather short, not quite a buzz job. Of course, we already had a run-down on his qualifications from Doctor Arquilla; he fit the profile I imagined from his description. Doctor Arquilla had already given him a briefing; there wasn't much that he didn't already know.

Doctor Tranquada's greeting was, "I've been looking forward to this meeting with a great deal of interest. I'm eager to know more about this case."

Daniels said, "We've been eager to meet you, too, Doctor. We had heard a lot about you and feel that with your background in the field of diabetes, you will be extremely helpful to us."

Daniels handed him a copy of our victims' medical records and said, "I think these records are fairly conclusive, but if there is anything else you need to know, just call me or Lieutenant White and we will see that you get it."

Doctor Tranquada thumbed through the book. "You fellows certainly have done a lot of work on this case, and from the looks of things, you have been very thorough."

"Doctor, we would like you to peruse that book, interview members of each victim's family for a more complete record, then send us a copy of your findings. Time is critical; we have a date for the Grand Jury hearing and it is getting close."

"Give me three or four days to look this over, and I will call you. I can spare a couple hours a day around noon to interview family members."

"Good, Doctor. Marty Deiro will make the appointments when you are ready."

Both Daniels and I were extremely impressed with Doctor Tranquada. We knew that we had three of the most qualified expert witnesses in the country. No one knew more about our suspected cause of death of our victims than Doctor Edward Arquilla, Doctor Robert Tranquada, and Doctor Grace Thomas.

I submitted the following memo to Undersheriff William H. McCloud:

"On June 6, 1967, the Criminal Complaints Committee of the Los Angeles County Grand Jury agreed to hear the case against William Dale Archerd. This hearing will start nine-thirty a.m. on July 5, 1967, and is expected to last three weeks."

At that time, the Los Angeles County Grand Jury consisted of twenty-three jurors, including the foreman, and was charged with hearing selected criminal cases, as well as being the watchdog over local government agencies.

We had to crank our paper trail up a couple notches in order to be ready July 5th. Daniels had the court issue subpoenas for one hundred eight witnesses, plus subpoenas *duces tecum* for medical, hospital, and bank records. In addition to the files that Marty and I had already copied on the six victims for our medical experts and other doctors who had treated each victim, we copied statements taken from some witnesses. This was to refresh their memories about events that, in some cases, had happened over twenty years earlier. It took two of us to haul everything over to the post office and mail them to each individual. Luckily, all witnesses received their copy on time. Arrangements were made with law enforcement agencies to get subpoenas served in the area where each witness lived. Somehow, they were all served on time, and the returns sent to the issuing court.

The next problem was getting the witnesses before the Grand Jury. Obviously, we needed more help. Daniels got a lady investigator from the district attorney's office to arrange transportation and housing for our out of town witnesses. I recruited Dick Keyes, and later Janet Stewart to help Marty shuffle witnesses from the airport to their hotels, then to the Grand Jury, back to their hotel, then to the airport.

Keyes, who worked the Metro Detail, was about six foot four, two hundred twenty pounds, athletic, and blonde. He was a good choice; he and Marty worked well together. I wouldn't want to meet the two of them in a dark alley.

Janet was a good-looking redhead who had lots of experience around the department. She, too, was a good choice. Following the Grand Jury hearing, she did a good deal of investigation for us. Thank God for good help! All the witnesses were ready and eager to testify. Although we did have to do a little shuffling, we eventually got it done.

My job was to sit outside the hearing room and keep the witnesses ready and in order. Daniels and the witness testifying were the only people in the hearing room other than the jurors.

The jury foreman, Lynn Franz, swore in the court reporter, then stated to the jury:

"The name of the defendant is William Dale Archerd, a.k.a. James Lynn Arden. Matter to be considered in connection with the above named possible defendant: a detailed opening statement will be made at the commencement of the hearing. However, in brief, there will be evidence presented at this hearing that the defendant murdered six persons by injecting them with an overdose of insulin. The motive in most instances was either some kind of an attempted insurance fraud or other type of attempted fraudulent monetary gain. The victims include three wives, his fifteen-year-old nephew, and two male associates. Three of the victims died in Los Angeles County and are the subject matter of three counts. Alleged in this indictment, one death occurred in Fontana, California, and two in Las Vegas, Nevada. These are being offered on the issue of identity, intent, motive, and common plan, scheme, and design.

Any member of the Grand Jury who has a state of mind in reference to the case or to any of the parties involved which will prevent him from acting impartially and without prejudice to the substantial rights of any of the said parties will now retire.

Let the record show that twenty-two qualified jurors are present after the foreman's statement."

Daniels followed with his forty-three and a half page opening statement, laying out in detail what each witness would testify to. It was the same speech he had tried on Marty and me on the way home from Vegas. At the end of his statement, the foreman called a five minute recess. Daniels met me in the lobby and said, "Whitey, I think the jury is ready to indict right now. They are going to get the full treatment, just like we planned all along. We want to get it all on record, so there can be no doubt in anyone's mind that Archerd is guilty of all six murders."

"Hang in there, Ray; we have half a dozen witnesses waiting and more on their way from LAX. Deiro and Keyes are trying to put Super Shuttle out of business."

"Walk with me down to the men's room. There are a few things I want to talk to you about."

"No, Ray, I'll pass on that. I'll talk to you anywhere but the restroom. You are not going to pull that L.B.J. crap on me!"

"Whitey," he laughed, "I didn't even think about that. I'm sorry; we'll get together about four thirty, okay?"

Daniels had told me a story that he had heard some-where that L.B.J. would only talk to some of his underlings while he was sitting on the throne. I don't think there is any truth in that story at all.

After eleven days of testimony, and a thousand three hundred twenty-seven pages of transcript, with two-hun-dred-three exhibits, and a hundred-eight witnesses, the Grand Jury returned a true bill, charging William Dale Archerd with three counts of first degree murder.

In anticipation of this true bill, I assigned Marty Deiro and Dick Keyes to set up a surveillance of Gladys' house,

as we knew Archerd was back living with her. The surveillance crews observed Archerd leaving the house and going
to Children's Hospital in the morning and returning in the
afternoon.

Daniels was still a little leery about his chances of a conviction, since most of our evidence was circumstantial. Doctor Arquilla had not completed his research project on the
brain tissue of Mary Arden. He wanted to have every base
covered and was taking no chances of not following the letter of the law. The three of us sat down and went over, line
by line, what we were going to do when we arrested our
suspect.

24
The Arrest

Daniels had written out his version of the Miranda decision, and said, "If he wants to talk to you after you have read him his rights, by all means listen and take good notes. If he wants to make any phone calls, let him. If we don't have enough to convict him now, we never will."

Daniels continued, "Just to make sure everything is on the up and up, the minute the defense demands everything we have under 'discovery,' we'll give it to them." The defense was sure to demand my notebooks, so I had already copied them.

On receipt of the Superior Court warrant, July 27, 1967, Deiro, Keyes, and I went to 314 West Adams Street in Alhambra where Archerd was living. We observed no activity. Deiro and Keyes remained at the location while I met Captain Etzel and Daniels in the office of Donal Meehan, the Chief of Police of Alhambra. The Chief gave us written authorization granting Archerd's arrest, and assigned Officer Ben Twitchell from his department to assist us.

At 5:05 p.m. July 27, Twitchell and I joined Deiro and Keyes at the West Adams Street address. I knocked loudly on the door and received no response. Deiro and Twitchell approached the house from the north side, looked in the bedroom window, and saw Archerd lying in bed in his underwear. I went around to the window and yelled, "This is Lieutenant White from the Sheriff's Homicide Bureau! I have a warrant for your arrest!"

Archerd awoke, walked to the front door, and admitted us. I told him that he was under arrest for the crime of murder. He replied, "Well, it took you long enough!"

The Arrest - Photos

The Arrest: Archerd in handcuffs, Marty Deiro to Archerd's left;
Dick Keyes, Lt. Harold White

Hospital Aide Jailed In Murders By Insulin

(Other Photos, B-4)

LOS ANGELES (AP)—Six persons close to William Dale Archerd died mysteriously over the past 19 years.

In each case, says the district attorney's office, injections of insulin were suspected.

The dead included his seventh wife—Mary Brinker Post Arden, author of a novel, "Annie Jordan," of which a million copies were sold—and his fourth wife, Zella Winders Archerd.

Archerd, 55, a gray-haired hospital attendant with a penchant for flashy clothes, was arrested at his suburban home late Thursday and booked on three counts of suspicion of murder.

He was jailed without bail being set, and his arraignment was set for today. A County Grand Jury issued a secret, three-count murder indictment after hearing 120 witnesses over the past three weeks. Sheriff's deputies then took Archerd into custody at his home in Alhambra, a suburb northeast of Los Angeles.

The grand jury indicted Archerd on charges of murdering his 15-year-old nephew, Burney Kirk Archerd, and his fourth and seventh wives.

He Learned Use Of Insulin In Hospital At Camarillo

The man who stands accused of murder with insulin in Los Angeles apparently learned about the use of the drug when he was a psychiatric technician at Camarillo State Hospital.

William Dale Archerd, 55, who was arrested at his home in Alhambra yesterday, indicted for three murders and suspected of three others, worked at the hospital from Dec. 1, 1939, to August 17, 1941, according to hospital Personnel Officer Guy Craig.

Archerd spent most of his time at the hospital assigned to the ward where insulin shock treatments were given, Craig said.

Insulin shock was a method of treating mental illness in which the patient was given a controlled overdose of the drug by the physician. Later, the method was replaced by electric shock.

Craig said shock treatment is largely outmoded today, and has been replaced by drug therapy.

Craig was the leadoff witness when the Los Angeles County grand jury started looking into the Archerd case July 5. He said Archerd wasn't fired, but quit. He apparently lived on the grounds when at the hospital. At that time, the title "psychiatric technician" hadn't been developed, and the job he held was called hospital attendant.

Another witness before the grand jury was Ventura County pathologist Dr. Gerald K. Ridge. Dr. Ridge was questioned about the autopsy in one of the suspect deaths, that of Archerd's fourth wife, Zella Winders Archerd, who died in Covina in 1966.

Archerd claimed a bandit wielding a hypodermic needle had broken into their Covina home, robbed them and then gave his wife a shot.

At that time, Dr. Ridge was a deputy medical examiner in the L.A. coroner's office, and it was he who read the microscopic slides in the Zella Archerd death.

He said that after microscopic and toxological examinations, the death was signed by the coroner as "terminal bronchial pneumonia due to coma of undetermined origin."

Some of the other deaths, Dr. Ridge said, were ascribed to hypoglycemia (low blood sugar) without an assigned cause for the condition.

Dr. Ridge said he understood that the investigation of Archerd is one of the most intensive ever conducted by the Los Angeles County Sheriff and District Atorney's offices.

Insulin, which is the substance used regularly by diabetics, is obtainable without prescription.

By the time Archerd and his seventh wife had met, investigators said, Archerd had changed his name to Arden. She died Sept. 5, 1966, in Pomona Valley Community Hospital at the age of 60.

Mrs. Arden was a sister-in-law of Manfred B. Lee, one of the authors of the famed Ellery Queen mystery stories. It was her death that set off the investigation of the bizarre slayings, it was reported.

Lynne A. Frantz, the jury foreman, said the 130 witnesses included 50 physicians, nurses and hospital laboratory technicians.

In each case, medical testimony reportedly disclosed that hospital laboratory reports showed hypoglycemia, an abnormally low level of sugar in the blood or spinal fluid. This may be the direct result of the presence of insulin, whose main function is to lower the level of blood sugar.

The indictment returned against Archerd did not mention the other deaths which occurred outside Los Angeles County. The dead were his fifth wife, Juanita Plum Archerd, 46, of Monrovia, Calif., and Frank Stewart, 34, of El Monte, Calif., both of whom died in Southern Nevada Memorial Hospital, and William Edward Jones Jr., 24, who died in a Fontana, Calif., hospital.

WILLIAM DALE ARCHERD

Newspaper clipping: Hospital Aide Jailed In Murders By Insulin

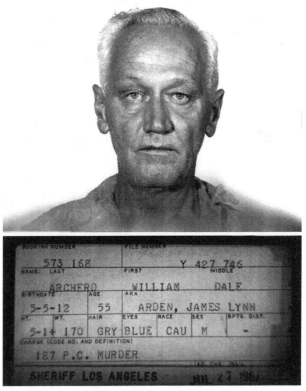

William Dale Archerd

I felt like hitting the evil son-of-a-bitch right in the mouth. But then, I stood back and looked at that emaciated creature. *Can this miserable looking excuse for a human being be the same glib, self-assured, neatly dressed person Thornton and I interrogated back in 1961 when we started the Burney investigation? Is this the same guy that masterminded all those insurance frauds and conned those poor victims into conspiring with him to commit fraud by unwittingly causing their own deaths?* I looked at his skinny white legs, scarred by osteomyelitis. *Is this the guy that had all those poor unwitting, lonely, love-starved ladies going ga-ga over him? I found it hard to believe, but we had built up such a strong circumstantial case, that there could be no doubt in my mind that here stood evil personified.*

At the same time, I felt nothing but sadness.

I advised him of his Constitutional rights: "Mister Archerd, at this time it is my duty to inform you that you have certain Constitutional rights according to the law.

"First, you have the right to remain silent. As you know, we are deputies from the Los Angeles Sheriff's Department, and if you decide to talk to us about this case, or to any other police officers or members of law enforcement, anything you say can and will be used against you.

"Secondly, you have the right to consult with an attorney before you talk to anyone, and thirdly, you have the right to have an attorney present during any questioning by the police or other members of law enforcement.

"And also, if you are unable to afford an attorney, an attorney will be provided for you free of charge before you talk to anyone, including ourselves or any other members of law enforcement, and this attorney will be present during any questioning by the police.

"Do you understand that these are your Constitutional rights?"

Archerd answered, "Yes."

"Do you also understand that you can talk to us about this case without first consulting or talking to an attorney and without having an attorney present while you talk to us, if you wish to do so?"

"Yes."

"Now, do you want to remain silent, or do you want to talk to us about this case?"

"No, I don't want to talk about it," Archerd replied.

We searched the entire premises for any evidence relevant to this investigation, and photographs were taken. Three hypodermic needles were found in the pocket of a top coat belonging to Archerd. There were also two suitcases with miscellaneous bills, receipts, checkbooks, and letters from Mary Arden, pleading for his return and expressing her undying love for him. One letter in particular, the final one mailed by Mary, told Archerd of her automobile accident. We believe this was the letter that brought Archerd home, as his subsequent actions mirrored those preceding the deaths of Burney and Stewart.

During the search process, Archerd was allowed to use the phone; he made several calls to his attorney, but couldn't make connections. He finally called Gladys at work. She returned home shortly, and was able to contact the attorney. She recognized me, and said, "What's going on?"

"We've just arrested Mister Archerd for the crime of murder." She did not seem surprised.

Archerd was handcuffed, and transported to the Temple Sheriff's Station, where he was booked. Then we took him to the San Gabriel Community Hospital where his extremities were examined by Deputy Carl Copping of the Narcotics Bureau, for any needle marks. The deputy was unable to find any needle marks indicating that the suspect had recently been using hypodermic needles upon himself. Urine and blood samples were taken and delivered to the Sheriff's Crime Lab.

Back at Temple Station, Daniels, Deiro, Keyes and I got together and reviewed the action taken during the arrest and booking procedures. I told Daniels, "You didn't have to worry, Ray. Although I felt like it, I didn't hit the s.o.b."

"Whitey, I knew you weren't going to hit him, but I don't know what I would have done."

On July 28, 1967, Archerd was arraigned in Department 100, Superior Court, before Judge Robert Feinerman. At that time, he was represented by Deputy Public Defender Lawrence Nagie. Further proceedings were continued and defendant ordered to return September 1, for plea.

✬ ✬ ✬

25
The Investigation Continues

Just because we had a Grand Jury indictment and had our suspect arrested and arraigned in Superior Court didn't mean the investigation was over. There were many things we didn't have all the answers to. It wasn't clear in our minds what effect certain barbiturates would have, if taken in large quantities, on the sugar content of a person's blood. We had several medical experts backing us up, but had to do some research of our own in order to know what questions to ask them.

Daniels and I were to spend many hours at the Los Angeles County medical library. I wasn't a lot of help; my knowledge of medicine was limited to aspirin and Maalox. I guess I was along just to keep Daniels company.

While we were at the library, Marty was back in our hidey hole, inventorying evidence we had taken when we arrested Archerd. Marty was good at that. He filled several legal pads with all items listed in their proper category. Believe it or not, Archerd still had a copy of the deposit slip when he deposited the five thousand dollars he withdrew from his and Zella's account to his own account in 1956! When Marty found that deposit slip, he about fell over. He couldn't wait for us to get back. We were greeted with a big grin and punch on my shoulder. "What do you think of that scheming bastard? He has held on to that deposit slip for eleven years. I wonder if he got his jollies by taking it out and gloating over his cleverness."

"You might have a point there, Marty, but dammit, do you have to punctuate each sentence with a punch on my shoulder?"

"Sorry, I got carried away. Guess it doesn't take a hell of a lot to make my day after going through all that crap in those suitcases."

Daniels contributed to the banter, "Marty, I'm glad you came on board. You're a stickler for details, and finding that deposit slip adds a new dimension to Archerd's profile. We're are learning more and more about his mental makeup each day. And, by the way, take it easy on Whitey. He's kind of fragile, you know. We're going to need him for a while longer, Yuk, Yuk!"

It was moments like this that made our long, drawn out investigation bearable.

Of course, we already had a Xerox copy of the slip from the bank records, and it had been entered into evidence at the Grand Jury hearing, along with bank records of Archerd's and Zella's joint account. That account had been opened June 1, 1956, at the Bank of California in Covina. There had been the usual small deposits with relatively small checks written on it up until Zella deposited $10,187.45 from the sale of her home in South Gate.

On that same date, July 13, 1956, Archerd wrote a five-thousand-dollar check which he deposited into his own checking account at the Bank of America in Covina. He had opened his account June 19, with a deposit of $15.28.

He listed his address as 4910 North Citrus, Covina. This was Archerd's address before he married Zella; they had been living at 530 Stewart Drive, Covina since June 1. There were no deposits or checks written on his account until July 13, when he deposited the five-thousand-dollar check from their joint account. Archerd wrote a check on his Bank of America account August 7, for $5,014.71, thus closing out that account.

On July 24, Archerd wrote a counter check for a thousand dollars on their joint account, so we know that from the time the $10,187.45 was deposited until Zella's death, he got away with over six thousand dollars from Zella's estate. That also accounted for the large amount of bills in Archerd's wallet when he gave Zella's son, Robert Winders, Jr., gas money so he could go to see his ailing mother.

There were other things of interest in the suitcases: all the letters Mary had sent him, pleading for him to come back to her. She told him how much she loved him and his adorable ass; that she loved him no matter how he felt about her. She kept sending him money, which she could ill afford, as they had filed for bankruptcy. He never answered her letters or telegrams which she sent through his attorney and other acquaintances until a telegram she sent October 29, 1966, "Smashed up Fiat and myself. Broken nose, black eye, head injuries. Imperative you call me immediately. Terribly sick. Love." And what do you know, right after the telegram, Mary called and asked Mrs. Fields, her neighbor across the street, to take her to get a rental car. She told Mrs. Fields, casually, that "Jim" was home.

As Marty, Daniels and I went through those lonely, pleading letters, I said to them, "Jesus Christ, guys, this son of a bitch knows only one script! The moment he knew of Mary's auto accident with head injuries, he headed home straight as the crow flies. Here was a ready-made situation that he could capitalize on, just like all his other victims.

Burney, Stewart and Archerd had a dilated left eye; all his other victims had grand mal seizures. What a perfect pattern!"

"Yeah! And we have his statements to Mary's friend, Paul Lewis, that Mary was jerking and thrashing around all evening after he had given her a sleeping pill and bourbon. He told the same thing to Mrs. Fields!" Marty cut in eagerly.

Daniels countered with, "And that he laid right there and watched her die, knowing that she had gone past the point of no return with no hope of recovery, before he called the ambulance. Just like he watched Jones, Zella, Juanita and Burney die."

I contributed, "He probably gave her a booster shot of insulin when he was alone with her in ICU. I wonder why Mary's left eye wasn't dilated."

"Hell, he probably ran out of atropine," Marty chortled.

Mister Fields took Mary to get the car rental and watched her drive into her garage and close the door. The Fields didn't see Mary until the following afternoon. As they drove by Mary's house, Archerd and Mary stopped them. Archerd said, "I want to show you some pictures." Then he fanned out several Polaroids of Mary's wrecked Fiat, and the location of the accident, as well as photos of her skinned nose and black eyes. Mary was alert and talkative; she said she was much better. The next day she would be dead.

Mrs. Fields was always positive in her statements to us. It was apparent that she and Mary were very close; she had lost one of her closest friends and would miss her terribly.

✵ ✵ ✵

26
Dr. Crue

Daniels flipped open his three-ring binder and started thumbing through it. "We have lots of loose ends to clear up, here. We need to talk to Doctor Crue about his examination of Archerd following the alleged hit-and-run. I know we have talked to him before, but I need to know more in order to establish a time frame in reference to Burney's death as well as Stewart's death.

"Doctor Crue testified at the Grand Jury hearing that Archerd was re-admitted to the Huntington Memorial Hospital on November 8, 1960, and discharged on November 25. Thereafter, he personally treated Archerd, known to him as James Arden, until September 18, 1961. Archerd claimed he had intermittent headaches of the right occipital area. At that time, Doctor Crue noted that Mister Arden seemed lethargic and withdrawn. His left eye was quite dilated and fixed to light, but the disc margins were sharp and there were good pulsations.

"Let's go out to the hospital and see if we can help Doctor Crue remember anything else strange about Mister Arden," Daniels said.

Marty was ready to go. He was eager to get out of the office and be right in the middle of things. He was tired of shuffling papers and acting as a travel agent for our out of county witnesses. I called Doctor Crue; he had about an hour of free time right after lunch.

Daniels greeted Doctor Crue, "Doctor, I'm sorry that it might look like an invasion with the three of us, but we are all deeply involved with this investigation. It helps us in our brain-storming when we are back at our office."

"That's not a problem, Mister Daniels. I'm involved pretty deeply, myself. After all, this creep has had me and my colleagues stumped with that dilated left pupil. We didn't know what to make of it. We almost did a paper on it. I'm sure glad we didn't!"

We went over the Arden/Archerd records again, minutely. It wasn't long before we hit pay dirt. "When was the last time you saw Mister Arden, Doctor Crue?"

"According to my records, it was September 18, 1961, in my office. He stated that he was continuing to have headaches, even though he had continued to take his prescribed Ergomar and Seconal at night, as well as Bufferin. He said in the last two months, he had had eleven episodes of severe headaches. This type of pain is usually seen after a neck injury. He said the Ergomar helped ptosis – droopy eyelid – and dilated pupil, as well as the double vision. An interesting aside is the fact that this patient, with his unusual post-traumatic dilated pupil, had a mother in Long Beach who was taking care of his cousin's son, a six foot tall, fifteen-year-old boy. The patient came in that day with the story that about three weeks previously, the boy had been hit by a pick-up truck in a hit-and-run accident. He was knocked down, but got up and walked home. They noticed that one

pupil was much larger than the other. Mister Arden, knowing that we believed that he had a brain clot when he had
such a big pupil, insisted that the boy be taken to Long
Beach Memorial Hospital where Doctor Ross-Duggan, a
neurosurgeon, was called in on consultation. According
to the patient's story, they did not think it was necessary to
operate. However, that night the boy stopped breathing. A
craniotomy was done, but no blood clot was found. Eleven
days later, the boy died of cerebral edema. The patient
stated that he got into his car and drove home to tell his
mother about this. He found his mother dead in bed. On
the day of his physical examination, the patient had no evidence of ptosis."

"Is there anything else that seems to be out of place with
Mister Arden/Archerd's alleged injury?" Daniels asked.

"No, I think his whole story is a figment of his imagina-
tion. Frankly, gentlemen, I think we had been had. Mister
Arden certainly had us going in circles. I want to thank you
fellows for helping us straighten this mess out. We certainly
didn't know what was going on."

On the way back to our cubbyhole, none of us said a
word. We knew that we had just driven another nail in Old
W.D.A.'s coffin.

Back at the office, I said, "That's at least three instances
where there has been a 'dilated left eye' in his insurance
scams. No! Make it four. The first was back in 1936 when
he allegedly fell at the Children's Hospital and hit his head.
He collected workman's comp and a small life-time pension. Then on October 10, 1960, a phony hit-and-run,
where he had a dilated left eye and was treated at Huntington Memorial. Six days later, Stewart's phony slip and
fall at McCarran Field. Stewart allegedly had head injuries,
causing a dilated left eye."

"You're right, Whitey, there are four instances where the dilated left eye shows up."

"One thing for sure though, fellows, Archerd never collected his fifty thousand as the victim of his hit-and-run, thanks to Stella Morin."

Marty was just sitting back with a sneaky grin on his face. "You know, if we keep piling up all this circumstantial evidence, we may not need any direct evidence."

Daniels was sensitive to that remark. "Marty, you know circumstantial evidence is kind of like icing on a cake. You have to have a little cake to make the icing stick. We are going to keep digging; we'll come up with something. By the way, we have an appointment to see Doctor Arquilla at nine a.m. tomorrow. Maybe he has some good news for us."

"I know you're right about the circumstantial evidence bit, Ray, but there have been cases made on circumstantial evidence before; the L. Ewing Scott case, for instance. They never did find a body, and he was convicted of murdering his wife," I told him.

"We're not going to worry about it right now, though. We'll just keep digging," he replied.

Marty said, "Let's get back to Doctor Crue for a minute. Do you think the doctor got his information about Archerd's cousin's fifteen-year-old son mixed up in his mind, or do you think Archerd twisted the facts a little?"

"It really doesn't matter; there is enough truth in his statement for a rational person to know that Archerd was talking about Burney. I'm surprised that he ever mentioned Burney's case to anyone," Daniels replied.

"I think the s.o.b. was in effect gloating over the fact that he was so smart, he could get away with anything. Remember, Burney had died just twelve days prior to Archerd's last visit with Doctor Crue," I reminded them.

There wasn't much more that we could do for the rest of the day, so we decided to call it a day and relax a bit. I don't know what Daniels did; he was probably playing with his 3-ring binder. We knew that at 7:30 the next morning, he would be ready and have the day planned out.

Marty and I headed for Li Po's, our favorite watering hole in Chinatown. We hadn't been there since we started this phase of our investigation. As usual, several men from Homicide were there, relaxing with Uncle Wally's cheap booze. Some had a couple days growth of beard and droopy eyes, indicative of having spent about forty-eight hours without a bath, shave, or change of clothes.

We were greeted with, "You fellows still traveling all over the country on county money? When are you coming back and giving us a hand? We're about run ragged! Everyone in the Bureau is racking up overtime like there's no tomorrow."

They knew that Marty and I were also racking up an excess amount of overtime and were worn out; it was the same story whenever we happened to stop by the office to keep Captain Etzel up to date on how we were doing. After a quick couple of vodka and tonics, we headed for the barn. Maybe we could have dinner with our families for a change. There hadn't been many of those during the past two years.

27
Brain Slides

Even after spending a quiet evening at home, seven-thirty a.m. came mighty early. Marty already had a fresh pot of coffee made when Daniels and I came in. A couple teams of investigators who had been out all night working on new cases were sitting there sipping coffee, getting their thoughts in order so they could dictate their reports as soon as a steno came in. They looked like I felt on many occasions: two days growth of beard, ring around the collar, and sweat circles under the armpits, knees and seats of their trousers stretched out of shape. They didn't have much to say to us, though, as they were rapidly running out of gas. They didn't even ask how we were doing with our case; they had problems of their own. That's the nature of our business.

We checked our messages and decided that there was nothing that couldn't wait until afternoon. Daniels grabbed his worn briefcase with his binder in it, and we all headed out to U.C.L.A. Medical Center to see Doctor

Arquilla. Things hadn't changed; we still had a hell of a time finding our way through the maze of a building up to his office. The doctor was still in a happy mood, tossing his handball in the air. He wore a baggy sweat shirt that had BRUINS across the chest. The armpits were still damp with salt rings round the outline.

"Looks like you just got off the handball court, Doc," I said with a smile. I remembered the time back in 1941 when I literally got thumped at U.C.L.A. I was on the wrestling team at Fullerton J.C. I've forgotten my opponent's name, but I'll never forget the licking I took during my first attempt at collegiate wrestling.

"I like to get in a couple sets each morning before I settle down to work. Keeps the cobwebs out," Doctor Arquilla answered.

Daniels was never one to waste time; he got right to the point. "Doctor, how are you coming along with your examination of Mary's brain tissue?"

"I have some slides all set up on the microscope. Why don't you have a look while I explain what you are looking at?"

Doctor Arquilla told us how he prepared the brain slides from tissue taken from Burney and Mary at autopsy, how the camera was mounted on a microscope and each slide was photographed, both in black and white and Kodachrome, at different magnifications. Then he went on to explain the difference between the damage to Burney's brain and Mary's. In short, the damage to Burney's brain had occurred over a much longer period of time than Mary's.

Daniels and Doctor Arquilla chatted for a couple hours; Marty and I just sat and listened. Daniels was busy making notes, preparing the questions he would ask the doctor at Superior Court trial.

Finally, Daniels asked, "Doctor, how are you coming with the radioimmunoassay of Mary's brain? I think the results of that test will be the key to our entire case."

"I'm making progress. I'm sure I'll have some answers for you before trial. I'll tell you this though, it looks very encouraging."

We left Doctor Arquilla with mixed feelings. We knew we had a first class scientist working for us and felt that he was on to something, but didn't want to talk about it yet. This was to hold true until he finally testified at the trial. We had to agree that the doctor was exercising his prerogative not to make his decision until he had all the facts. This, we respected.

28
Dale Culbertson

When the transcripts of the Grand Jury hearing were released, we asked the press to ask anyone who knew of William Dale Archerd, a.k.a. James Lynn Arden, to please call us. We received several calls, all of which amounted to nothing, except one from an ex-prison mate of Archerd's.

We found him at home in Hermosa Beach. Dale Culbertson was a Native American about forty years old, five foot nine, one hundred fifty pounds. We sat in the living room of his small apartment, and listened while he told his story. I wondered what he wanted in return, but he never asked for favors of any kind, and the more he talked, the closer we listened. We were skeptical. Here sits an ex-con who called us with some information in response to a news release asking anyone with any information about William Dale Archerd, a.k.a. James Lynn Arden, to contact us. In my twenty-plus years of law enforcement, this was unheard of.

Culbertson started out by saying, "Just let me tell you my story, then you can ask anything you want."

He didn't miss a beat. If he detected our skepticism, he didn't show it. "I first met Archerd in Chino in 1954, when we both worked in the prison hospital. In August, 1956, I met Archerd at the Handy Pantry Bar, now named the Gladstone. It's located at Vernon Street and Gladstone Avenue in Azusa. That was the first time I had seen him since I got out of prison. I gave him my home address, and about a week later he came by my house in the evening. He told me that his wife had just died and that he had suddenly come into some money from her estate. He claimed to have thirty to forty thousand dollars. He was dressed in a suit and tie, and flashed a lot of money. He was driving a Cadillac convertible, black with a white top. He said his T-Bird had been repossessed, due to some misunderstanding."

I was about to interject a question, when he held up his hand and said, "Let me finish, please, and then you can ask all the questions you want."

Marty was busy taking notes. He stopped and grinned at me, as if to say, "Let him talk, Whitey."

I told him to continue; he did.

"On the morning of February 6, 1957, Archerd picked me up at my house and drove me to a house at 322 Prospect Avenue in Monrovia. He told me he would give me five thousand dollars if I would set fire to that house. His girlfriend lived there and was getting a divorce. He also told me that he would give me ten thousand dollars to kill his girlfriend's husband who was living in Huntington Park. We drove to Huntington Park, and Archerd pointed out the house where the husband lived, then by the factory where the husband worked."

I asked him how and where he wanted the husband killed. "He said he would get me a .45 or a shotgun. A shotgun would be better; that way I couldn't miss. He said he knew the husband's routine. The best time would be about ten p.m. at the husband's apartment. 'If a girl that lives there gets in your way, shoot her down, too.'

"I saw Archerd again late that afternoon when he came by my house again. I told him the deal was off."

Culbertson appeared to be running down a bit, so I quickly asked, "How do you remember that exact date?"

"Because that was the date my parole papers arrived, and I didn't want to foul up and go back to prison."

"When did you next see Archerd?"

"About two days later. I told him the deal was still off. He said for me to think it over and he would check with me later."

"Did you see him again, later?"

"Yes, he wouldn't give up. He kept at me. He came by again in the early part of April and drove me by 322 Prospect. This time, he opened the door with a key and showed me where and how to set the fire. He said all I had to do was put some lighter fluid in a soap dish next to the towels in the linen closet next to the electrical wires, then light the fluid with a match and close the closet door. The fire would burn the wires and it would look like an electrical short had caused the fire."

"What else did he tell you about what he wanted done?"

"I asked him, do you want all her furs, jewelry, furniture, as well as your own clothes to burn, too? He said he wanted everything to burn, as his girlfriend had it all itemized with the insurance company. He said that they would collect from sixty thousand to seventy thousand dollars from the insurance company. Then I asked him, how come I'm getting only five thousand dollars to set the fire? His answer was, 'don't worry, you will get more later.'"

Marty asked Culbertson, "Did he say anything about a previous fire?"

"Yes, he said the insurance company covered that fire and would cover this one, too, because both fires, being electrical, would tie them together as far as insurance coverage."

Marty and I didn't really know what to make of this. Culbertson knew all the facts surrounding the fires. We wondered why he knew so much. Could it be that he set both fires? No way is he going to tell such a tale and be found guilty of arson. Food for thought!

On July 30, 1967, we let Culbertson direct us from his home to 322 Prospect in Monrovia. It was apparent that he knew the way perfectly. He had described the house to a T, and even pointed out changes that had been made by the new owners. He directed us to the linen closet where Archerd had wanted the fire set. The present owners were courteous and eager to show us around; they had been following our case on television.

On the way back to Culbertson's house, he talked freely, without any prompting from us. I learned a long time ago when someone wants to spill their guts, let 'em go and don't interrupt. Marty and I still couldn't believe what we had just heard.

Back in our 'hall closet' next to the duplicating machines, Marty and I went over the story that Culbertson had told us. "Marty, Zella wasn't even cold yet when Archerd was living with Juanita, driving her Cadillac and soliciting Culbertson to torch Juanita's house!"

"Yeah, whoever set the first fire didn't get the job done to Archerd's satisfaction. Juanita only realized $1,781.10 from that fire. Three months later, the second fire was set. This time Juanita collected over seven thousand dollars," Marty replied.

"I'm sure Archerd set the second fire on May 7, 1957. Remember Marie Allen at the Monie Marie Motel? She told us that Archerd and Juanita stayed at the motel on the night of the second fire. Juanita told her that Archerd had gone back to Los Angeles for some reason. While he was gone, Juanita got a call about one-thirty a.m. from a neighbor, telling her that her house was on fire. Archerd came in about an hour and a half later. That's how Mrs. Allen remembered Archerd and Juanita when they checked in on March 10, 1958. Three days later, Juanita was dead."

"I'm with you on that, Whitey. I think it's a possibility that Juanita conspired with him on those fires to collect the insurance. But I don't think she expected to die as a result."

"It's the same old M.O., Marty. He conspired with Frank Stewart on his slip and fall, and with Burney on the hit-and-run. They didn't expect to die, either. Too bad someone didn't inject him in the ass with a massive shot of NPH U80 when he faked his own hit and run accident with Stella."

"We're getting it down there, Whitey, let's keep tying up all the loose ends and we'll convict that diabolic sociopath," Marty answered, as he was about to slug me on the shoulder.

There was one other inquiry: Marty took a phone call from a Mister Howard Heyn from the Los Angeles office of the Associated Press. Mister Heyn said he had been plagued with phone calls from the Honolulu press. They were trying to verify that William Dale Archerd was the same person involved with the briefcase containing dynamite which was found at the Honolulu Airport in 1963. Apparently, the Honolulu press had information from an insurance company that Archerd had taken out a large amount of flight insurance on himself, naming his twin sons, William and Robert, as beneficiaries.

That was the first we had heard that Archerd's sons were beneficiaries of the flight insurance. When Marty heard this, his comment was, "Yeah! That s.o.b. got shit in his neck and didn't have balls enough to blow up that plane load of people with him in it."

All I learned from the F.B.I. in 1963 was that Archerd was suspected of placing the dynamite laden briefcase in a locker in 1961. At the present time, 1967, we had never received a requested copy of their report.

✲ ✲ ✲

Victims Gallery

William Edward Jones

Zella Winders Archerd

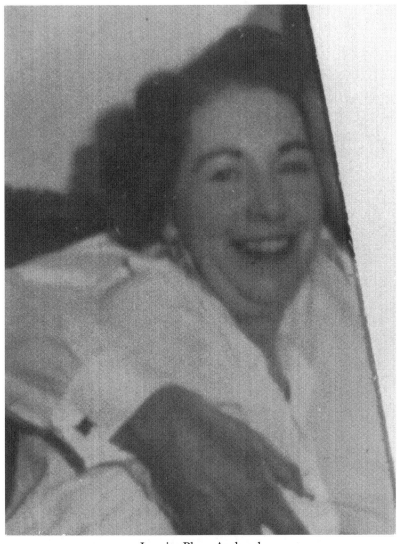

Juanita Plum Archerd

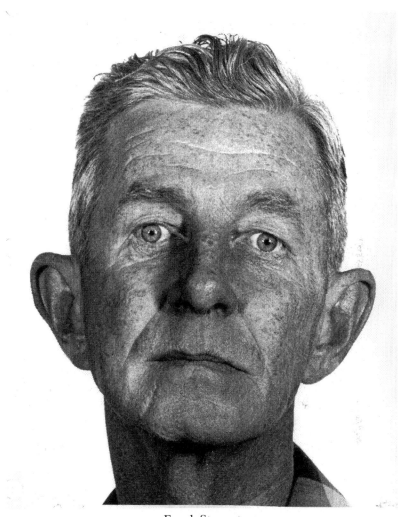

Frank Stewart

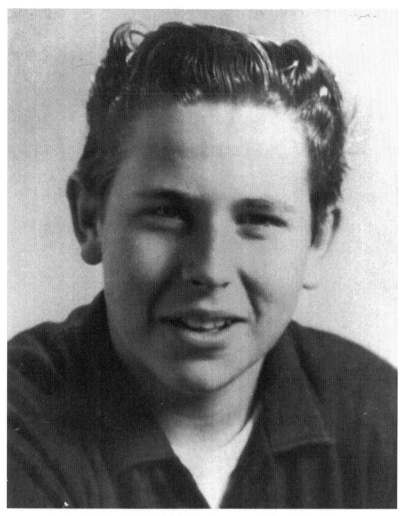

Burney Kirk Archerd

Mary Brinker Post Archerd

29
The Trial

Archerd went through the arraignments and pleas that go along with these sorts of crimes. The public defender opted out of representing him, citing a conflict of interest. Eventually Phillip Erbsen was appointed by the court to represent Archerd.

The first thing he did was to file several motions:

For the appointment of a co-counsel, this was denied.

For funds to hire experts in the field of pathology, which was granted.

For funds to hire investigators, which was granted.

Erbsen also asked for a writ of discovery of all evidence and reports surrounding his investigation. Thanks to Marty's talent for organizing our paperwork, he had all the asked for reports and notes, as well as evidence, ready. Finally, Judge Shauer ordered that there be no release of information to any news media regarding this case. He set the date Archerd was to enter a plea: October 5, 1967.

On that date, Archerd appeared with his attorney in Department 100. At the hearing, the District Attorney

alleged two prior felony counts. Proceedings were continued until October 23, 1967, in Department 102 for pur-
poses of a California Penal Code 995 hearing and plea. A
995 Penal Code hearing is held before a Superior Court
judge to determine if there is sufficient evidence to pro-
ceed with the prosecution of the subject charged with the
crime in question. Erbsen's motion to dismiss the charges
against Archerd was denied. Archerd was ordered to
appear in Department 100 of the Superior Court October 30,
for the purpose of setting a trial date. Erbsen requested
that Archerd be examined by a psychiatrist. The Judge
appointed two doctors to perform the examination: Doctor George Abe and Doctor Alfred Boner.

Finally, the Superior Court trial began December 4,
1967, in Department 25 before the Honorable Judge
Adolph Alexander. He was a man eminently qualified to
preside over a trial of this nature. Born and brought up in
the Hell's Kitchen area of New York, he practiced law there
from 1928 to 1934, and then moved to the Los Angeles area
where he had a private practice until 1942. He joined the
Los Angeles County District Attorney's office, where he rose
to the position of Chief Deputy. For a time, he was actually
the acting District Attorney, and was prosecutor in several
notable criminal trials, including those for Fred Stroble,
John Crocker, and Barbara Graham, who was the next-to-
last woman executed in California. Her story was made into
a movie starring Susan Hayward, *I Want to Live.*

Alexander returned to private practice and was later
elected Beverly Hills Municipal Court Judge. In 1961,
he was appointed to the Superior Court by Governor Pat
Brown.

At the time this case was making its way toward trial,
Judge Alexander was sitting in Department 25, a civil court.
Appointed by the presiding judge to hear Archerd's trial,

he was the choice of Ray Daniels, the prosecutor, and Phillip Erbsen, attorney for the defense.

The first thing that happened in Department 25 was a request from Erbsen for a co-council. The judge agreed, and appointed Ira K. Reiner, who later became Los Angeles City Attorney, and finally, Los Angeles County District Attorney. Reiner was a tall, handsome, well-built man with tight curly hair, graying at the temples. He possessed a loud, clear baritone voice, of which he was extremely proud. The court room had no trouble hearing every word he said. He is, by the way, a very capable attorney.

Erbsen, on the other hand, was quite dapper, in his late forties; about five foot ten, salt and pepper hair. He was rather cocky, a fighter and proud of it. He always gave his clients all he had. He can still be seen in some movies of the late '60s and '70s, playing the part of – what else – an attorney.

Along with Ray Daniels, that was the cast of characters that would determine the future of William Dale Archerd.

Archerd and his attorneys decided on a court trial rather than a jury trial. I think they were afraid there would have been too many lonesome widows on the jury, lying in wait for Archerd. They didn't want to take any chances! Judge Alexander had an outstanding reputation on both sides of the fence. Each of these attorneys was walking in the judge's footsteps. He had been there before them.

There are a few others in that cast that bear mentioning. Of course, I was right beside Daniels from the first day. I kept track of witnesses, evidence, and any other thing that Daniels needed. He had four huge three-ring binders with all the witnesses he intended to call, listed in order of their appearance and what they could testify to. There was Marty, and Dick Keyes, along with Jan Stewart, to see that our out-of-county and out-of-state witnesses had transportation and lodging.

The transportation detail was responsible for getting Archerd to court on time, and back to the county jail. The deputy in charge was "Sweet Sugar" Charlie Sharp. I didn't know about the nickname until a couple years later when Charlie came to work in the Homicide Bureau. My daughter, Janet, worked the radio room. Somehow, she and I were talking shop, and I mentioned Charlie. She did a double take and said, "You don't mean 'Sweet Sugar' Charlie Sharp?"

"If he is a six foot tall, one hundred seventy pounds, blond, blue-eyed, good ole boy from down south, yeah, I do."

She got a big kick out of that. "The girls in the radio room think he is cute. They hung that label on him."

When Charlie came to work the next day, I walked over and said, "Good Morning, Sweet Sugar!" His jaw dropped; he sputtered, "W-w-who told you that?"

I wouldn't tell him. I had him and he knew it. I never told anyone else that story and never mentioned it to him again. He wasn't aware that Janet was my daughter, and isn't aware of it to this day.

Then there was the bailiff. I can't recall his name, but he had been a bailiff for several years. They loved the eight-to-five job with weekends and holidays off. I think they backed up to the pay window. If they had a mantra, it most likely would be, "just leave me be; don't ever transfer me."

Finally, Judge Alexander, in his long black robe, emerged from his chambers, climbed two steps and stood behind the bench. The bailiff pounded his gavel and said, "All rise!" The packed court room stood at attention. "Superior Court Number 25 is now in session, the Honorable Judge Adloph Alexander presiding. Please be seated."

Right off the bat, Erbsen came up with three motions: 1) that Archerd was denied due process of law since some of the charges against him had occurred previously many years ago and he was denied the right to a speedy trial; 2) that the three murders that had occurred outside of L.A. County not be allowed into this trial; 3) that separate trials be held on all three counts of murder that Archerd was charged with. All three motions were denied.

I took out my yellow legal size pad and a couple of sharp pencils, so I could make notes and keep track of the evidence we planned to introduce. I had another legal pad listing the names of our witnesses in the order we expected to call them. Naturally, the best of plans do not always turn out the way you hoped. Some witnesses had to be called out of order. In this case, it didn't matter too much; we did not have twelve jurors and two alternates that could have had trouble following the testimony and evidence as it was presented. With a court trial, our only concern was convincing the judge that our evidence and testimony spoke for itself.

I sat back with a sigh of relief; finally, after several frustrating years, we were getting our case to court. I'm sure that sigh could be heard all over the court room. Daniels leaned over and asked, "Whitey, are you ready?" All I could do was nod.

"Well then, let's get this show on the road!"

Then he began his opening statement. By this time, he had the twenty-one page typewritten statement pretty well memorized. He started out by laying out Archerd's background from birth up to the murder of our last known victim, plus all the related scams Archerd had run through the years. He painted a picture of Archerd's employment record and training as a practical nurse; his employment at Camarillo State Mental Hospital and training in the treatment of schizophrenic patients with insulin shock therapy. Then, Daniels told what some witnesses would testify to regarding Archerd's training for duties on the insulin shock ward. He named the doctor in charge of that ward,

Doctor Grace Thomas, and what she would testify to; also two of Archerd's fellow students and co-workers, Evalynn Briggs and Leo Bradley Miller. Both attended the same class with Archerd that taught them their job in the treatment of mental patients, that they knew Archerd well and recognized him as the same person they had worked with.

Daniels took each death we investigated in order and told the court what we would prove and how we would prove it in each case. Occasionally, he would refer to his notes, but generally he spoke off the cuff; after all, he had been living with this case for almost two years. In fact, Marty and I had been his sounding board as he practiced his speech many times on our long trips to Las Vegas, San Francisco, and other northern California cities.

The defense reserved the right to make their opening statement later on.

The first witness called was Guy Craig, personnel officer for Camarillo State Hospital. Mister Craig brought with him copies of Archerd's employment records, showing that he had worked there from December 1, 1939, to January 2, 1941. Erbsen vehemently objected to the admission of those employment records, but Judge Alexander overruled him.

The next witness was Leo Bradley Miller. Mister Miller brought the original notes he took while he, Evalynn Briggs and Archerd were training in the insulin shock classes. Erbsen objected to Miller's testimony and the admission of his notes as evidence. Again, the judge overruled him. These were the same notes that Miller, Daniels, Marty and I spent half a day looking for in Miller's basement.

Another shocker for the defense was when Daniels asked Mister Miller, "How well did you know Mister Archerd?"

"Well enough to baby-sit with his twin sons, William and Robert, when he and Mrs. Archerd wanted a night out. Mister Archerd lived in the house in front of mine; we would get together often after working hours."

"Have you kept in contact with Mister Archerd all these years?"

"No, we corresponded for a while, and then I lost contact with him. I still exchange Christmas cards with Eleanor, his wife at the time."

Doctor Grace Thomas, the supervising physician in the insulin shock ward, was not called to testify at this time. Daniels had established through the personnel officer and the testimony of Briggs and Miller that Archerd was, in fact, employed as a nurse and did inject patients with the proper dosage of insulin, and that he did complete the required training to assist in the treatment of mental patients.

Daniels moved on to Jones' death, and called Mary Engelmann, one of the three sisters of our first known murder victim. She testified that her brother was a very good friend of Archerd's, and that they often socialized together.

Another of Jones' sisters, Thelma Glenn, told about Jones' mother, sisters and friends raising money to pay off the family of a babysitter that Jones allegedly molested. Between the two sisters, Daniels was able to establish that Jones had been arrested on that charge and was out on bail. According to the sisters, the family had raised about ten thousand dollars, which was given to Archerd to pay off the sitter's family. He also established that Archerd was with Jones constantly while Jones was in the hospital.

He was able to show that Archerd bought a 1934 Buick for three hundred dollars from Sam Knox, a friend and golf partner. Knox testified to the sale, and that he later learned that Archerd gave the car plus three hundred dollars to the babysitter's parents, then ushered them across the state line.

This was later verified by two of the babysitter's sisters. They did not know about the ten thousand dollars paid to Archerd to get the family out of town.

The next witness was Dorothea Ford Henes Archerd Sheehan, the woman Archerd was married to when he met Zella Winders, our second known murder victim. Reiner asked the judge to advise Dorothea of her Constitutional rights under the Fifth Amendment.

Judge Alexander advised her, "You have the right to decline to answer any question that you feel would incriminate you."

"I understand my Constitutional rights, Your Honor. I'll answer any question anyone asks."

She did just that. She was not about to let Erbsen or Reiner bulldoze her. She told the same story she told to Andre in 1956, to Thornton and me in 1961, and to Daniels and me in 1966. Dorothea was an outstanding witness.

After court that day, as we walked back to the Hall of Justice, I said to Daniels, "Dorothea sure as hell wasn't intimidated by 'The Voice,' was she?"

"Not one bit, Whitey. 'The Voice' is an appropriate name for Reiner! He's really proud of it."

☆ ☆ ☆

30
Research

Daniels, Marty and I would rehash what went on that day, decide what witnesses we were going to call the following day, and what we expected them to testify to. Sometimes, those afternoons turned into several hours into the night. We were about to call it a day after an especially long and trying day when Charley Sharp dropped by. I think he had just returned from having a hit or two at Li Po's in Chinatown. He said, "Here's a nugget you might get a kick out of. This morning, when I was hooking Archerd up in high power, Jack Kirshke was being hooked up for court, also. He said to Archerd, 'I sure am glad to see you come along. Now maybe the press will lay off my ass!' Jack Kirshke was formerly the District Attorney in charge of the Long Beach branch of the District Attorney's office. He was an outstanding prosecutor and well regarded, until he was charged with the murder of his wife and her lover.

Charlie continued, "By the way, I need a little more help with Archerd. Would you see what you can do?"

"What's the matter, Charley, can't you handle that spindly-assed creep?"

"It's not him, Whitey; it's all the other bullshit that goes on up there in the Gray Bar Hotel. That damned place is a zoo."

"OK, Charley, I'll get you some help. I don't want to see you over-worked."

"Up your ass, Whitey, you know I wouldn't ask it if wasn't necessary!"

"Yeah, I know, Charley, I just had to gig you a tad," I answered.

Traditionally, civil cases have never drawn many spectators. Occasionally, a celebrity such as a movie star or a politician would become involved in a civil matter that would end up in court. These cases always drew many spectators and a larger courtroom would be made available to accommodate them. It seems that almost any murder trial would draw the curious, and the older retired people that had nothing better to do. Since this case had no celebrity status and no bloody crime scenes that involved firearms, or butcher knives, there were relatively few spectators on the opening day of the trial. It looked as if we were going to escape the crowded courtroom scene of many high profile trials that had been held in the old Hall of Justice.

The quietness of Department 25 was shattered on the second day; good criminal reporters such as Mary Neiswender of the *Long Beach Press Telegram*, and Ron Einstoss of the *Los Angeles Times*, assisted by Bill Hazlett, all wrote outstanding stories outlining the nature of the six murders Archerd was charged with. This brought out the usual courtroom watchers and more of the morbidly curious that were always looking for a new wrinkle in the art of one human being killing another human being. Well, they were about to get the full story of one cunning sadistic, sociopathic killer. From the second day of testimony until the end of the trial, there was never an empty seat in that court room. The defense attorneys made sure their wives had front row seats.

Reporters from the *Saturday Evening Post, Time Magazine, News Week* and other national news media showed up and did a credible job of reporting. Mary Neiswender was by far the best news reporter of the group. She reported on the case from the time Archerd's nephew, Burney, was killed. I think she had a special interest in the case, as Burney lived in Long Beach, and died in Long Beach Memorial Hospital.

Mary did a great story of her interview with Archerd. He tried his charm on her; she wasn't having any of it. Mary is a very street-wise lady, and is hard to fool. Archerd repeated to her the story that Charley Sharp told about Kirschke saying to Archerd, "I'm sure glad you came along, now maybe the press will lay off my ass." Mary also followed Kirschke's trial. She has given me encouragement to complete this attempt at telling the story from the investigator's point of view.

The second day it was standing-room only, due to the television and press coverage of the first day. It started with the wrap-up of Dorothea. She was still being badgered by Reiner, but held her ground. She did not change one word of her testimony. Daniels took her on re-direct examination and was able to bring out that she had called Juanita Plum, and told her not to marry Archerd; that she had suspected that Archerd had injected his previous wife, Zella, with insulin; and that he would likely do the same to Juanita.

Reiner, on his re-cross, asked sarcastically, "Mrs. Sheehan, are there any other activities that you can remember when you were involved with Archerd?"

"I can't remember much about my activities with him. I've spent ten years trying to forget this," she replied.

Doctor Alvin Sanborn, medical director of the Kaiser Hospital in Fontana, was the next witness.

Daniels asked, "Doctor Sanborn, did you treat Mister Jones in your hospital?"

"Yes, the attending nurse called me and said that Mister Jones wasn't doing well, and would I come and check him."

"Did you go check on Mister Jones, and if so, what did you find?"

"I found Mister Jones in a comatose condition, sweating profusely. I checked his chart and noticed that his blood sugar was extremely low, so I ordered glucose injections intravenously. There was no response. We corrected the hypoglycemia but there was other damage. I believed that there had already been permanent brain damage. He was in an irreversible state of hypoglycemia."

"Was there any record of any type of injection given him that would cause this state of hypoglycemia?"

"No sir! Neither anyone on my staff nor myself gave him anything that would cause that extreme low blood sugar."

Doctor, was Mister Archerd in or around that hospital room?"

"Yes, sir, he was in and out of that room all night."

Daniels took Doctor Sanborn line by line through Jones' hospital chart; when he was through, Doctor Sanborn was still of the opinion that Jones died as a result of a massive injection of insulin. Neither Erbsen nor Reiner was able to change the doctor's testimony. He was an excellent witness.

Daniels went down the list of witnesses in the Jones murder in order as they appeared on his hospital chart. This included all the nurses that attended Jones from admission until death. He then called all the lab technicians that had anything to do with checking the body chemistry. I was amazed at the knowledge Daniels had acquired since we initially talked to them. I think Daniels could have operated the auto-analyzer as well as the technicians could. There was no doubt in anyone's mind that he had a good understanding of how hospital labs operate. Of course, I may be a little bit prejudiced; my admiration of his capacity to absorb technical facts involved with our investigation grew steadily as we prepared for trial. Along with his medical knowledge, his legal expertise was likewise exemplary. He was the perfect prosecutor for a case with all the medical and technical knowledge required for the successful prosecution of our six murders, as well as the insurance scams Archerd pulled over the years.

While the three of us walked from the court house back to our fifth floor broom closet, I told Daniels, "Ray, there is not a doubt in my mind that we are going to prove Archerd guilty of all six murders. We have done a complete investigation and you have started out charging like an angry bull. With that latent finesse that comes through, you are winning major points already. I'm proud to have had the opportunity to work closely with you. I no longer feel the pressure that I have heaped upon myself ever since George Walsh called me and told me about Mary's death. I know that we can't count on convicting Archerd in the Jones, Juanita, and Stewart cases, but we'll prove him guilty, anyway."

"Thanks for those kind words, Whitey. I need a little boost right about now. You know we have all put a lot of effort into this case for the past two years, and frankly, I'm tired as hell. I'll surely be glad when we finally wind this trial up. By the way, I talked to Doctor Arquilla this morning. He didn't come right out and say it, but I believe he is about to make medical history with the results of his research on Mary's brain. He is a little reluctant to testify to his findings. Something about setting a precedent."

"Is there anything Marty and I can do to help you? I know the issue of barbiturates will come up and we haven't answered our own questions about what effect they have when a person is drinking alcohol. Erbsen in sure as hell going to allege that Mary and Juanita took barbs with considerable booze, and that is what caused their low blood sugar, followed by sweating and grand mal seizures."

"I've done a little extra work on that and have been referred to some medical journals and other publications, but haven't had time to check them out. Why don't you come in Saturday morning and we will go back to the Los Angeles Medical Library and find those references."

"I'll meet you about ten a.m. I want to have breakfast with the family for a change."

"That's fine with me, Whitey. I'll appreciate the company. I've got some legal research to do before we head into the final week of the trial. We'll have to go to the Los Angeles County law library to Shepardize old cases with similar legal problems, although I don't think we'll find too many such cases. This one is unique in itself, and we'll also be making legal history."

Marty didn't have much to say, but he wasn't about to head home until we did. Daniels and I both were pleased that Marty was with us all the way, and that sometimes, he pre-empted our decisions with remarkable insight. Both Daniels and I let Marty know how much we appreciated having him do the great job he did.

✲ ✲ ✲

31
Stella Testifies

As planned, Daniels and I went to the Los Angeles County medical library on Saturday. He quickly located and photocopied the articles that referred to barbiturates and their effect on the human body when taken while drinking alcohol. He said, "I'll need this information in case the defense alleges that low blood sugar and grand mal seizures are caused by mixing barbs and booze. I'll be ready for them."

We went back to our niche and did a postmortem, so to speak, of the trial so far.

"You know, Whitey, it's amazing what triggers the human mind. The cross-examination by the defense of some of our witnesses has brought out information that we didn't know about!"

He meant the testimony of Ruth Coutts, Zella's sister, when she volunteered that Archerd's brother, Everett, told Zella that she shouldn't marry Archerd, and that he was a lying bum. That was the second time one of the victims was told that Archerd was no good. Dorothea told Juanita to be careful or he would inject her with insulin, just like he did to Zella. Darlene had told us that Zella told her that Archerd was treating her with iron shots. He was just conditioning her for what was to come – her death.

Daniels said, "Oh, by the way, Whitey, find out the dates of the Battle of Midway. Archerd told Coutts that he went to Midway to work as a medic so he could earn enough money to complete his MD degree, and that he was shot up pretty badly in both legs. I think those alleged wounds were actually the osteomyelitis sores that he has had most of his life."

Archerd had collected Workmen's Comp for injuries to his legs, allegedly when he was riding a bus from Los Angeles to San Francisco, just before he went to Midway.

"Let's get back to Everett and Jennie May," I said. "They both died without benefit of an autopsy, and were cremated very shortly after death. Stella told us that Archerd bragged about 'taking care of anyone who crossed him.' Could it be that Archerd got even with Everett for telling Zella not to marry him, and that Jenny May found out that he sacked Burney's bank account, and she accused him of doing harm to Burney?"

"All that's entirely possible, Whitey, but there's no way we can prove it at this point. Let's just forget about that and get on with the cases we know we can prove."

"Okay, Ray, but you'll have to agree that it's a possibility. What did you think of Velma Roseneau, the nurse Archerd hired to care for Zella? She sure stuck to her guns and didn't let Erbsen get to her on cross examination. She backed up Doctor Chambers when pressed by Erbsen that when she first saw Zella, she was comatose and only had two needle marks on her buttocks. Later, she saw four. Doctor Chambers hung right in there and wouldn't back down, either. He scored some points when he said he told Archerd that Zella needed to go to the hospital where she could receive the care that she needed. The doctor made it clear that Archerd didn't want that; he wanted to make sure she didn't regain consciousness. He wanted her to die!"

Tom Hughes, the Covina Police Department sergeant who was first on the scene, flew in from Texarkana, Texas. We had very little time to talk to him before he went on the witness stand. He proved to be a very important witness. He laid out the story Archerd had told many times about the robbery. Hughes examined both Zella and Archerd, and found no needle marks on Archerd's skinny ass. There were two marks on Zella's buttocks, both still oozing blood. He talked with Zella and she asked him if he thought it was possible that her husband could have injected her.

The light dawned on Zella; she remembered Dorothea telling her that she should be careful because Archerd might inject her like he did Jones. The dawn came too late. Hughes was called back to the Archerd residence the next night. Zella was dead with four needle marks on her buttocks.

Daniels and I did not leave our broom closet until about nine on that Saturday night. We had our witnesses lined up for Monday morning.

Midge was already in bed, sound asleep. I warmed up some left over goulash, washed it down with a couple glasses of milk, and hit the sack. Midge didn't even stir, but I doubt if she was asleep. I didn't want to talk about anything. I was asleep before my head hit the pillow.

When I woke up the next morning, Midge was watching the Rams on TV. I poured a cup of coffee, leaned back in the recliner, and slept until noon. Thank God for an understanding wife!

We wound up the Zella case the next court day, with the testimony of Doctor Gerald Ridge, the autopsy surgeon. He was a fine pathologist whose testimony was necessary, but not spectacular. Daniels fed him some hypothetical questions;

his testimony was, in essence, "If I had been aware of the facts you have stated, I would have to conclude that Zella Archerd died of hypoglycemic shock due to an injection of insulin."

I stopped by the Homicide Bureau to keep Captain Etzel up to date. He said, "Damn it, Whitey, I haven't got time to listen to that bullshit, I have a dozen other cases that aren't anywhere near to being wound up! Write a memo to the assistant sheriff. He's been asking what's going on with your case." [1]

It was customary at that time that any correspondence from the Detective Division to the corner pocket originate from the chief of detectives. Seldom did the captain of the unit dictate memos.

At seven-thirty the next morning, Daniels, Marty and I were having a quick cup of coffee in the coffee room on the third floor of the Hall of Justice. The coffee was a little stale, but we drank it anyway; we were too wrapped up in preparing our program for that day's testimony. We had wrapped up the Zella case, except for the testimony of our expert witnesses and, possibly, the recall of some witnesses to clear up a point or two.

Before we got down to the nitty-gritty of the task at hand, Marty handed me a letter from Doctor Ross-Duggan, who wanted to know if the county was going to pay for his flight back from Fiji. "Shall I tell him that since he was subpoenaed before he left for Fiji, we could only authorize a round trip ticket from his home in Florida, and that he would have to pay for his Fiji trip himself?"

"That seems fair enough to me, but tell him that when he gets here, maybe we could make some sort of adjustment. He's too valuable a witness to risk alienating him. Without him, we might have trouble with the Burney case," Daniels replied.

"Yeah, it's not like a neurosurgeon would be a charity case. He might be just a tad tight. I remember when I saw him earlier at his divorce hearing, I had to pay for lunch. Anyway, he's too nice a person to squeeze us like that. We can expect him here on the date he is supposed to appear to testify," I said.

"By the way, Marty, how are things going with your "travel agency"?" I was referring to Marty's job of booking flights and housing arrangements for our out-of-state witnesses. "So far, we haven't had any major problems. We've had to make a few small adjustments, but were able to get it done, thanks to the help of Jan Stewart and Dick Keyes. They are good help and are doing a hell of a job."

"Ray, I found the information about Midway Island. I checked the Workmen's Comp files we had on Archerd. I found that he reached Midway December 4, 1941. He was examined by a Doctor Terts December 23. The doctor found osteomyelitis in his legs and one elbow, and had him returned to Honolulu. He arrived there January 2, 1942, and was examined by Doctor Alsup. He saw the doctor again January 29 and 30. Archerd returned to the States February 17, where he was examined by Doctor Floyd Parks. All three doctors concluded that Archerd's 'injuries' were, in fact, osteomyelitis. I could find no record of any military action on Midway before the Battle of Midway in June of 1942. Archerd had been back in the states for four months by the time of the battle."

"Thanks, Whitey, and now I remember. Didn't he collect about twelve hundred dollars in a compromise and release settlement?"

"That was his second industrial accident settlement that we know of. The first was from his fall at Children's Hospital back in 1936, the beginning of a long string of insurance frauds."

"Well, there's not much we can do about it now, but let's keep it in mind for future reference," Daniels stated with finality.

By this time, we were walking across Broadway up Temple Street to the 'new' court house. Every seat in Superior Court #25 was occupied and several people were waiting outside in the hall. Marty went down the witness list and scanned the crowd. "It looks like all our witnesses for today are present or accounted for."

The bailiff called for order, Judge Alexander took the bench, and said, "Mister Daniels, call your first witness of the day."

Daniels called Virginia Bemmer, a neighbor of Juanita Plum's. Mrs. Bemmer testified that Archerd was an employee of her husband's, that she introduced Archerd to Juanita in October 1956, and that, shortly thereafter, he moved in with her. She said that Juanita's personality changed after that; she was always sweet and very religious until then. Juanita gave Mrs. Bemmer a note to give to Juanita's ex-husband in June of 1957. The note read, "Dale is giving me some kind of shots for migraine. I want you to know in case something happens." Mrs. Bemmer said, "I put the note away and gave it to Mister Plum at Juanita's funeral."

Myron Plum, Juanita's ex-husband, testified that he and Juanita ended their twenty-one year marriage, and as a settlement, he gave her their thirty-five thousand dollar house and furniture, a thirty-four-hundred-dollar promissory note, three thousand dollars in savings bonds, eleven thousand cash, and a car; and agreed that she remain beneficiary on his twenty-four-thousand-dollar life insurance policy, plus five hundred dollars monthly alimony. Daniels was trying to show that from the time Archerd and Juanita met, Archerd had depleted all of Juanita's assets, plus money collected from the insurance as a result of two fires that had done considerable damage to her home.

Our next witness was Dale Culbertson, the ex-con who had met Archerd in Chino state prison. The defense objected to the admission of any testimony by Culbertson. He testified that Archerd had asked him to set fire to Juanita's house and that Archerd had offered him ten thousand dollars to kill Myron Plum. After considerable arguments by both sides, Judge Alexander ruled that there was no evidence that Archerd knew Juanita was the beneficiary of Myron's insurance policy; therefore, Culbertson's testimony was ruled inadmissible.

32
Archerd's Heart Attack

Stella Morin was safely in a motel in Chinatown. Marty decided that she should be housed somewhere close by so we could talk to her before she was to testify. Apparently, some of the single men in Homicide heard she was staying near our watering hole at Li Po's. I wasn't too surprised when Marty and I walked in late Friday afternoon and found her surrounded by Homicide dicks. The guys sure knew how to make a witness welcome.

As I walked in, Stella stood up and waved. "Hi, Lieutenant White, it's good to see you again."

"Nice to see you too, Stella. Have a nice flight?"

"Couldn't have been better. Janet picked me up at the airport and brought me straight here. Wasn't that nice?"

Janet Stewart sat there with an amused smile, as if to say, "I done good, eh, Whitey?"

I bought the two ladies a drink, and then asked Stella, "Can you direct me to the car owner's house and to the location where you left the car?"

"I know the general area; I know I can identify the house when I see it. We dumped the car in the parking lot of a big grocery store. I don't know if I can find where I met him after I got the car."

"Well, we'll give it a try tomorrow morning, if Janet will pick you up and meet us at the Hall at nine-thirty." Janet's smile disappeared, like, Oh, hell, more overtime! She said, "We'll meet at your cubby hole at nine-thirty sharp, Whitey, won't we, Stella?"

"Okay by me, I don't have anything planned, Lieutenant. It will give me a chance to get out of my hotel room."

At nine-thirty sharp that Saturday morning, I pulled in the parking lot just as Janet and Stella arrived. I drove; Stella sat in the passenger seat, Janet in the rear. We drove out to Altadena, north on Lake Street. Just as we were about to pass a Market Basket supermarket, Stella said, "Stop! That's the grocery store I was telling you about. Archerd told me to park right over there in the rear of the lot."

I drove into the lot, and Stella directed me to the exact stall. "He told me to be sure and wipe everything I touched. I told him that I was wearing gloves and had never had them off since I got in the car. He took out a handkerchief, wiped off the door handles inside and out. He threw himself against the fender and bent the antenna and moved the windshield wiper straight up, stepped back and said, 'that ought to do it!' We got back in his car and he drove to where my car was parked. I went on home."

"Do you know the location where the fake hit-and-run was to have taken place?" I asked.

"I think so. I forgot to tell you that he had me drive him around a bit and he pointed out a place near a school."

Stella directed us to Lake and Boston. "Turn left here, up just a little bit. That's it, just across the street from that barber shop." Of course, I already knew where it allegedly took place. Archerd had called Pasadena Police Department to report the "accident." Since the location was in county area, traffic accidents were the business of the California Highway patrol. Archerd ended up in Huntington Memorial Hospital, where he completely baffled the neurosurgeons with his dilated left eye syndrome.

The barbershop was owned and operated by the father of Division Chief Vic Riseau. Archerd made his call, reporting his accident from the pay phone inside that barbershop. Small world!

I drove to La Cañada toward the home of Joseph Crossley, the owner of the car that allegedly hit Archerd. I told Stella to point out the house where she picked up the car when we came to it. I turned up Fairview Street; as we approached 1152 Fairview, Stella said, "That's the house right up there. It hasn't changed a bit."

I dropped Janet and Stella at the hall and headed home. I had promised Midge that we would shop for a Christmas tree in the afternoon. Our family had shopped together for our Christmas tree every year since the kids were small. Even the Christmas before the kids left home, I had still enjoyed playing Scrooge. I would wait until we were standing within ear shot of a live Santa, then lean over and whisper loudly, "Janet, say hello to the nice Santa." When she stopped believing in Santa, I made the same statement to her. She replied, too loudly, "That old coot doesn't look like Santa to me!"

The Santa said, "Just for that, little girl, I'm bringing you a bundle of switches!" Janet was embarrassed but took it good naturedly, and all of us, including Santa, had a big laugh.

That was about as short a weekend as I have ever seen, other than no weekend at all, and too many weeks with no break for the past two years. Those extra days and hours were beginning to show. I was short tempered and barked at Midge and the kids for no reason. I looked in the mirror and saw a thin-faced man with a gray pallor that I hardly recognized. If it hadn't been for the red birthmark on my nose, I would have sworn that I was looking at another man. I stepped on the scales and was surprised that I weighed only 205 pounds. No wonder I had to take up my belt a couple of extra notches! The last time I remembered weighing myself, I weighed 230. My pants looked like a Bull Durham tobacco sack, there were so many wrinkles around the waist. Oh well, that's what long hours, eating on the run, and very little sleep will do to you.

Monday morning, Stella was ready to testify. In fact, she was eager to get it over with. Daniels went down her statement that Thornton and I took from her back in 1962. She told the same story about the Frank Stewart case and the alleged hit and run case that she had helped Archerd stage; she held nothing back. Daniels did a great job of getting every bit of information from her that she had. She was a hell of a witness.

Stella's testimony set the stage for our medical experts to explain why Stewart's death was caused by an injection of insulin. There was a question about the rupture of the cerebral artery. This was explained by Doctor Leona Miller, the head of the diabetic ward at U.S.C. Los Angeles County Medical Center. In her opinion, Stewart suffered from severe arteriosclerosis. The injection of insulin to such a patient would increase the blood pressure, causing the patient's brittle arteries to rupture, thus causing a massive hemorrhage.

✫ ✫ ✫

33
Heart Attack Confirmed

The following day Doctor Jack Cherry was called to the witness stand. He was the autopsy surgeon of both Frank Stewart and Juanita. He had barely begun his testimony when Archerd appeared to become distressed and slumped over in his chair at the counsel table. Doctor Cherry quickly stepped down from the witness stand and briefly examined him. "Your Honor, I can't tell if this man has had a heart attack or not. I don't have the equipment necessary to do an examination."

Archerd was taken by ambulance to the jail ward at U.S.C. Los Angeles County Medical Center. Judge Alexander recessed the trial until nine-thirty a.m. the following day. Neither Daniels nor I believed that Archerd had had a heart attack. We had returned to our 'phone booth' of an office where we kicked around several ideas and finally decided that we would go to the jail ward and check on him. Archerd seemed to be okay; in fact, he looked better than he did when we arrested him. The charge nurse said we could have ten minutes with him. Daniels had barely asked one question when we heard from a distance, "Don't answer that!" It was Erbsen and Reiner. They, too, were there to check on Archerd.

Erbsen said to Archerd, "You don't have to answer any questions, and I advise you not to."

There was a short verbal altercation among the three attorneys, then Daniels said, "Come on, Whitey, let's get out of here, we aren't going to learn anything here."

On Christmas Day, I was able to contact Doctor Margaret McCarran at Los Angeles General Hospital. She told me that the enzyme tests she had ordered had not been completed, due to the holidays. She also said if those tests proved negative, Archerd would be able to appear in court on the twenty-seventh.

Doctor McCarran called me at nine a.m. December 26, and told me that the enzyme tests were essentially negative, indicating that there had been no heart attack. However, Archerd was still complaining of chest pains. The doctor believed that Archerd would be able to appear in court the next day, but she wanted him returned to the jail ward daily, so he could be monitored. Both Daniels and I were of the opinion that Archerd had faked the heart attack so he could be sent to the jail hospital where there were fewer inmates, better food, and clean sheets.

On the twenty-seventh, Doctor Cherry resumed his testimony on the Juanita case and completed his direct examination. This included Daniels taking him step by step through his examination of Juanita before death and her autopsy.

During cross-examination, Reiner attempted to show that Juanita's cause of death could have been other than from an injection of insulin. He cited the finding of large amounts of barbiturates in her stomach and the fact that she had been drinking prior to her admission into the hospital. "Doctor Cherry, could the barbiturates and alcohol have caused Mrs. Archerd's death?"

"It's possible," he answered.

Reiner then succeeded in getting Doctor Cherry to admit that long time, excessive alcohol usage could produce an enlarged liver and spontaneous hypoglycemia.

I passed a note to Daniels: "That trip we took to the medical library really paid off!" He poked me in the ribs, smothered a little smile, and a gave me a quick wink. He was ready for the re-cross.

When Reiner finished, Daniels said to Doctor Cherry on re-direct: "Doctor, when you said it was possible to cause hypoglycemia by mixing barbiturates and alcohol, how much alcohol and barbiturates would it take to cause hypoglycemia in a person about the same size as Juanita?"

"It's hard to say, but it would take a lot more barbiturates than I found in her stomach, and she would have to have been consuming alcohol for a long time without having eaten anything."

Doctor Cherry then stated that Juanita's death was not caused by an overdose of barbiturates. He believed her cause of death was shock due to the convulsions that were caused by an injection of insulin.

When Doctor Cherry completed his testimony on the Juanita case, Daniels asked the court to call him out of order for the Frank Stewart case. He cited the fact that the doctor had been called from his home and practice twice. Judge Alexander allowed Daniels' request, with little or no opposition from the defense.

Doctor Cherry stated that he had never seen Stewart until he was asked to do an autopsy on him. He was told by the mortician that Stewart had fallen and struck his head on a cement floor. Doctor Cherry had received no hospital report or other medical information about Stewart's physical condition.

Daniels asked, "Doctor Cherry, is there a portion of your autopsy referring to your examination of Mister Stewart's skull? You may refresh your memory from your autopsy report."

"There was a small abrasion on the right side of the skull about two inches to the rear and to the top of the right ear."

"Did you reflect the scalp?"

"Yes."

"What, if anything, did you find?"

"There was no ecchymosis of the scalp, which surprised me. I expected a hemorrhage, and there was none. So the man could not have fallen and had an injury to his head. Also, the skull was removed and it showed no fracture."

"You mention that the dura was opened and showed no evidence of a fracture, but a large hematoma was found involving two-thirds of the right brain. The hemorrhage was traced directly to a branch of the cerebral artery which was found to be severely sclerosed. What was your conclusion?"

"That the patient suffered from arteriosclerotic disease, and death was caused by cerebral hemorrhage."

Daniels had Doctor Cherry explain arteriosclerosis, then asked, "Did you have access to the hospital records of Frank Stewart from the Southern Nevada Hospital, or his records from the L.A. County General Hospital?"

"No, I did not."

"Doctor Cherry, have you had an opportunity to review Mister Stewart's hospital records from the Southern Nevada Memorial Hospital?"

"I saw them for the first time at the Grand Jury hearing back in July."

Daniels took him line by line through Stewart's hospital records. He pointed out where Stewart had been examined by Doctors Sutherland and Ver Brugghen, at which time Stewart had an episode of full-blown convulsions. He died at 10:35 p.m. March 17, 1960.

When Doctor Cherry was made fully aware of the entire hospital records, Daniels posed his patented hypothetical question: "Knowing all this in the form of a hypothetical question, do you have an opinion as to his cause of death?"

"It would be my opinion that he was injected with an overdose of insulin, which brought on convulsions which preceded his death."

"Doctor, when a person is injected with insulin, does that have any relationship with the blood sugar level?"

"Yes, it lowers the blood sugar and it increases your blood pressure."

"Knowing the pre-existing physical condition of Mister Stewart prior to March 17, 1960, would you for any reason inject Mister Stewart with insulin?"

"No, sir."

"What would be the damage of injecting such a person with insulin?"

"Well, the danger would be, the man would go into convulsions and, in this case, he would have a hemorrhage of the brain."

"Exactly as you found in the autopsy report of Frank Stewart?"

"Yes."

"I have nothing further," Daniels stated.

Reiner took Doctor Cherry on re-cross, asked a few questions that were aimed to re-establish his idea that Stewart's death was not caused by an injection of insulin, but that Stewart died from a cerebral hemorrhage caused by Stewart's severe arteriosclerosis; a natural death. Apparently, he had not done his homework; his arguments were not the best I had ever heard.

We then started on the Crossley matter, the alleged hit and run that Archerd faked with Stella Morin's help. Stella had completed her testimony and was on her way back to Florida.

Don Nightingale testified that he had never been to the Sal Sagev Hotel in his life. He knew Archerd; in fact Archerd tried to talk him into taking the fall before Stewart agreed to it. Archerd was probably trying to get back at Nightingale for refusing to help him pull that scam. Stella had already testified that she registered at the hotel under the name of Mr. and Mrs. Don Nightingale.

Joseph Crossley was next on the stand. He told the story of a tall, dark-haired lady coming to his house to try out his 1957 Plymouth he had advertised in the Pasadena daily paper. His testimony was short and sweet. Daniels asked very few question on direct examination; Erbsen asked even fewer.

Due to the interruption caused by Archerd's 'heart attack,' we had to call several witnesses out of order. We used as many local witnesses as we could until Marty's travel agency was able to get our out-of-county witnesses back on line. On this court day, we put on witnesses from the Juanita, Burney, and the alleged hit and run. That could have been enough confusion for any trial judge, but it did not seem to bother Judge Alexander. He did not have a problem understanding what each witness was testifying to.

It crossed my mind that the defense had deliberately staged the whole heart attack incident to confuse the court.

Other witnesses followed that established that Archerd had conspired with Frank Stewart by having Stewart buy flight insurance on his life in the amount of sixty-two thousand five hundred dollars, making Gladys the beneficiary, and another policy naming Jennie May, Archerd's mother, beneficiary. These claims were dismissed with prejudice in January, 1964. This came about through the investigation by Thornton and me after we had talked to Stella in 1962.

Witnesses, including Stella, testified about the phony hit and run accident where Archerd was the alleged victim. According to Stella, Archerd set up his hit and run so he could have time off to pursue his scam involving Frank Stewart's death.

Doctor Benjamin Crue, from Huntington Memorial Hospital, testified that Archerd was his patient, and that he had remarkably similar symptoms that Burney had from his accident; notably, a dilated left eye. Doctor Crue was convinced after reviewing Archerd's hospital records and consultation with other neurosurgeons that Archerd was an outright fraud. Archerd collected three thousand dollars workmen's comp as a result of that 'accident.'

We were able to establish that of the seven thousand dollars awarded to Burney following the death of his father, Archerd succeeded in replacing Jenny May as trustee, and then he systematically sacked the account. At the time of Burney's death, there was no money left. All withdrawals were made by Archerd, except for a hundred fifty dollars.

At the time, Thornton and I theorized that Jenny May was on to her son, and when she braced him with her suspicions, he killed her, too. However, she had already been cremated when we started the Burney investigation.

Since the trial had been delayed, and our pre-arranged schedule was out the window, there was nothing we could do but ad lib. All this time, Archerd sat there rather stoic, showing little emotion. He looked better than ever and was even able to play chess with his attorneys.

Thankfully, our local witnesses were happy to fill in. We had a bit of luck when a witness we had not counted on showed up. Mrs. Chauvet Boven was the widow of Juanita's personal physician, Doctor Bernard Boven. She testified that Juanita called her the day following her marriage to "Bill," as she called him, and wanted the doctor to come to Las Vegas to see her. Juanita told her that she and Bill had had a quarrel, and that she was concerned about something.

Doctor Boven was ill and unable to make the trip. Mrs.
Boven learned of Juanita's death a few days later.

Myron Plum was recalled to testify about Juanita's
health. The only problem that he was aware of was migraine
headaches.

34
The Trial Continues

January 2, 1968, we received another low blow. Just when Marty and his crew of travel agents had made arrangements to schedule our remaining witnesses, I received a call from Doctor Margaret McCarran. "Lieutenant White, after re-evaluating the tests I ran on Mister Archerd, it is now evident that he did have a heart attack. I feel it imperative that he be confined to bed for at least two, or possibly three weeks."

I thanked her, but it was difficult. I don't know how well I hid my disappointment. I immediately called Baby Jane and dictated a memo to the boss.

Next, I called Daniels and told him about Doctor McCarran's call. "Ray, do you think we were just a tad harsh in doubting Archerd having a heart attack?"

"I'm still not convinced, Whitey. Just look at his past record of fooling the medical profession. He's been pulling crap like that for years, but who are we to dispute the doctor's findings? We'll just have to go along with it. We'll take advantage of the extra time to assess where we stand now, and re-contact our expert medical witnesses to make sure everything is ready to go."

I was hoping for a little time off to renew acquaintances with my family; it didn't happen. I hadn't had a vacation in over two years, and I needed a rest. I ended up asking to defer my vacation until after the trial was over.

Daniels spent his time either in the Los Angeles County medical library or the law library. I tried to ease the load on Marty's shoulders in handling the travel agency. He was also a little weary and welcomed any help I could give him.

Finally, Daniels completed his legal research and medical library exploration. He came in one day and said, "Let's get Doctor Thomas on the phone and make sure she has reviewed all the material we sent her, and has interviewed the family members of all our victims."

I hit it lucky! I got her on the first try. She was usually hard to locate; she had several irons in the fire involving other commitments that required her expertise in psychiatry. She was happy to hear from us, saying, "I've been following the trial in the paper every day. I hope you are getting a little rest while Mister Archerd recuperates from his heart attack."

"Thank you, Doctor. We aren't working as many hours as before, but I'm afraid rest is out of the question. There are always loose ends to tie up in cases like this."

That lovely, busy doctor was really concerned about our well-being. That scored a lot of points with us. It isn't often that a witness feels empathy for prosecutors or investigators.

We tried to get doctors Arquilla and Tranquada together for a luncheon meeting, but couldn't find a time that they both would be free at the same time. First, we met Doctor Tranquada in the cafeteria at U.S.C. Los Angeles General Hospital. The lunch was so-so, but the coffee was good. The doctor told us that he had completed his interviews with family members of our victims, as well as review of all their hospital and medical records. He was ready for trial. Doctor Arquilla asked us to come by his office at UCLA. We still had trouble finding him in the maze of offices. He ran through his research on the tissues taken from Zella, Burney, and Mary. He stated that he was ready for trial.

Daniels asked him, "Doctor, could you tell us specifically about your results of the examination of Mary's brain?"

"Well, I have completed my radioimmunoassay of her brain tissue and am in the process of writing my report. I must say that this process seems to be favorable to your case. I'll have a more definitive answer by the time I'm called to testify."

Daniels wasn't happy with that reply; he wanted a solid yes or no answer. It was obvious that Doctor Arquilla wasn't going to commit himself until he was absolutely sure of his results. To me, the fact that he hadn't flatly said no was pretty darn close to a yes; the test results were positive.

January 30, 1968, I received information from the jail ward that Archerd would be released from the hospital to the main security jail within two or three days.

Daniels and I met with Inspector Ralph Welch of the Jail Division. The inspector had worked with me at Biscailuz Center, a juvenile detention facility, in 1952. He did not object to my calling him by his first name; we had been good friends all through the years, even though he had surpassed me in rank.

"Ralph, we are concerned about security problems with Archerd. We have already had two uniformed deputies assigned to transport him to and from court. As you know, our trial has been held up several weeks due to a heart attack. We would like you to isolate him in a private cell in the main security jail hospital where he can have close medical observation."

Inspector Welch readily agreed, and said, "Since he is in pro per, I'll furnish him with a telephone, typewriter, desk and any other materials he needs, including law books."

"Thanks, Ralph.   We surely do appreciate your cooperation."

"Think nothing of it, Whitey, that's what we're here for, to help any way we can. When you finish this trial, come up and have lunch with me. I can't guarantee that lunch will be as good as it was during our old B/C days, though."

The three of us walked over to Department 25 and told Judge Alexander that we would be able to continue the trial in a day or two, and that we had some security and medical concerns with Archerd. We then told him of the plan we had agreed on.

Just then, Erbsen and Reiner walked in. Dead silence. The silence was broken by Judge Alexander. "These fellows are here to tell me we can resume the trial in two or three days, and that they have some security concerns. They have outlined a plan, and I concur with it." Erbsen and Reiner exchanged strange looks, but said nothing.

On our way back to the Hall, Daniels said, "We can expect the defense to make an issue of our meeting with the judge."

"You can count on it," I replied.

✫ ✫ ✫

35
Dr. Chapman

The trial continued Monday, February 5, 1968. We were all set for another month of testimony, providing there were no other disruptions.

Doctor Kenneth Chapman performed the post-mortem examination of Burney. Originally, his cause of death was ascribed to cerebral edema and pulmonary congestion with early bronchopneumonia due to cerebral concussion with facial cerebral hemorrhage. Daniels asked him, "Doctor, at the time you did the post-mortem examination on Burney Archerd, were you in possession of his hospital chart?"

"No sir, I was not."

"Have you since perused that hospital chart?"

"Yes sir, I have."

"Now that you have had a chance to review Burney's hospital records, do you have an opinion as to the cause of his death?"

"I believe there was nothing organically wrong with Burney that could have caused his death as revealed by the autopsy anatomic findings, microscopic section, and clinical history. His cause of death was consistent with coma and hypoglycemic shock caused by an injection of insulin."

Doctor Chapman, a tall blond, shy man talked in a quiet sort of mumble that was difficult to understand. The defense attorneys had little success in their cross-examination. They may have mistaken his quiet, shy attitude as incompetence. If so, that was a huge mistake. They never shook his testimony.

I was fortunate to have had Doctor Chapman as the pathologist on several murder cases I had investigated. He was an excellent pathologist and was always prepared when he appeared on the witness stand.

I never could get used to walking through the coroner's laboratory and seeing pathologists and their assistants having coffee and doughnuts while watching an autopsy through the windows in the next room, particularly when an over-ripe cadaver was brought in.

We were successful in getting Doctor Ross-Duggan back from his vacation and on the witness stand. His testimony was that when he was called to examine Burney, he was stunned to find his left eye dilated. He did not believe that Burney's injuries were severe enough to cause such a symptom. The doctor was also puzzled about his extremely low blood sugar. A head injury that would cause one eye to dilate would not ordinarily cause such low blood sugar. It was apparent to him that his patient was critical and something had to be done. He then drilled burr holes in Burney's skull to relieve any pressure. He found nothing to indicate that there was ever any head injury.

Daniels completed his direct examination of Doctor Ross-Duggan with a similar hypothetical question that he was to use when examining attending physicians and our medical experts to establish the cause of death of each victim.

✳ ✳ ✳

36
Whitey

I was the next witness called to testify. I told about our investigation involving Burney's death. It was mostly about the alleged hit and run that was supposed to have caused Burney's death; specifically, that Thornton and I did a thorough canvass of the neighborhood where the 'accident' took place. It took us several days to complete that chore, as people's work habits differ from home to home. We were unable to find anyone in a five square block area that had seen or heard of such an accident. We had determined that the red truck involved in the so-called accident had not been off the used car lot in several weeks due to mechanical difficulties.

I also testified that the pictures of the various hospital rooms occupied by Burney during his stay at the Long Beach Memorial Hospital were located in such a position that a patient could not be seen from the nurse's station. In fact, for anyone to have seen Burney in his bed, they would have had to walk to the door and look in. This testimony was to show that Archerd, who visited Burney throughout the day, could have done anything to Burney.

I had to concede that the pictures taken at my direction were taken in May, 1967, and not at the time of Burney's death. Therefore, the positions of the beds in those rooms could have been different, as well as the nurse's station. This was after Erbsen had spent an hour or more on cross-examination.

There were several nurses that attended Burney from the time he was admitted until his death. They all made specific notes on the hospital charts: "Uncle visiting throughout the day." They all testified that the locations of the rooms in relation to the nurse's station as well as the location of the beds in each room were essentially the same when the photos were taken, as when Burney was there.

Other witnesses who talked with Burney, such as hospital volunteers, candy stripers, and friends, placed Archerd in Burney's room several times during his stay, therefore giving Archerd the opportunity to zap Burney with his needle of death.

✲ ✲ ✲

37
Dr. Grace Thomas

M idge and I picked up Doctor Grace Thomas at LAX and delivered her to the Mayflower Hotel. There was a reason of some significance, unknown to us, why she requested that particular hotel. We wondered, but did not ask her. We had the impression that it meant a great deal to her, and if she wanted us to know, she would tell us. She never did.

Doctor Thomas was our first witness the next day. She walked with a limp and carried a cane to help her with her balance. She took her seat in the witness chair after being sworn in, refusing help from the bailiff. Her mannerisms immediately made one forget any frailties she might have, as she exuded intelligence and competency. She was examined by Daniels:

Q: Please state your full name for the record.

A: Grace Fern Thomas, M.D.

Q: Are you a physician licensed to practice in the State of California?

A: I am.

She took her time, then methodically stated her education and medical background. Very impressive.

Her biography appears in the National Directory of Medical Specialists, in Who's Who in the West, Who's Who of American Women, and in the Directory of International Biography.

As she described her medical studies and career positions in the fields of neurology and psychiatry, it became evident that we had selected the proper witness for this prosecution.

Very important to this case was her special training in insulin shock therapy for the mentally ill under Doctor J.P. Frostig, who at the time, 1939, was state head of the Insulin Shock Therapy Department for the California State Hospital system.

All the time she was presenting her qualifications, there was not a sound of distraction in the courtroom. The only thing audible was her exceedingly clear voice.

Daniels had Doctor Thomas identify Archerd as one and the same person she had worked with while treating mental patients with insulin shock therapy while at Camarillo State Mental Hospital.

She went on to describe in great detail the procedures of treating mental patients, demonstrating that Archerd and all the attendants were thoroughly schooled in the procedures and were qualified to assist in the treatment.

When she had finished explaining the insulin shock treatment, she straightened her skirt, folded hands together as if to say, "Let's get on with it, Mr. Daniels."

Daniels flashed her a quick smile, and asked for a short recess.

The first thing Daniels said at the break was, "Whitey, I have never had an expert witness as qualified as Doctor Thomas – and what a wonderful lady." He then quickly continued, "Do we have all the medical records of all six victims?"

After the break, Daniels continued his questioning of Doctor Thomas.

Q: Now, in preparing for your testimony today, starting off with the case of William Edward Jones, Jr., I would ask you whether or not you have read and become familiar with the contents of the hospital record of William Edward Jones showing his admission to the Kaiser Hospital in Fontana in October of 1947?

A: Yes, sir, I have.

Q: Have you also considered the autopsy report of the same William Edward Jones?

A: I have.

Q: Have you also reviewed the hospital records showing Jones' admission at a prior time to the Santa Fe Hospital?

A: Yes, I have.

Q: Now, I would like to ask you a hypothetical question concerning Mr. Jones with the idea, at the completion of the question, of having you interpret the neurological signs appearing in the hospital record of Mr. Jones, and also giving us your opinion as to the cause of the last illness of Mr. Jones which resulted in his death.

So, with that in mind, I would ask you to assume the following hypothetical factual situation:

Assume that a Mr. W.J. was admitted to the Kaiser Permanente Hospital in Fontana at approximately one a.m. on the morning of October 11, 1947; that he died at the hospital at approximately ten-thirty a.m. the following day, October 12, 1947; that all the acts, conditions, and events which occurred surrounding the time that Mr. W.J. was in the hospital

are identical in all respects to the hospital record of
William Jones that you have before you;

Furthermore, that an autopsy was performed on
the body of W.J., and that the findings at autopsy
were identical in all respects to the autopsy report of
William Jones,

Furthermore, that W.J. had been in the Santa Fe
Hospital prior to that time, and that his acts, conditions, and events during his stay at the hospital were
identical in all respects to the contents of the file,

And, furthermore, that the aunt and sister of
Mr. Jones, a Mrs. W.H. and a Mrs. T.G., state that in
their opinion, having known Mr. Jones for approximately thirty-three years of his life until his death at
or about that age, that to their knowledge he was
not a diabetic and had none of the symptoms of
hypoglycemia, such as fainting, loss of orientation,
hunger, et cetera, nor, to their knowledge, had he
ever used insulin.

Based upon that hypothetical situation, do you
have any opinion as to the cause of the last illness of
Mr. W.J.?

A: Yes, I do. I think the cause of his last illness
was hypoglycemic shock due to the injection of insulin.

Q: Now, would you please explain the basis of
your opinion?

A: I have reviewed all of the material available to
me very carefully, and I note that at the time of the
admission the patient was conscious and talking and
was described as somewhat nervous, complaining of
severe headache and hunger, symptoms which are
consistent with the early stages of hypoglycemia.

And I note from the hospital records that shortly
after his admission he was given food, consisting of

eggs, toast and hot milk, and also medication, consisting of codeine at one-thirty a.m. and Demerol at five-thirty a.m. The immediate morning after midnight – he was admitted, I believe, at twelve-forty a.m. on 10/11/47, and when he again complained of severe headache, he was given these medications for relief.

Then at nine a.m. on 10/11/47, he voided involuntarily, indicating that he was semi-conscious or unconscious, and the nurses' notes report muscular twitching, irregular respirations, strong and irregular pulse, and the patient was also described in the hospital records as perspiring freely, and all of these enumerated signs indicating advancing insulin coma.

Then, at eleven a.m. on 10/11/47 a spinal puncture was done, and the blood pressure was found to be low, namely, 100/70 and a little later 100/80. Fifty-percent glucose was given intravenously at that time, and a lab report on a specimen of spinal fluid was reported as 36 milligrams, the normal being 60 to 90 milligrams, and the blood sugar on the same lab report taken before the man was given food was 51 milligrams, and normal being 80 to 100 milligrams. I.V. glucose was given, and after it was given his blood sugar was recorded as 80 milligrams, and yet there was no response, indicating to me that the intravenous glucose was then not effective because brain damage had already occurred.

At two-thirty-five p.m. on 10/11/47 – we are still talking about the same day – the patient was given considerably more glucose, 100 ccs of fifty percent solution, but didn't recover consciousness even with that. And later a thousand ccs of a ten percent solution of glucose, which, of course, is a form of sugar, was then given intravenously, slowly, also without response, and at three-thirty-five p.m., the nurses' notes indicate that there was muscular twitching and involuntary urination, all indicating a deepening coma, and by six-forty-five p.m. on the same date, 10/11 47, the blood pressure had fallen to 104/60, and by eight-twenty-five p.m., to only 80/55, which is extremely low.

Respirations were then recorded as very irregular, indicating that the patient was now in precarious condition, such that oxygen was actually administered within a short time.

Then, from two-twenty a.m. to three-twenty-five on 10/12/47, after midnight of the day of the admission, convulsions occurred at frequent intervals, according to the record, but were controlled for a time by the administration of sodium luminal, after fifty-percent glucose and magnesium sulfate given intravenously had no effect. And this, of course, was at a time when the patient had been unconscious for many hours.

He was described as quiet and relaxed at eight-thirty a.m. but still unconscious, and at nine-thirty a.m., the blood pressure was very low, 100/96, and was associated with rapid pulse, 104, which was recorded as irregular at times.

At ten-thirty a.m., his blood pressure rose to 150/80 with a stronger pulse, and there was an increase of mucus secretion from the nose and mouth, which is frequent in deep insulin coma, and at ten-forty-five the patient was recorded as being in acute respiratory distress, and he didn't respond to resuscitative measures and died at eleven a.m.

It is my opinion that this man was given either a large dose of slow-acting insulin, such as protamin zinc insulin, or whatever kind was available, shortly before his hospital admission, or else that he was multiply injected with regular insulin during his hospitalization, and the administration of food and glucose and other medications such as hypnotics, sedatives and anti-convulsives, slowed the process of the insulin coma for a time. Of course ordinarily early convulsions, if they occur at all, do so in two or three hours after insulin injection, unless it is a slow-acting injection, but late convulsions have an entirely different cause and a different prognosis, in other words, they are collapsed phenomena, and I think that this man did die of insulin shock coma.

Q: Now, was there one portion in the hospital records wherein the blood pressure was very low and then it took a sudden rise?

A: Yes, sir, I believe there was. I found on examining the records that occurred – I believe that occurred after he began to have convulsions. Yes, it did. At ten-thirty a.m. his blood pressure rose from the former level which was taken at 9:30 and found to be 96/60 to 150/80, which would indicate that he was secreting adrenalin within his own body trying to counteract the effect of the insulin, and also that he was having strong extensor spasms, that is, strong extensor movements like this (demonstrating), which would tend to raise the blood pressure, also.

Q: Now, assuming that all of the facts as set forth in the hypothetical situation of W.J. are the facts surrounding the death of William Jones in this case, would your opinion be the same as to the cause of the last illness and the cause of death of Mr. William Jones, being hypoglycemia due to injection or injections of either regular insulin or long-acting insulin?

A: Yes, it would be.

Daniels moved on to our next victim, Zella Winders Archerd. Doctor Thomas testified that she had read the autopsy report on the body of Zella, as well as her hospital records, when she was treated at St. Francis Hospital in Lynwood on two separate occasions. She had also interviewed several members of Zella's family, and found no indication that Zella had ever been treated for diabetes. Nor had she ever used insulin in any form.

Daniels laid out the facts as reported by the investigators that originally handled the case. This included Archerd's statement about the alleged robbery where both he and Zella were injected in the buttocks by the alleged robbers. He also included the statements of Velma Rosenow, the "nurse" Archerd hired to see to Zella while he was away. Then he went into the details of Doctor Chamber's testimony about his initial examination of Zella and his finding her comatose with two needle marks in her buttocks, and his second examination after her death, where she had four needle marks in her buttocks. Daniels further included a recap of the testimony of Zella's daughter, Darlene Lopez, and her son, Robert Winders.

Then he posed the familiar hypothetical question to Doctor Thomas:

Q: "Now assuming that hypothetical situation to be true, do you have an opinion as to the last illness of Zella Archerd which resulted in her death on July 25, 1956?"

A: "Yes, I do. I would be obliged to assume, in view of all the recorded evidence that has been made available to me, that Mrs. Zella Archerd died as a result of coma due to injection of insulin."

"Do you wish to state the basis of your opinion?"

"I have carefully read all the material that has been made available to me, most of which I believe was covered in your hypothetical question, and my professional opinion would be based on the following points."

Doctor Thomas was on a roll now, and Daniels let her continue without interruption. It is a real pleasure for a prosecutor to have witnesses the caliber of Doctor Thomas who knows instinctively the questions that need answering and do so in a logical, intelligent, and professional manner. She went on for several minutes, emphasizing each point, only to be interrupted by Daniels when he believed further explanation of a medical or technical point needed to be clarified so that there would be no doubt that she knew what she was talking about. She finally ended her testimony with, "It is my professional opinion that Zella Archerd died as a result of insulin shock coma due to injection of insulin over dosage."

"Thank you, doctor." Then, to Judge Alexander, "Your Honor, may we have a fifteen minute break?"

"So ordered," replied the judge. He was ready for a break in the action, also.

Following the recess, Doctor Thomas resumed her testimony, looking more relaxed and at ease. She took her time and settled down, eagerly awaiting Daniels' questions regarding the cause of death of Juanita Archerd.

Daniels took her through Juanita's hospital records from the Southeast Nevada Memorial Hospital, and the autopsy report. Finally, he asked Doctor Thomas:

"Do you have any opinion as to the cause of the last illness which resulted in the death of Juanita Archerd?"

"Yes, I do. It is my opinion that Juanita Archerd died of insulin coma due to injected insulin in large over dosage."

"Rather than due to any barbiturates?"

"Yes."

She then went on to pinpoint each instance that pointed to her professional opinion. There was no doubt that she was sure that Juanita died as a result of an injection of insulin. She discounted any pretense that barbiturates and booze had anything to do with her death. In fact, any barbiturates which were administered probably prolonged the convulsions. That shot a hole in the claim by the defense that Juanita died from an overdose of barbiturates, chased by booze.

Daniels moved on to Frank Stewart's death, and posed the same hypothetical type questions. Doctor Thomas' opinion was that Frank Stewart died of insulin shock coma due to administered insulin, which caused sudden generalized convulsions, causing a recurrent brain hemorrhage in the area of old damage and, subsequently, death within a few hours.

Daniels then asked her:

"Doctor, was there anything in Frank Stewart's hospital records about the condition of his arteries?"

"Yes, Mister Stewart's arteries were severely sclerosed."

"Is there any relationship between the injection of insulin and the blood pressure as it might affect his circulatory system?"

"Yes, the injection of insulin would tend to originally bring the blood pressure down and then in an effort to combat the insulin coma, secreted adrenalin within the body, the pressure would come back up, as the hospital records show that it did in Mister Stewart's case. This man was atherosclerotic, and by no means in normal condition. The blood pressure probably fell, and then rose again. Because of the old damage and the convulsions initiated by the insulin coma, he bled again from this old, weakened area."

This was a good place to stop for the day, as Doctor Thomas was visibly tiring and we had two more victims, Burney Archerd and Mary Brinker Post Archerd Arden. They would have to wait until the next day.

Judge Alexander banged his gavel and stated, "This court will stand in recess until nine a.m. tomorrow."

Marty and I gathered up Daniels' three-ring binders and the three of us headed back to our cubby hole in the Hall of Justice, where we did our usual autopsy of how things were going. We all agreed that Daniels was on a roll and headed in the right direction.

Daniels said, "Whitey, I don't think I have ever had an expert witness that was as well prepared as Doctor Thomas. She is sure something! What a wonderful lady."

"Yes, Ray, she is good, and such a lady. There's no doubt in her mind that all of our victims were injected with fatal doses of insulin. The defense is going to have one hell of a time discrediting her testimony. She will eat them alive!"

I ducked just in time to evade one of Marty's eight inch jabs to the shoulder as he said, "Damn! I think we're on a downhill pull now, and we have two other medical experts to back her up."

"Marty, what about Doctor Tranquada and Arquilla? Are they ready to go?" Daniels asked.

"All I have to do, Ray, is give them a couple hours' notice and they will be here. They are as ready as they will ever be. I don't think we have any worries there."

"Thanks, Marty, I knew we could count on you to keep things rolling. You are one hell of an organizer. By the way, I got a copy of Doctor Arquilla's final report today. He called me to tell me he had sent it. He is still a little reluctant to testify to his findings; something about setting a precedent."

"Well, I'll tell you, I'm not a bit worried about Doctor Arquilla. He is a dedicated scientist and he'll be fine," I told Daniels.

"I agree with you, Whitey, this report is a first! He will be sending it to all the medical journals for publication.

"Marty, I'm going down to check in with the boss to let him know we are still around. Maybe I'll run into someone that will recognize me after being away for so long. Want to come along?"

Marty and I went down to the Homicide Bureau; the place was almost empty. Norm Peterson, from Missing Persons, and our head secretary, Baby Jane Sawai, were the only ones there.

Marty said, "Let's go down to Li Po's for a quick one, then head home for a night with the family." That suited me fine, since I hadn't had a meal with my wife for a long time!

Doctor Thomas took the witness stand promptly at nine a.m. ready to begin her testimony regarding the death of Burney Kirk Archerd. She had previously submitted a four-page report outlining the pertinent case history from the time Burney was admitted to the Long Beach Memorial Hospital at four-thirty p.m. August 21, 1961, until his death September 2. Her report was concise and to the point. She listed twelve points that she based her opinion on. Her final conclusion:

"It is my professional opinion that Burney Kirk Archerd died as a result of prolonged insulin coma, produced by multiple injections of insulin in large overdoses. My opinion is based on the patient's condition at the time of hospital admission, and the sequence of events during his hospitalization."

After a short recess, Doctor Thomas, looking somewhat refreshed, took the witness stand again. She seemed eager to finish her testimony about the death of Mary Brinker Post Arden Archerd. Daniels laid out Mary's case, step by step, as he did the five other deaths. Then he asked:

> "After hearing all the facts stated in my hypothetical question and assuming them to be true, do you now have an opinion as to the cause of death of Mary Post Arden Archerd?"
>
> "It is my professional opinion that Mary Post Arden Archerd died from hypoglycemic coma induced by the injection of a large overdose of insulin, probably a long acting insulin such as NPH or Protamine-zinc insulin, injected several hours prior to hospital admission and probably repeated one or more times following hospital admission. My opinion is based on the pertinent case history, the records of the patient's visit to Doctor Smilkstein's office, and the hospital records."

"Thank you, Doctor. I have no further question."

The defense tried to give Doctor Thomas a bad time, but she was up to the task. I think she rather enjoyed the verbal sparring with Erbsen and Reiner. Finally, they decided they were getting nowhere, and ended their cross examination.

Daniels said, "Your Honor, may this witness be excused?"

"There being no objection, you are excused, Doctor Thomas. Thank you for your testimony."

✲ ✲ ✲

38
Dr. Tranquada

The next witness was Doctor Tranquada. He was one of the three expert medical witnesses who examined medical records, hospital records, and interviewed family doctors and family. Daniels examined him as follows:

Q: Will you please state your full name for the record, sir?

A: Robert E. Tranquada—T-r-a-n-q-u-a-d-a.

Q: And state your profession.

A: Physician.

Q: Are you a physician licensed to practice in the State of California?

A: Yes, I am.

Q: Do you have some particular specialty?

A My specialty is internal medicine with a sub-specialty in diabetes and hypoglycemia.

Q: Doctor, I wonder if you will outline your general education and experience and qualifications, particularly in the field of diabetes and hypoglycemia.

A: I have an M.D. degree from Stanford University of Medicine in 1955.

I was an intern in medicine at the U.C.L.A. Medical Center, and the following year had an Assistant Residency in internal medicine at U.C.L.A. from 1956 to 1957, an intermediate residency in medicine at the Los Angeles V.A. Hospital in 1957 and '58.

In 1958-59 I was a Fellow in metabolic diseases and diabetes at U.C.L.A., and the following year a Fellow in diabetes at U.S.C. School of Medicine.

I have been on the faculty full time at the U.S.C. School of Medicine since 1959, and am presently appointed as Associate Professor of Medicine and chairman of the Department of Community Medicine and Public Health.

I have been a member of the American Diabetes Association since 1959, of which I am a member of the board of Directors, Chairman of the Committee on Emergency Care for the American Diabetes Association, Chairman of the Assembly of State Coordinates and Affiliate Representatives of the same organization.

I am a member of the Diabetes Association of Southern California, and past president of the Clinical Society of that organization, and a member of the Board of Directors of that organization. I have over 35 publications in the field of diabetes, and four of these are specifically in the field of hypoglycemia.

Q: All right, doctor. Now, I intend to ask you questions specifically related to the last illnesses of William Edward Jones, Jr., Zella Archerd, Juanita Archerd, Frank L. Stewart, Burney Archerd, and Mary Arden, and I would like to have you tell us, first of all, what hypoglycemia is, tell us the different types, particularly those which are or are not fatal types in relationship with any investigation that you have done and concerning the particular described persons that I have just enumerated for you, with the idea in mind of eventually giving an opinion as to your opinion of the cause of their last illness and the cause of the death. Will you do that for us?

A: I will certainly try.

Hypoglycemia is a condition specifically related to a very low blood sugar. The only nutrient that the brain can utilize is glucose, or sugar, as it is usually referred to in the blood, and when the blood sugar falls below a certain critical point—this may vary from patient to patient, and it will vary depending upon the laboratory that does the determination of the blood sugar and the method that is used, but generally speaking, on the average blood sugar below 50 milligrams percent, the unit of measure that is used, will result in a variety of symptoms, which may include severe and prolonged states in which the blood sugar is maintained low for a long time in death.

The causes of hypoglycemia, of which there are many, can be categorized relatively well in several ways, but I would suggest for this purpose we think of them in two or three major categories: One, there are a number of causes of hypoglycemia which have never been reported as being responsible for death. I don't know whether it is necessary for me to enumerate all of these, except to say that certain kinds of what we call self-reactive hypoglycemias, which are the most common kinds that doctors find in patients, result from mild, self-limited symptoms and have never been a cause of death in and of themselves.

There are a certain number of drugs, that is, medicines that have as a side effect on rare occasions a mild lowering of the blood sugar, a mild hypoglycemia. These, too, have never been noted in the literature to be responsible for death. This might include such drugs, for your information, as aspirin in very large doses, certain of the antihistamines, also in very large doses, and a few investigative drugs that simply don't come in contact with patients outside of research hospitals.

There is another group of causes of low blood sugar, or hypoglycemia, that occur only in infancy and childhood that have never been reported above the age of 6 to 10 for these varieties, which can be severe, but which, however, are not of interest to us today since they simply don't occur above the age of 10, and certainly not in adults.

There is a group there that we are most interested in of potentially fatal causes of hypoglycemia, and these I think we can divide conveniently into two categories, those that are obvious causes in which there is always a recognizable cause, that is, easily recognizable cause, and a group of more obscure causes of hypoglycemia in which it may be difficult to determine exactly what the cause is, but in which the cause can inevitably virtually always be determined.

Now, the obvious causes of potentially fatal hypoglycemia include severe liver disease of a variety of causes. It has been reported in liver disease following prolonged heart trouble. It has been reported in liver disease resulting from severe terminal or pre-terminal cirrhosis of the liver. It has been reported in patients who have tumors of the liver, that is, tumors from other parts of the body that have moved to the liver. These are always associated with very obvious changes, usually with rather marked deep jaundice, which no physician would miss in the patient; inevitably with a very large liver, which at the time of examination or postmortem would be clearly obvious to the autopsy surgeon; and all of these causes would be quite obvious to anybody who examined either the patient living or dead.

A second more obvious cause is that related to failure of the adrenal glands or the pituitary gland. Among other effects, these may result in sensitivity to low blood sugar, the mechanisms of the body losing their normal control, and the blood sugar may fall spontaneously, and this is a potentially fatal condition. However, both of these endocrine changes are accompanied by other symptoms and signs which are clearly obvious to the practitioner – low blood pressure, episodes of fainting, changes in skin color, changes in the texture of the skin, changes in the level of energy for periods of months. These are not things that happen suddenly. These are things that happen over a period of months and years, and in all cases these would have to be described as obvious causes.

Not only that, but at examination by the autopsy surgeon, these would be causes that could not be missed. There would be an obvious disease present, either a disappearance of or a markedly diseased condition of the adrenal glands or the pituitary gland. So again we would classify this as an obvious cause.

The third obvious cause of potentially fatal hypoglycemia is a group of rare tumors that have been reported. There are perhaps 80 of these now in the literature. These consist mostly of tumors that we call fibro sarcomas. These are always large tumors. There is not a single one that is less than grapefruit size. So they either cause, in addition to being responsible for causing low blood sugar that can be very severe, they usually are responsible for symptoms resulting from their size. The tumors occur in the chest and the abdomen and the pelvis, and they usually interfere with bodily function. They could not possibly be overlooked by an autopsy surgeon, they are so large.

There is a very much smaller and rarer group of tumors of the adrenal glands, of the lung and of the stomach that have been reported to be causes of low blood sugar. These, too, are very obvious conditions. They always cause symptoms related to their primary location in the lung or the stomach, and these are things that could not be overlooked.

There are two major causes of obscure—that is, obscure causes of potentially fatal hypoglycemia. One of these is a small tumor of the pancreas called the islet cell adenoma. This may vary; this is a tumor that can either be benign or malignant, that may vary in size from half an inch to several inches in diameter, and may be very difficult to ferret out. In life this is a difficult diagnosis to make. However, at autopsy, it is always possible to determine whether or not such a tumor had been present.

The other category of obscure causes of fatal hypoglycemia is the administration of drugs. There are two known drugs that can result in fatal hypoglycemia, the major one being insulin. As you know, insulin is the product of the pancreas, extracted from the pancreas of animals. It is used for the control of diabetes, and its major function in diabetes is to lower the blood sugar.

If an overdose of insulin is given, the blood sugar falls too far, and a variety of symptoms ensue. If an overdose persists long enough, death will be one of the possible results.

This may be impossible to detect except by exclusion of other causes. It is, in fact, now possible, within the last couple of years, for us to detect this by chemical means when tissue or blood is obtained early enough and properly processed. However, these are research techniques.

The other categories of drugs that can cause fatal hypoglycemia are the oral drugs that are used in the treatment of diabetes, and there are now, I think, four of these on the market. These would have to be given in very large doses.

There are perhaps four or five cases of attempted suicide recorded with these drugs, two or three of which were successful.

Spontaneous hypoglycemia, that is, low blood sugar, in patients who are using normal amounts of these drugs, is rarely fatal.

I think, Mr. Daniels that outlines the basis of this discussion.

Q: Doctor Tranquada, you enumerated some obvious causes of hypoglycemia that could possibly cause death.

Did you consider those obvious causes in determining the cause of death of the six victims which are the subject of this trial?

A: Yes, of course. I looked for any other possible cause of death. Those obvious causes, such as tumors of the pancreas, and severe liver disease, were not found in any medical record or autopsy of any of the subjects of this trial.

Daniels then posed his patented hypothetical question with the facts leading up to the illnesses and deaths of each individual victim.

It was Doctor Tranquada's professional opinion that all six of our victims were killed by an injection or injections of insulin resulting in prolonged hypoglycemic coma and death. There was no other apparent cause of death for any of our victims.

Erbsen and Reiner were almost speechless when Daniels finished his direct examination of Doctor Tranquada. There was a valiant attempt at cross examination, but they soon realized they were getting nowhere and excused the witness.

If the defense thought the two previous witnesses were tough, they had another think coming. Our next witness was Doctor Edward Arquilla, who was the key to our being able to file this case in the first place. Daniels and I had talked with Doctor Arquilla on several occasions and were taken by his straight forward approach to our problem of trying to prove that Archerd had killed at least six people. We were pleased that he so eagerly took our information and ran with it. The results of his scientific endeavor was about to make history in the field of pathology.

I kind of felt sorry for the defense team. *Yeah, right!*

✳ ✳ ✳

39
Dr. Arquilla

Doctor Edward Arquilla was our next medical expert to be called. His calm unassuming attitude could be misleading to anyone not familiar with his qualifications. As soon as the doctor was settled comfortably in the witness chair after being sworn in by the clerk, Daniels asked him, "Doctor, what is your full name?"

"Edward Robert Arquilla."

Q: Your occupation?

A: I am a pathologist, professor of pathology at UCLA.

Q: Now, Doctor, would you please state your formal education and training.

A: I have a B.S. degree from Northern Illinois University and as part of my military training I acted as an interpreter in Military Government School for the Army. From there I went to the University of Illinois, got a Master's Degree in physiology and then I had a combined M.D. and PhD program at Western Reserve University at Cleveland.

Q: Did you receive both an M.D. and PhD?

A: Yes, I did. The PhD was in anatomy and I was teaching anatomy at the Western Reserve University Medical School. I am a Board certified pathologist in anatomic pathology. I have been awarded several fellowships, one for the Arthritis and Rheumatism Foundation, and I had an award for research activities in the Department of Anatomy at Western Reserve University. I have had a number of teaching positions in anatomy and physiology as a research assistant. I was an Assistant professor of Pathology at UCLA.

Q: Doctor, I don't want you to be bashful. Do you have any professional memberships, and if so, would you mention a few, particularly in relation to the field of diabetes?

A: Well, I am on the Board of Directors for the American Diabetes Association, and I am also on the Board of Directors for the Southern California Diabetes Association. I belong to the American Diabetes Association. I am a member of the American Association of Immunologists, and a member of the American Association of Experimental pathologists, and a member of the American Association of Pathologists and Bacteriologists, which is sort of a senior group.

Q: Do you perform any editorial services as part of your duties?

A: Yes. I review articles for Science, Journal of Clinical Investigation, Archives of Internal Medicine, and the official Journal of the Diabetes Association.

Q: Have you participated in any Lilly insulin symposiums?

A: Yes. I have been to the last three or four. They have them every two years, and the symposiums are involved with people interested in insulin action in diabetes, and they invite about twenty people from all over the world. It is every two years we have those, and I have been to the last three of those.

Q: Now, have you received any research grants at UCLA?

A: Yes. I have about twenty-five grants. There is a total of about a half a million dollars over the past ten years.

Q: Have any of these grants pertained to the immunological studies of insulin, or insulin in general, or research on insulin?

A: Yes. That has been my major field of interest for the past fifteen years, actually.

Q: Can you state some of these grants?

A: There is the United States Public Health Service on Immunological Studies of Insulin. That began actually in '59 and it has been continuous ever since. It averages about forty thousand dollars per year. I have had sort of an open-end grant. Eli Lilly Company always gives me money when I am a little short.

Q: Approximately how much?

A: It is about five thousand dollars every time I sort of need it or want it, and it has been very useful.

Q: You have certain grants, USPHS grants, is that right?

A: That is the United States Public Health Service. That is from the National Institute of Health.

Q: What is the approximate amount of each of these grants?

A: On the average, about forty thousand dollars a year.

Q: Does that have to do with research on insulin?

A: Specifically, yes, insulin, insulin action, and its relationship to diabetes and the treatment and care of diabetes.

Q: Now, have you written or published any research papers on insulin and diabetes, and if so, how many?

A: I must have twenty-five or thirty papers on insulin, I guess, and the rest of them are in related fields of endocrinology and immunology and protein chemistry.

Q: Will you tell us where they were published, what publications?

A: The Journal of Clinical Investigation, the Journal of Immunology, the Journal of Laboratory and Clinical

Medicine-most of them science-Journal of Experimental Medicine, which is a very good journal.

Q: Have you ever worked together in publishing this material with Doctor Robert Tranquada?

A: Yes. We had a paper together when I was publishing "Diabetes" in '62.

Q: Have you published any abstracts on insulin research and diabetes, and if so, how many?

A: Oh, about twenty abstracts, and they were presented at various meetings and they have been published, most of them, and the Federation of Experimental biology and in the diabetes meetings.

Q: Now, doctor, did you perform some type of microscopic examination of the brain slides of Burney Kirk Archerd's brain?

A: Yes. I examined all of the brain slides and all of the tissue that was mounted in wax and of which slides were made.

Q: Did you also examine microscopic sections of the brain slides of Mary Arden?

A: Yes, I did.

Q: Now, at the conclusion of the examination of these particular brain slides, did you cause photographs to be made?

A: Yes. Photomicrographs of microscopic sections.

Doctor Arquilla then took each brain slide of Burney's brain, described the damage and explained what causes that type of damage. He was able to pinpoint when the damage occurred, about nine to ten days before he died. All sections of Burney's brain showed the same severe damage which meant the insult was really profound. Therefore, insulin must have been given in a very, very large dose.

He discounted any possibility that such profound damage could have been caused by anoxia or any other cause.

In Mary Arden's case, Doctor Arquilla stated that it was probable that she received insulin about six to eight hours prior to coming to the hospital, and that the dose must have been rather massive.

Q: No, Doctor, what type of brain damage is reflected in the photographs of the microscopic sections of Burney Archerd's and Mary Arden's brain?

A: This could be classified as a toxic necrosis to the neocortex, technically. It means that there has been some metabolic event take place which resulted in the death of the nerve cells themselves in the cerebral hemispheres. These cells are the most sensitive of the cells in the brain, central nervous system, to metabolic insults.

Q: Now, was there any of this brain damage as shown by the photos of Mary Arden's or Burney Archerd's brain indicative of trauma or any type of injury in that regard?

A: No sir. There is no evidence whatsoever of trauma to the head in the case of Burney.

Q: Was there any evidence, as shown by those photographs of Mary Arden's brain, of trauma-type damage?

A: No, sir.

Q: What type damage was shown by those photographs of Mary Arden's brain and Burney Archerd's brain?

A: It is damage that one sees secondary to metabolic insults, such as hypoglycemia and anoxia, or carbon monoxide poisoning is another.

Q: Have you familiarized yourself with the hospital records of Mary Arden?

A: Yes.

Q: I am particularly referring to the history given by the husband of convulsions and the opisthotonus position, et cetera.

A: Yes, I have.

Q: Was there any history of anoxia?

A: There was no history, and, furthermore, the objective signs for anoxia were not present at admission. She came into the hospital, she was apparently breathing, she was not cyanotic, and there was no evidence to believe she had any oxygen deficiency.

Q: Was there any history of hypoglycemia in the hospital record?

A: No, none in the hospital record or in the attending physician's records.

Q: Including the laboratory reports, et cetera, was there a history of severe hypoglycemia?

A: There was both a blood sugar that was low and a cerebrospinal fluid sugar that was very low.

Q: Does the lack of a history of anoxia and the presence of a history of hypoglycemia, as shown by Mary Arden's hospital records, aid you in determining the causation of the brain damage indicative of hypoglycemia as shown by the photographs of the microscopic sections of Mary Arden's brain?

A: Yes. In view of the autopsy findings, there is an absence of an insulin tumor, there was no evidence of anoxia, there was toxic necrosis to the cortex, and there was hypoglycemia which was well documented, two samples, both in the cerebrospinal fluid and in the blood. One is left with only one conclusion, that she had received a rather massive dose of insulin exogenously administered to her.

Q: What does that mean?

A: It means that somebody took a syringe and gave her a large shot of insulin.

Q: Was there anything shown in Mary Arden's hospital records to indicate that she had been administered any insulin in the hospital?

A: No, none.

Q: Making the same analysis of the hospital records of Burney Kirk Archerd, have you familiarized yourself with those hospital records?

A: Yes, I have.

Q: Have you also familiarized yourself with the autopsy report of Burney Kirk Archerd?

A: Yes, I have.

Q: Was there any history of anoxia as set forth in the clinical history and the acts and conditions and events as set forth in Burney Archerd's hospital records?

A: No. And I think this is particularly important because he was under surveillance for head injury and his vital signs were being taken every two hours and documented, and at no time for the two or three days before he went into the coma while he was under this strict surveillance was there any evidence of anoxia taking place at all.

Q: Was there any history of hypoglycemia as set forth in the pertinent history and the acts, conditions, and events of the hospital record of Burney Kirk Archerd?

A: Yes. There were, I think, two blood sugars and one cerebrospinal fluid sugar. All three samples had abnormally low blood levels of glucose.

Q: With this clinical absence of any history of anoxia and the clinical history of severe hypoglycemia, as shown by Burney's hospital records and the acts, conditions, and events thereof, does this aid you in determining the cause of the brain damage as shown in the photographs of the microscopic sections of Burney's brain?

A: Yes. He received multiple injections of insulin in the hospital, and I think most of the brain damage that we see there can probably be attributed either to one or two injections administered sometime on the twenty-third of August, I guess, 1961.

Q: Based on your examination of the hospital record of Burney Kirk Archerd, the report, and on your examination of the slides of the microscopic sections of the brain of Burney Kirk Archerd, do you have any opinion as to the cause of Burney Archerd's death?

A: I think he died because of brain damage, the result of hypoglycemia which was caused by multiple injections of insulin.

Q: Any particular type of insulin?

A: I suspect he was given several types during the course of this thing, but the most instrumental, the one that did the most damage, was a long-acting insulin, probably administered in the late afternoon of the twenty-third.

Daniels addressed the court, "Your Honor, may we have a short recess?"

"The court will stand adjournment for fifteen minutes."

Daniels and I debated whether or not Doctor Arquilla would testify to his findings when he tested Mary's brain for the presence of excessive insulin. "Why don't you give it a try, Ray? It might be a good idea to discuss it with him before he resumes the stand."

"Whitey, that's why I called for this recess. I'm going to tell him it's time to fish or cut bait. I think he really wants to talk about it, but is afraid it would sound like he was bragging."

Daniels took Doctor Arquilla aside to discuss the report the doctor had prepared. He showed me a restrained smile and a quick wink just as the doctor resumed the witness stand. "We're on, Whitey; he's going to tell it like it is!"

"Doctor, I have here a four-page report prepared by you at our request," Daniels said as he walked toward the witness stand. He handed two copies of Doctor Arquilla's report to the defense, even though we had previously supplied them with copies, then handed the original to the doctor.

"Doctor, in the interest of time and clarity, would you read into the record this report that will be marked for identification only."

"Yes. The following are the facts upon which I based my professional opinion concerning the cause of Mary Arden's death.

Mary Arden was well and able to communicate between eleven p.m. and midnight the night before she was admitted to the hospital. At four a.m. she was noted to have had severe convulsive seizures. At approximately eight-thirty a.m. she was admitted to the hospital in coma with a low blood glucose level (48 mgm percent). Slightly thereafter (ten a.m.) an electroencephalogram was taken showing severe cortical depression, indicating that between midnight the night before and about ten a.m. Mary Arden's higher brain centers had been virtually destroyed. In view of the low blood sugar, the precipitous development of the convulsion, and the generalized nerve cell necrosis of the neocortex noted at autopsy, it was considered most likely that the causative factor was an overwhelming dose of insulin administered about midnight prior to the morning that she was admitted in coma to the hospital.

Alcohol should not be considered as being in any way involved in the hypoglycemia and brain damage which was noted in this case. Alcohol-induced hypoglycemia requires between forty-eight and seventy-two hours of fasting prior to ethanol consumption. Furthermore, a relatively large amount (two to three ounces of 100 proof whiskey) taken in a very short period of time (five to ten minutes) is required for the onset of hypoglycemic symptoms. Mary Arden had not been fasting for even twelve hours prior to drinking. In such cases the symptoms of hypoglycemia have not been noted for at least eight hours after the last drink of alcohol. The suddenness with which the symptoms appeared approximately four to five hours after Mary Arden had her pre-bedtime drink mitigates against alcoholic hypoglycemia as a causative agent in Mary Arden's death.

The additional findings of a very severely depressed spinal fluid glucose level of 14 mgm percent and a very low blood glucose, 37 mg percent (taken twenty-four hours after the first blood glucose determination) in spite of having received glucose infusions over a period of twenty-four hours is additional indication that she had been administered an overwhelming dose of insulin.

In addition, we measured the insulin level in brain tissue taken from Mary Arden's body at autopsy. This tissue had been preserved in formalin for a period of more than one year. In order to add validity to our tests, it was necessary to test the effect of formalin on our measurement of insulin. Insulin was added to formalin and allowed to stand for a period of days to months. The effect of formalin upon the biological activity of insulin and also on the radioimmunological measurement (one, two, three and four) of insulin was then evaluated. These experiments indicate that after being in formalin for a period of days, about 30 percent of the biological activity insulin can still be discerned when injected into alloxan-diabetic mice. Additional tests using a radioimmunological method for the measurement of insulin were in agreement with the biological tests, indicating that anywhere from 30 to 50 percent of the insulin molecule was still intact after exposure to formalin and could be detected by both of these assay procedures.

The next series of experiments consisted of extracting the insulin from brain tissue. This involved a number of trial experiments after which we felt confident that insulin could be extracted from brain tissue which had been in formalin for days and months. The extraction procedure was a modification of the method which is currently employed by pharmaceutical industries for making insulin. Eight grams of Mary Arden's brain were submitted to this extraction procedure which involved the homogenization of the brain in acid-alcohol, taking the supernate, removing the alcohol, and measuring the insulin recovered by the radioimmunoassay and also biologically by injecting it into allowance-diabetic mice. Two radioimmunoassays were performed; both indicating elevated insulin levels in the brain tissue from Mary Arden. One of these assays was performed in parallel with control brain tissue from a patient of roughly the same age as Mary Arden.

After the extracted fluid from the brain tissue of Mary Arden and from the brain of the control patient was concentrated, seven mice were injected with the material from Mary Arden's brain and six mice were injected with the material from the control brain. The average blood sugar depression of the mice injected with the extract from Mary Arden's brain was 145 mgm percent. In the case of the six mice injected with the control brain extract, a 71 mgm percent decrease in blood sugar was noted. In both cases the mice had been made diabetic and their initial blood sugars ranged between 500 and 660 mgm percent. Statistical analysis of these two samples showed that the extract from Mary Arden's brain contained significantly more insulin than did the extract from the control brain. Therefore, by biological assay and by radioimmunological assay the brain tissue from Mary Arden contained elevated levels of insulin compared to the brain tissue of a randomly selected person who came to autopsy. These findings, in conjunction with the fact that Mary Arden had well-documented low blood glucose and low cerebral spinal glucose, strongly imply that she was administered a large dose of insulin.

My opinion is further supported by the fact that a normally functioning pancreas usually does not secrete insulin when the blood sugar is very low, as was the case with Mary Arden. There is every reason to believe that Mary Arden had a pancreas which was functioning normally. It had a normal gross appearance at autopsy and two sections taken of her pancreas were also within normal limits. Furthermore,

there is no history, even with close medical supervision, that
Mary Arden had any pancreatic aberrations which would
lead one to believe that she might have had abnormal insulin secretions. Therefore, in all probability she had a normally functioning pancreas. The elevated insulin level in
her brain tissue in the face of a very low blood sugar can in
my opinion be explained only by a massive dose of exog-
enous insulin administered the night that she went into
coma and perhaps a subsequent dose of insulin while in
the hospital.

It is my opinion that the sudden onset of convulsions
and coma, the low blood glucose, the massive toxic necrosis of nerve cells in the neocortex which occurred almost
at one point in time, in conjunction with the elevated levels of extractable insulin in brain tissue from Mary Arden's
body, force me to conclude that her death was caused by an
overwhelming injection of insulin given either as a single
or multiple doses."

As Doctor Arquilla read, there was not another sound
to be heard. His voice was clear and there was no mistak-
ing his expertise. Daniels leaned over as he smothered a
smile, and said, "Whitey, we have not only set a precedent,
but we have made medico-legal history, thanks to Doctor
Arquilla and all of our expert witnesses. This is the first
time that murder by injection of insulin has been proven
in this country!"

We could discount that case in England where a male
nurse injected his wife with insulin just before she took a
bath. She passed out in the bath tub and drowned. Insulin
from the injection site was recovered.

With the completion of Doctor Arquilla's testimony,
Daniels said, "Your Honor, the prosecution rests."

Erbsen began a long tirade about how some witness'
names and addresses were withheld from him by the prosecution; also that Archerd was denied a speedy trial by not

being charged with the crime of murder immediately after each death had occurred.

Daniels cited points and authorities regarding "Violation of due process by deprivation of a speedy arrest and trial" as outlined in Witkin's California Criminal Procedure, page 297 et seq, and several other sources. The right to a speedy trial commences only upon either the filing of an information or the return of an indictment by the Grand Jury, and not before. (See Witkin-Cal Criminal Procedures, page 304). There were several other points and authorities mentioned, all with the same conclusion, which indicated that Archerd was not deprived of the right to a speedy trial.

Daniels explained to Judge Alexander that the defense had been supplied with a complete witness list pursuant to the discovery motion filed by the defense. He explained that at the time the first five victims died, there was no known method proving a criminal cause of death where the victims were injected with insulin. He further explained that he and I had interviewed three hundred to four hundred potential witnesses during the past two years. As a result of our investigation we were able to establish the similarities of each death, therefore making a strong circumstantial case. We felt it was not strong enough for a conviction. It was not until we located Doctor Arquilla and the completion of his scientific examination of Mary Arden's brain tissue that we felt there was enough cause to prosecute Archerd.

Erbsen also complained that my investigative notebooks were withheld from him. Daniels produced an itemized list of every article we had planned to introduce as evidence, including copies of all my investigative notes.

Judge Alexander agreed that Archerd was not deprived of a speedy trial, and said, "Gentlemen, let's move on."

At this point, Daniels moved that all 150 exhibits be entered into evidence. After objection from the defense on the acceptance of a few of the exhibits, all were entered.

Included in the evidence were all hospital, medical and autopsy reports of each victim; bank records that showed Archerd in a position to receive or had received money as a result of the death of each victim; insurance records showing that Archerd had received workmen's comp money as the result of some self-inflicted injury or ailment.

There were twelve letters written by Mary Arden, pleading with Archerd to come back to her. These were the letters we found in Archerd's luggage the night we arrested him. Archerd had drained Mary financially, forcing her into bankruptcy. She had no more money; therefore, she was useless to him, as well as being a clinging vine type that he could not tolerate.

The first letter was written Tuesday, September 27, 1966. To quote in part, "You see, I love everything about you. I love your legs and thighs and your delightful ass. I have a special feeling about your precious wounded ankle". She was referring to his osteomyelitis infected extremities that he attributed to war wounds received in the Battle of Midway.

There were other letters imploring him to come back to her. One could imagine the tears flowing from each pathetic sentence. This woman was thoroughly and completely, hopelessly in love with "Jim." The last letter was written Wednesday, October 26. She had almost resigned herself that he wasn't coming back; still she sent him a twenty-five-dollar check for the shoes he wanted! Apparently, he was receiving those letters regularly, but had no intention of going back to her. Why should he? He was back leaching off Gladys!

Then on October 28, 1966, Mary rear-ended another car and received minor injuries, including a bruised nose and a black eye. "Jim" shows up about October 30; Mary goes to the hospital at eight a.m. on November 2, and died the following day. We never learned how Archerd heard of Mary's accident or how he got home. The only thing that brought him back was that Mary had a visible head injury: the same MO as Archerd, Burney, and Stewart.

Regarding the death of Zella: she, too, was hopelessly in love with Archerd, and so proud to be married to an "almost doctor." She trusted him totally, to the extent that she allowed him to inject her with iron shots. This she wrote in a letter to her sister and her daughter.

Even Juanita was completely in love with Archerd. However, she had her suspicions; Dorothea had warned her that Archerd would inject her with insulin, "just like he did to Zella." This caused Juanita to write a note to her ex-husband. She gave the note to her best friend to hold, and give it to her ex-husband if something happened to her. What a hold this evil bastard had on his women!

At the end of that court day, I prepared a memo from Captain Etzel to Undersheriff McCloud:

"After twenty-seven court days and testimony of over 130 witnesses, the prosecution has rested its case. The defense will commence the presentation of witnesses and evidence on 2/20/68."

✷ ✷ ✷

40
The Defense

Defense Attorney Phillip Erbsen told the court that he would call only a few witnesses. He further stated that Archerd would testify in his own behalf when the defense began its case.

The first witness called was Gladys Stewart-Archerd-Arden. Under direct examination, Erbsen was able to get Gladys to say that Archerd had bad taste in women. Archerd sat there in his new gray suit with a fresh haircut, looking as if he were about to preach a sermon. He really cut a dashing figure with his silver hair and a confident smile; a far cry from the bewhiskered, bleary-eyed drunk that we had arrested two years earlier on July 27, 1967.

It was obvious that Gladys was still in love with him, but she did have a little trouble explaining his "poor taste in women." She reluctantly went on to say that she had found several nude pictures of one of his girlfriends in the glove compartment of his car. The pictures were of Stella, who

had earlier testified for the prosecution as to her involvement with Archerd.

"It showed her just as she is, skinny legs, and skinny bust.
Just ugly, just an ugly naked woman!" she said. Archerd
could contain himself no longer. He laughed out loud,
which drew a strong rebuke from Judge Alexander.

Gladys' demeanor and attitude on the witness stand told
volumes about the love she still had for Archerd. There was
no doubt that she was still totally committed to him in every
way, even after Bob Chapman and I told her back in 1962
that she could be a victim of Archerd's proclivity for killing wives by injecting them with insulin. She had been in
court every day and had heard all the testimony that would
eventually lead to Archerd's conviction. I asked myself how
could she not know that he was a killer?

Archerd's twin sons had been sitting in the audience
throughout the trial; one of them testified as to what a loving, kindly father Archerd had been. He also stated that he
had heard Juanita say that she was only leaving Archerd one
dollar in her will. This was to dispel any proof that Archerd
was to gain monetarily from her death.

Erbsen called Rex Kramer, an attorney, who testified
that he had drawn up the last will for Juanita Plum, but had
never seen Archerd until he walked into the court room.
This was to rebut the testimony of Joan Plum Diaz, Juanita's daughter, who had testified earlier. She said that at
the reading of the will she had accused Archerd of killing
her mother. Archerd gripped her shoulder roughly, and
spoke quietly but forcefully into her ear, "If you value the
life of that kid of yours, you'll keep your mouth shut." Mister Kramer testified that no such meeting ever took place.

There is still a lingering doubt in my mind whether
there was a reading of Juanita's will as described by Joan
Diaz. There must have been some occasion where Archerd
and Diaz were together when facts about the will were dis-

cussed. Since we had already proven that Archerd did gain considerable money from his marriage to Juanita prior to her death, the matter of the will was relatively unimportant.

Finally, Archerd took the witness stand in his own defense. He carried with him his glasses and a legal pad, and reminded me of a kindly old uncle. Anyone not familiar with the facts of the six murders, plus all the other scams he pulled, would have had a hard time believing that this sophisticated, kindly looking person could ever be guilty.

Defense counsel started out by asking Archerd about his friend, William Edward Jones. He testified that he had only known Jones for a few months, and they were not close friends, but they were friendly since they both belonged to the same organizations. He went on to state that Jones was accused of raping a babysitter, and that Jones came to see him at the Kaiser Hospital in Fontana. He asked Archerd to help him get out of the criminal charge.

"Just what did he want you to do to help him get out of the criminal charges?" Erbsen asked.

"Well, he told me the babysitter's family wanted to go back to Indiana and that he wanted me to arrange for them to leave."

"Did you collect any money from Mister Jones or his family to help the babysitter's family leave the state?"

"Yes, I got exactly five hundred dollars from the Jones family with which I bought them a truck to use for their trip."

"Did you ask Dorothea Henes or anybody else to buy insulin so you could inject Jones to simulate an injury?"

No, sir, I did not."

"What were you doing the day Jones died?"

"It was a Sunday and I was playing golf. I later babysat for my twin sons."

Erbsen then questioned Archerd about Zella's death. Archerd told the story about a home robbery which occurred as he and Zella were preparing for bed. A man suddenly appeared at their bedroom door. He had his face covered with Archerd's robe which was held by one hand; in the other hand, he held a gun.

"I told Zella, don't get excited but we have company. A second man came in and forced me to leave the room at knife point. That man jabbed me twice with the knife, then he tied my hands and feet. The robbers took my wife's purse and my wallet, but they left her watch as well as mine."

Monday, February 26, Archerd resumed the witness stand. Erbsen continued his direct examination. He testified that he had married Juanita Plum Archerd twice; once in Mexico and once in Las Vegas, and in no way did he benefit from her death. He denied that the reading of her will ever happened, and stated that he never threatened harm to Joan Diaz' son. He said that he and Juanita had separated but decided to try again, so they went to Las Vegas and were remarried. That same night Juanita washed down a couple of sleeping pills with bourbon. The next day she became ill. He took her to a doctor who told him she was merely drunk. He took her back to the motel and she became ill again. He called another doctor, who admitted her to a hospital where she died the next day. While telling this sad tale, Archerd wiped away an imaginary tear, and allowed his voice to crack.

Finally, Erbsen wound up his direct examination. On cross examination, Daniels tore into Archerd like a bull dog. First, he showed him Jones' hospital records, and made him admit that he knew the nurses on duty during Jones' stay. He pointed to an entry that mentioned Archerd's presence while Jones was having convulsions, then asked, "Is that your name on this man's record as attending him while he is having grand mal seizures?"

"That's my name, but I wasn't there. I was babysitting my twin sons."

"Can you think of any reason anyone would place your name on such a document?"

"No, sir, I can't."

"Mister Archerd, do you know Dorothea Sheehan?"

"Yes, I was married to her at one time."

"Do you remember her testimony that you were at the Kaiser Hospital Sunday, October 12, between the hours of seven a.m. and eleven a.m. when William Edward Jones died, and that you were in the room where Mister Jones was having continuous convulsive seizures?"

"Yes, I remember that testimony. I was not there."

"Do you remember the testimony of Wilnora Harrison, Mister Jones' aunt and a supervising nurse at Kaiser Hospital, and that she testified that you were, in fact, in and out of Mister Jones' room several times that Sunday morning?"

"Yes, I remember her testifying that she saw me there, but I was not. I played golf that morning and babysat with my sons that afternoon."

Daniels went over the testimonies of all the Jones' family members about the money each contributed to help get the babysitter's family out of town. Archerd still maintained that he only got five hundred dollars from the family and that he bought the babysitter's family a truck with it. It was actually a 1934 Buick sedan; Archerd paid Sam Knox three hundred eight dollars for it.

Archerd still maintained that he never profited from the death of any of the six victims covered by our investigation. He was shown bank records from his and Zella's account showing the deposit of $10,187.45 July 13, 1956, and his deposit of a five-thousand-dollar check three days later at another bank. Six days after the five-thousand-dollar check, he wrote another check for a thousand dollars. The records showed that their joint account went from $10,187.45 July 16 to a balance of $791.19 July 25, the day of Zella's death.

Daniels continued down the list of victims. He showed that Archerd had actually made six withdrawals from a bank account naming him and his mother, Jennie May Archerd, as guardians for Burney Kirk Archerd. This money was in trust from a workman's compensation claim arising from the death of Everett Archerd, Burney's father, while he was on the job in San Pedro. The total of these withdrawals amounted to $6,074.34.

That was better than the average yearly salary in 1961. I don't believe Archerd earned that much as an honest wage in any one year of his whole life!

It is interesting to note that Archerd's mother was found dead by his cousin, who he recruited to go with him to tell her that Burney was dying. Kind of makes a fellow wonder what caused her death; she was cremated before we knew about Burney's death. Oh! The suspicious mind of a homicide investigator! Also, was Burney's father's death really a heart attack? He, too, was cremated shortly following his death.

Walt Thornton and I had kicked those two deaths around from all sides back in 1961, but couldn't come up with any way to prove a criminal cause of death. It would have really been a stretch even for two very suspicious-minded homicide investigators.

Archerd had begun his testimony February 26. Erbsen advised the court March 1 that Archerd would be their last witness. Therefore, when Daniels completed his cross-examination March 5, the trial was, in effect, over. We had expected several medical experts to testify for the defense, but were surprised when none were called. The defense rested its case.

✲ ✲ ✲

41
Guilty!

Judge Alexander found William Dale Archerd guilty of three counts, first degree murder, in the deaths of Zella Archerd, in 1956; Burney Kirk Archerd, in 1961; and Mary Brinker Post Arden, in 1966; stating that these deaths were committed by the administration of poison (insulin) and by premeditation.

He further commented that the key to the entire case was testimony of one, Dorothea Archerd Sheehen, an ex-wife of defendant, who stated that she and defendant had contemplated writing a novel sometime prior to the death of Zella Archerd; and during this discussion with the defendant, he stated to her that insulin would be the perfect thing to use in the murder in that insulin could not be retrieved from the blood and tissue of the human body.

Let's face it, if it hadn't been for Dorothea, there probably would have been no trial at all. It was her continued insistence that Archerd had killed Jones, Zella, and Juanita by injecting them with insulin. Probably no one would have suspected that any of his six known victims were cold-bloodedly murdered by that evil sociopath.

Harry Andre had spent many hours, days, weeks, and months of frustration trying to prove a criminal cause in Zella's death. Then, Dick Humphreys tried his best to prove that Archerd had killed Juanita and Frank Stewart. Walt Thornton and I were similarly stymied when Burney died. It was not until Archerd killed Mary that Marty, Daniels and I were able to put together a circumstantial case that led to his conviction.

42
Arguments and Sentencing

Dorothea really was the key to the successful prosecution of Archerd. That, and a hell of a lot of hard work by all the investigators involved, an outstanding prosecutor, and of course, our highly-regarded medical experts.

The other three deaths presented at trial, but not charged, were the murders of William Edward Jones in Fontana in 1947, Archerd's fifth wife, Juanita Plum Archerd, in 1958 in Las Vegas, and Frank Stewart, Gladys Archerd's ex-husband, in Las Vegas in 1960. Those three murders were committed outside our jurisdiction, and were introduced to show common scheme and plan in the prosecution of Archerd on the murders of Zella, Burney, and Mary. These murders were allowed to be introduced in spite of Erbsen's impassioned argument that they were inadmissible. He also argued that the time delay from when the crimes were committed to prosecution was prejudicial to the defendant.

Judge Alexander stated, "I have to find because of the long delay there was some prejudice to the defendant. Was there a deliberate delay? I cannot say there was since under the facts of evidence the people could not have filed against the defendant without the scientific evidence of experts. I find no deliberate delay for the purpose of suppressing evidence."

Defense counsel Erbsen made a big deal regarding the competency of the doctors in this case. He alleged that they were incompetent and negligent, since insulin was discovered in 1921 and that convulsions, sweating and pinpointed pupils were in the medical books long before 1947. He went on to say, "If the British in 1957 could determine that insulin could be recovered from the human body in a criminal case, why couldn't the prosecution's doctors? Because their doctors are ill-equipped, lazy, negligent, or uninformed. He was suspected in the deaths of Zella, Juanita, and Burney, why wasn't something done? If doctors are that incompetent, you can't attribute that to the defendant! I think the testimony of Mrs. Diaz, Juanita's daughter, is so tainted as to become completely unbelievable, odiferous!"

Erbsen failed to say that insulin was recovered from the injection site of the victim who drowned before the insulin was assimilated by the body.

At the request of Judge Alexander, Doctor Margaret McCarran, the physician in charge of the jail wards at the General Hospital, was called to testify as to defendant's present physical condition. She testified that defendant had suffered a mild heart attack December 21, 1967, but had completely recovered from this attack, and that in her opinion the defendant could live for another twenty-five years.

At the end of Doctor McCarran's testimony, it was stipulated to by the defense and the prosecution that no further evidence would be presented as to the penalty phase of the hearing. Arguments on the penalty phase were reserved until nine-thirty a.m., March 7, 1968.

When Archerd appeared in court the following morning, Erbsen advised Judge Alexander that Archerd had suffered chest pains in his cell overnight. "Although they are not believed to be serious, they could be. Your Honor, I would like my client returned to General Hospital and examined by an independent cardiologist, Doctor Joseph Marx, of Encino. I believe that Doctor McCarran's testimony may have been influenced by the investigating officers."

Judge Alexander replied, "This man's life is involved, and I will do nothing to stop either side from presenting evidence to the court."

The judge then appointed Doctor Irwin Hoffman, Director of Cardiology at the General Hospital. He ordered both doctors to examine Archerd that evening, and suspended proceedings until nine a.m., March 8.

Archerd slumped in his chair and managed to look suitably pitiful for the judge's benefit, saying, "I had quite a few chest pains yesterday."

✡ ✡ ✡

43
Congratulations

When I got back to the office, there was a teletype message on my desk:

"L.A.S.O. Homicide Detail

Attn: Lt. Harold White

Congratulations on results of several years of hard work and dedication.

Sort of makes up for some of the overtime spent that seemed so fruitless.

Lieutenant Hal Barnett   Central Records Division

Frank Bland, Sheriff   San Bernardino County"

Hal and I had worked some murder cases that involved both Los Angeles County and San Bernardino County. In doing so, we became good friends and shared a mutual respect. I got him on the phone and thanked him for the quick atta boy. We agreed that we would meet soon at Li Po's in Chinatown to celebrate. There's no feeling like it when a contemporary from another agency congratulates you.

The next message was a telegram from Doc Parnell in Tulsa, Oklahoma. Doc was a brand-new deputy whose first assignment was on my shift at a juvenile detention center in East Los Angeles. I had just been promoted to sergeant when he showed up. Doc was working the metro squad during the time I worked the Archerd case, and was familiar with the history of my frustrations over the years. Doc had accepted a job of Chief of Security for Shell Oil Company. His message was, "I knew you could do it. Congratulations."

When I got home that night, the good news had preceded me. The Gannaways greeted me with a round of applause and I received a big hug and kiss from Midge. After things quieted down, Ralph said, "If you remember, we started this thing a couple years ago with dinner and a belt or two at the *Tally Whackers.* Why don't we celebrate the successful end of a hell of a lot of hard work?"

"That's fine with me, Ralph, but don't sandbag me like you did back then."

Everybody knew that admonition was not going to work. I had all weekend to recover. It turned out that I needed every bit of the weekend. What the hell! Wasn't I due for a little relaxation? The celebration was a tad premature; we had one more day to go before I could start to recover.

The next day I came into the courtroom a little worse for wear, slightly bleary-eyed, and a little out of joint. Daniels could hardly contain himself. "Kind of over trained a bit didn't you, Whitey? You look like you slept under a bridge last night. Just sit there and don't lose your cookies, it'll be over before you know it."

Both doctors were examined at great length by Daniels and Erbsen. Essentially, Doctor Marx stated that Archerd had suffered a heart condition; Doctor Hoffman testified that he didn't. That afternoon, prosecutor Daniels argued for the death penalty, stating that Archerd had led a full life and all he ever created was death, misery and heart-ache, not only for the people who died, but for their families. He watched his victim's progress with a cold scientific eye. Coldly and clinically he killed them, and his motive was greed.

Daniels cited the similarity between the deaths of two of his wives. He lived with each of them a year and a half. Unemployed, he lived off them until their money was gone, then he left them, to return only after they pleaded with him to come back. Three days later, they each ended up in a hospital; on the fourth day they were dead.

But Burney, Archerd's nephew, was the most pathetic of all. Archerd staged the accident, put drops in Burney's eyes and took him to a hospital where his condition worsened following each visit by the 'loving uncle' who stood there impatiently and coldly watching him die. "What kind of fiend are we dealing with? What is so precious about this man's life?" Daniels asked.

Erbsen argued for less than fifteen minutes, mostly condemning the death penalty and preaching about the abolition of it. "I'm not saying Mister Archerd deserves any medals for what he did, and I don't think we can concern ourselves with rehabilitation in this case, but this defendant can be punished by just not being able to be free."

Erbsen sat down as if he were dead tired. I knew that in his heart, Erbsen knew that Archerd would be sentenced to die in the gas chamber.

Judge Alexander, obviously under great strain, said, "I appreciate the fact that sentencing this man is my responsibility and mine alone...nobody can share that with me. Medical testimony introduced yesterday conflicted as to how long Mister Archerd could live. I was interested in his heart condition for one reason. I did not want to put the State in the immoral position of racing this man's God to claim his body.

"I agree with the defense attorney that times have changed and that many states have done away with capital punishment, but can a judge at a trial level do away with capital punishment? I hate the death penalty as much as anybody, but it is on the books and I have taken an oath to support the constitution and uphold the law. The Penal code and the legislature provide that one found guilty of murder in the first degree will suffer either the death penalty or life imprisonment. The legislature must have had some reason for the alternate sentence, and I can only assume that in aggravated cases the legislature intended the death penalty imposed. If there ever was an aggravated case, this is it."

The judge went on to tell of cases he had tried as a prosecutor, including Barbara Graham, the next to last woman to die in California's gas chamber. "I recall a good many years ago that I prosecuted a man who molested and brutally murdered a little girl. I felt that was the most evil man I would come in contact with. Later, I prosecuted three people on murder. Their theory was to leave no living witness behind, and I thought those were the most evil people I could ever come across. But then, it was my misfortune to meet Mister Archerd. I think he is more evil than any I had ever seen before.

It is a very, very difficult thing to tell a man he must die, and I certainly derive no pleasure in doing so…but if I do the other, I would be doing a cowardly act. It would be a cowardly act not to impose the death penalty in this case. Regardless of what he has done, he is still a human being and it is a difficult thing to tell a man, you must die, but in this case I must."

Judge Adolph Alexander is one of the very few judges in Los Angeles County ever to impose the death penalty after hearing the case without a jury.

When the judge concluded his remarks, Archerd leaned across the counsel table and congratulated Daniels, the man who had successfully prosecuted him.

Judge Alexander set March 18, 1968, to hear arguments for a new trial and to formally impose sentence. At that time, the defense motion for a new trial was denied; the arraignment for judgment was waived. The defense's plea for reduction of sentence to life imprisonment was denied. Archerd was sentenced to die in the gas chamber in San Quentin for the murder of each of the three victims in this case. A stay of execution until March 26, 1968, was granted at the defendant's request.

44
Thank God It's Over

Back in our broom closet of an office, Marty was waiting for Daniels and me to return from court. He greeted us with a big grin and a punch on my shoulder. Our quarters were so close that I didn't have room enough to avoid the punch, but kept me from hitting the floor. "Damn it, Marty, a hand shake would have been enough! You don't have to knock me on my ass every time you get excited. Remind me never to get you pissed off at me!"

"Ah hell, Whitey, I didn't mean anything by that. I guess I just got carried away. I'm so glad this ordeal ended so successfully. Now, maybe we can relax a bit. By the way, while I was waiting for you, I did a little research."

He handed me a three by five card, then continued, "I thought you'd get a kick out of this." During the eight months of trial, including delays due to Archerd's 'heart attack' and holidays, there were 5,476 pages of transcript, 134 prosecution witnesses, including twenty-one doctors, twenty-two registered nurses, seven lab technicians, two coroners, and one criminalist. The defense had seven witnesses all told, including two doctors, two attorneys and the defendant. Of this nearly eight months, there were only fifty days of actual trial.

One would have thought that the three of us would have gone out and celebrated a little. I think we had all been kept away from our families for too long and could hardly wait to get home and relax. We had had enough of William Dale Archerd to last a lifetime. I didn't want to spend another minute thinking about that sadistic monster; I wanted to get home and get reacquainted with my wife and friends.

By this time, Van was in the Army and headed for Viet Nam; Jan had married and was helping her husband through dental school. I didn't know what was in store for me; I had been loaned back to Homicide Bureau from Lakewood Station. As it worked out, Captain Etzel had retired and Captain George Walsh was the new Commander of the Homicide Bureau. Things were changing fast in the Sheriff's Department, and the Homicide Bureau was destined to grow dramatically. I was to be part of that expansion plan.

I started moving my gear back to the Bureau and was about to settle in when a teletype message was transmitted through Department communications:

SHERIFF'S DEPARTMENT BROADCAST
4-12-68   FILE NO. RB-50
TO – ALL PERSONNEL
I HAVE THIS DATE COMMENDED LIEUTENANT HAROLD WHITE AND DEPUTY MARTIN DEIRO OF OUR HOMICIDE BUREAU FOR THE PROFESSIONAL EXCELLENCE WITH WHICH THEY CONDUCTED THIS DEPARTMENT'S LENGTHY INVESTIGATION INTO THE "INSULIN MURDER CASE." THEIR UNTIRING EFFORTS RESULTED IN THE CONVICTION OF WILLIAM DALE ARCHERD ON MARCH 15, 1968, OF 3 COUNTS OF MURDER.

PETER J. PITCHESS, SHERIFF
LB SNDG   2030 PST

There happened to be five or six of my old colleagues in the office. Someone read it out loud. They all congratulated Marty and me for a job well done. They had all been following our progress from day one.

The only crack in that jar of euphoria was by my old friend and partner, Roy Collins, when he said, "Sheeit, Whitey, any one could have done it!"

You could have heard a pin drop. I knew he was yanking my chain again to get a rise out of me, and he nearly succeeded. After I composed myself somewhat, I replied, "Maybe so, Roy, you dip shit, but I did it! Of course, I didn't do it by myself; I had a hell of a lot of help. There were better detectives than me that had this case before I did. There was Harry Andre, who with the help of Ted Nissen, Archerd's parole officer, convinced Dorothea to come forward and tell us how Archerd had killed Jones and Zella. Harry did a great job with what he had to work with, but things weren't right at that time. Then Dick Humphreys had it for the Stewart and Juanita deaths. He also did a bang up job and documented his many hours of fruitless work. Then there was Walt Thornton and me on the Burney case. I think we came closer than anyone had so far because we knew that if we were ever going to prove all those people were murdered by Archerd, it would have to be done by circumstantial evidence. We had no crime scene, no smoking gun, no bullet or spent cartridge, no blunt instrument to match with wounds or any other physical evidence. In short, we had no direct evidence and no proof of a criminal cause of death; we had to rely on circumstantial evidence. In this case, Judge Alexander stated that our circumstantial evidence was overwhelming. But things weren't just right, even then. We felt that Archerd's next victim would be Gladys, and we told her so. I think that's why she is still living. We had to wait for one more victim.

"If it hadn't been for the greatest group of medical experts anywhere, we wouldn't have been able to file a single case against Archerd. Of course, I can't say enough about Marty, who held up his end and kept things in order. Let me tell you, he's going to be one hell of a homicide investigator because he has the patience of Job. He listens carefully and retains what he learns. He has a knack for gathering facts and placing them in chronological order, and he is a real stickler for detail. And Ray Daniels is by far the best prosecutor I have ever worked with. Without him, with his medical and legal expertise, we would never have made it. He was with us in the field all the way. I have never before seen a prosecutor leave his desk to give the investigators a hand. He may be small in stature, but he is surely a giant of a man. Yeah, Roy, even you might have been able to handle this one!"

I looked around to see a lot of smiles and winks, the best silent accolade one could imagine.

"Aw, shit, Whitey, you know I was just pulling your chain. I didn't mean to piss you off." Yeah, sure!

"That's okay, Roy, you kind of put me in my place, but I had to say what I did because none of us does it all by ourselves. We all have to depend on others for their help and guidance."

✷ ✷ ✷

Afterword

June 6, 1968

A letter from Wesley Grapp, Special Agent in charge of the Los Angeles office of the F.B.I. to Peter J. Pitchess, Sheriff of Los Angeles County:

Attention: Lt. Harold White, Homicide Division

"Dear Sheriff, A review of the Federal Bureau of Investigation file concerning the investigation of William Dale Archerd as a suspect in an investigation in 1962 and 1963 concerning a possible violation of the Federal Statute covering the destruction or the attempted destruction of aircraft reflected as follows:"

The letter goes on to tell of finding a brown leather briefcase in the dead storage area of the old Honolulu International Airport. This briefcase contained sixteen sticks of dynamite, a two-foot fuse with a dynamite cap attached, some galvanized wire, a box of ninety-nine number six dynamite caps, a large quantity of twenty-penny spikes, and two-inch finishing nails. The briefcase bore the initials W.J.A. on the locking flap. There was a baggage tag on the briefcase from the Alexander Young Hotel in Honolulu. Records indicated that the briefcase was placed in the airport locker between noon, September 30, 1961 and October 1, 1961.

The letter pointed out that Archerd had registered at the hotel as James Lynn Arden at 9:55 p.m., September 29, 1961. They also learned that Archerd had taken out a seventy-five-thousand-dollar flight insurance policy on his life, naming his twin sons, William and Robert, the beneficiaries. He was still actively pursuing his lawsuit regarding the death of Frank Stewart in 1960.

The letter described in detail their investigation and made note of the fact that I had assisted them. I had been investigating the death of Archerd's nephew, and was naturally interested in anything with which Archerd was connected.

Since this incident occurred less than a month after Burney died September 2,1961, a copy of their report could have been helpful in my investigation. Thankfully, we were able to convict Archerd without the help of the F.B.I.!

January 6, 1969:

I received in the departmental mail from the then agent in charge of the Los Angeles office of the F.B.I. a copy of the F.B.I. Law Enforcement Bulletin for that month. It featured the article I had written on the orders of the sheriff: "Proof of Murder by Insulin - A Medico-Legal First." Inside this bulletin marking the article was a 4 by 6 plain sheet of paper, dated January 6, 1969:

"Dear Harold: Great article. Congratulations. Robert E. Kerten."

It was signed, Bob, scribbled over the name Robert. That little note was enough to set things right, again.

I had worked with several outstanding F.B.I. agents over the years, and never before lacked for the exchange of information.

December 10, 1970:

The California Supreme Court handed down a fifty-eight-page decision that the "Judgments of conviction and the sentence of death are affirmed." All seven judges concurred.

February 1972:

Judge Adolph Alexander retired, leaving a huge void in the Los Angeles County judicial system.

October 29, 1977:

William Dale Archerd died in Vacaville Prison, allegedly from natural causes. His death certificate says that he died as the result of a cerebral-vascular accident, right anterior artery due to arteriosclerosis, moderately severe. Too bad it wasn't helped along with a heavy shot of NPH U 80 so he could have experienced the agony he caused his victims.

Mary Neiswender, the reporter from the Long Beach Press Telegram, supplied me with boxes of information she had accumulated on this case as well as sound advice and encouragement.

Ray Daniels left the District Attorney's office and joined the firm of F. Lee Bailey for a short time, then joined another firm. I had a note from him shortly after he joined Bailey. I hadn't heard from him again until 2004 when I called him at his home. He was semi-retired. Good prosecutors like him should never retire.

Marty Deiro finished his time in the LASD working homicides. After retiring, he worked for a while as a security specialist, and as a deputy U.S. Marshall. He was also security director for Lieutenant-Governor Mike Curb during his political campaign. Marty died October 10, 2008 – may he rest in peace.

Phillip Erbsen disappeared from my scope and I have lost track of him. Perhaps he is still practicing law and keeping his Screen Actors Guild card active.

Ira Riener served for a time as City Attorney for Los Angeles, then as District Attorney for Los Angeles County.

He may be seen at times on television as a legal consultant for a news reporter regarding some high profile crime.

Doctor Edward Arquilla moved from UCLA Medical Center to California State University at Irvine where he headed the pathology department. He still maintains an office there.

The other players in this drama are too numerous to mention, although most played a major role in our investigation.

I retired from the LASD in 1976 and became a recreational golfer, equestrian, avocado rancher and world traveler.

Midge, my first love and my wife of almost fifty-one years, had a fatal heart attack on the golf course, and died in 1993. We were blessed with two children, Jan and Van, six wonderful grandchildren, and so far eight great-grandchildren.

I found love again after friends introduced me to Mary. We were married in 1996. She has saved my life and made it worth living. I would never have finished the telling of this case without her constant support and encouragement, her typing, and her computer skills.

Mary and I walk two miles every day at a fast clip to keep the old heart pumping. When not tending my roses or traveling, I enjoy honing my writing skills.

The End.

✲ ✲ ✲

Appendix

Whitey with Marty Deiro

Lt. Harold White and Deputy District Attorney Ray Daniels

Awards Presentation, Archerd Case, April 30, 1968. Left to Right:
DA Evelle Younger, Deputy DA Ray Daniels, Dr Edward Arquilla,
Lt Harold White

Los Angeles County Hall of Justice

County of Los Angeles
Office of the Sheriff
PETER J. PITCHESS, SHERIFF
Los Angeles, California 90012

June 6, 1969

Quinn Tamm, Executive Director
International Association of
   Chiefs of Police, Inc.
1319 Eighteenth Street, N.W.
Washington, D. C. 20036

Dear Quinn:

It gives me great pleasure to nominate Lieutenant Harold W. White of
our Department's Detective Division, Homicide Bureau, for this year's
"Parade - IACP Police Service Award."

Lieutenant White, a twenty-two year veteran of the Sheriff's Department
and an outstanding member of the Department's Homicide Bureau, was
instrumental in bringing to a successful conclusion the infamous "Murder
by Insulin" case which was investigated by this Department in 1967.

Lieutenant White, then Sergeant White, received my personal commendation for his excellent and untiring investigation which was terminated
on March 15, 1968, with the conviction of William Dale Archerd on
three counts of murder.

The case required one of the most exhaustive investigations in the history
of the Sheriff's Department. It was a first of its type in this nation, and
only the second in the history of law enforcement throughout the world.
Because of Lieutenant White's tenacious investigation, the Sheriff's
Department received local, state and nation-wide recognition.

Letter to Quinn Tamm by Sheriff Peter J. Pitchess Nominating Lt.
Harold White for *Parade Magazine's* IACP Police Service Award

QUINN TAMM, EXECUTIVE DIRECTOR -2- June 6, 1969

During his investigation, Lieutenant White travelled in excess of twenty thousand miles, and interviewed more than four hundred persons. Of those 400, one hundred and thirty gave testimony before the Grand Jury, which resulted in the indictments that eventually led to the conviction of the defendant.

His willingness to spend untold hours doing medical library research in order to educate himself in the highly technical theory of insulin and its reaction on human tissues, reflects highly on his professional dedication to duty. His willingness to cooperate fully with the District Attorney and members of the medical profession is evidence of his outstanding sense of responsibility.

Because of Lieutenant White's extraordinary investigative accomplishments which brought this unusual case to a successful conclusion, I respectfully submit his name for nomination of this year's "Parade - IACP Police Service Award."

My kindest regards.

Sincerely,

PETER J. PITCHESS
SHERIFF

PJP/VJC/co/A

Quinn Tamm Ltr June 6 1969 p2

INTERNATIONAL ASSOCIATION OF CHIEFS OF POLICE, INC.

President THOMAS J. CAHILL SAN FRANCISCO, CALIF.	**First Vice President** CURTIS BRUSTRON ST. LOUIS, MO.	**Fourth Vice President** DON R. FANNING WINNETKA, ILL.	**Treasurer** PLISNARD L. JASMIRE TINSON, ARIZONA
Immediate Past President LEONARD G. LAWRENCE HAMILTON, ONT., CANADA	**Second Vice President** JOHN R. SHRYOCK KETTERING, OHIO	**Fifth Vice President** EDMUND L. McKADAY JEFFERSON CITY, MO.	Director of State and Provincial Police, General Chairman LEO J. MULCAHY HARTFORD, CONN.
Honorary President JAMES M. BROUGHTON CHESAPEAKE, VA.	**Third Vice President** GEORGE A. MURPHY ONEIDA, N.Y.	**Sixth Vice President** THOMAS REDDIN LOS ANGELES, CALIF.	

1319 EIGHTEENTH STREET, N.W. • WASHINGTON, D. C. 20036 • AREA CODE 202—TELEPHONE 265-7222

QUINN TAMM
Executive Director

June 16, 1969

Sheriff Peter J. Pitchess
Los Angeles County Sheriff's Office
Hall of Justice
Los Angeles, California 90012

Dear Pete:

Your nomination of Lieutenant Harold W. White
for the "Parade-IACP Police Service Award" has been
forwarded to the Editors of PARADE Magazine for their
consideration.

We appreciate your effort, and wish you success in
the judging of the nominations which will begin August 1.

Sincerely,

Quinn Tamm
Executive Director

JUN 18 1969

Quinn Tamm Letter to Sheriff Peter J Pitchess

78 1 SSI N25 8H-AD-32 5-66

COUNTY OF LOS ANGELES
SHERIFF 'S DEPARTMENT

DATE   4-8-68

OFFICE CORRESPONDENCE

FILE NO.

FROM: PETER J. PITCHESS   TO: Harold W. White, Lieutenant
      SHERIFF   HOMICIDE BUREAU

SUBJECT: COMMENDATION

I wish to extend my personal commendation for your excellent and most
untiring investigation which was terminated on March 15, 1968 with the
conviction of William Dale Archerd on three counts of murder.

The Sheriff's Department was highly complimented as a result of your
tenacious investigation. Not only was it one of the most exhaustive
investigations in the history of the Sheriff's Department; it was a
first of its type in this nation, and only the second in the history of
law enforcement throughout the world.

I have been informed that in your pertinacious efforts to locate
witnesses, you travelled in excess of twenty thousand miles, and
interviewed more than four hundred persons. Of these, one hundred
and thirty testified before the Grand Jury, which resulted in the
indictments that eventually led to the conviction of this heartless
individual.

Your willingness to spend untold hours doing research in medical
libraries in order to educate yourself in the highly technical aspects
of the theory of insulin and its reaction on human tissues reflects
highly on your professional dedication to duty. Your willingness to
cooperate fully with the District Attorney and members of the medical
profession is evidence of your outstanding sense of responsibility.

Again accept my personal commendation, and that of the entire Sheriff's
Department, for your extraordinary investigative accomplishments, which
were the result of a challenge to prove what you personally believed to
be true.

A copy of this memorandum will be placed in your performance file.

Sheriff's Commendation Memo Apr 1968

COUNTY OF LOS ANGELES
OFFICE OF THE DISTRICT ATTORNEY
600 HALL OF JUSTICE
LOS ANGELES, CALIFORNIA 90012

EVELLE J. YOUNGER, DISTRICT ATTORNEY

April 30, 1968

Lt. Harold White,
Homicide Bureau
Los Angeles County Sheriff's Department
211 West Temple
Los Angeles, California 90012

Dear Lt. White:

It gives me great pleasure, on behalf of the citizens of Los Angeles
County, to present you a commendation for outstanding service to
the community.

Your work in connection with the successful prosecution of William
Dale Archerd is deeply appreciated.

To recapitulate: You, Lt. Harold White, have been investigating a
series of homicides for approximately 10 years. And the death of
the latest victim triggered a new investigation by you in November,
1966.

The deaths covered a period of 20 years, and the investigation had
many setbacks and difficulties. This was because many persons
with information were either deceased or their whereabouts unknown.
In addition many vital documents were presumed missing or destroyed.

However, during the most recent investigation, beginning in January,
1967, most of the records were recovered by you and members of your
staff.

I am most happy to commend you for your efforts in this matter and
thank you for your assistance.

Sincerely yours,

EVELLE J. YOUNGER
District Attorney

pr

Evelle Younger Ltr Apr 30 1968

Thank-You Note from Ellery Queen

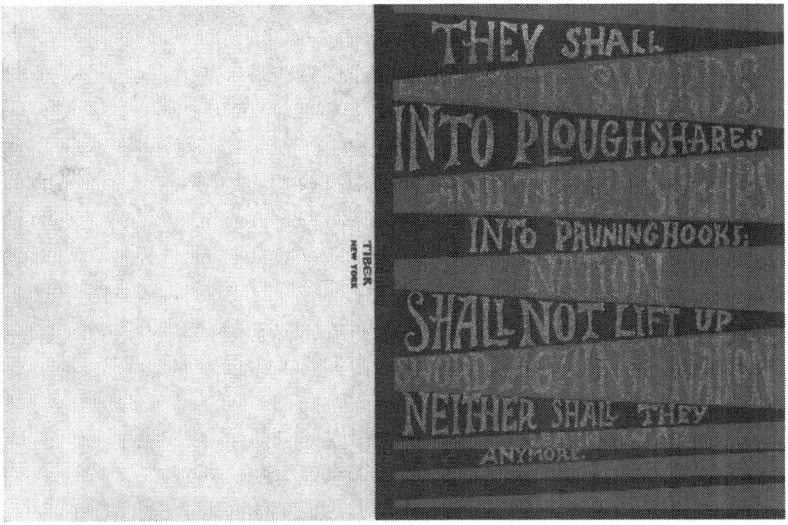

Card from Manfred Lee (Ellery Queen) and his wife, Kaye, who was the sister of Mary Brinker Post

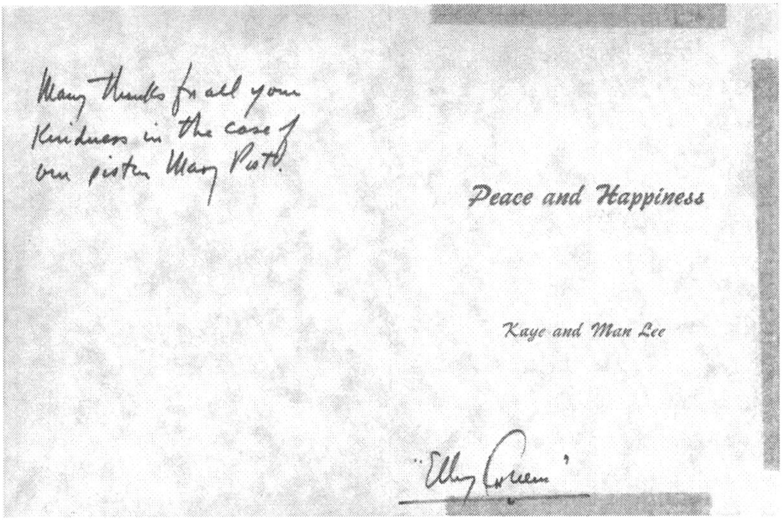

("Many thanks for all your kindness in the case of our sister Mary Post.")

✡ ✡ ✡

Endnotes

1 Baby Jane took my dictation. Ten minutes later, she
   handed me this memo:

SHERIFF'S DEPARTMENT

Date: 12-15-67
File No.   Y-427-746
Office Correspondence
From: F.G. Fimbres, Chief To: W.H. McCloud
Detective Division   Assistant Sheriff
Subject: ARCHERD CASE

Captain Etzel, Homicide Bureau, reports as follows:

As of 12-14-67, there have been a total of 39 witnesses
who have testified in this case. It is expected that testimony
will be completed regarding the death of Count #1 Zella
Archerd on 12-15-67, and some testimony will be presented
regarding the death of Juanita Archerd on 12-15-67.

On 12-14-67, the Defense brought to the attention of Judge
Alexander that the defendant was suffering from a painful
sore caused by his osteomyelitis and the Judge ordered that
the defendant be examined forthwith by a doctor. The insin-
uation by the Defense was that Archerd had asked for medical attention previously but had been denied same. In view
of this statement, Lt. White contacted Lt. Frazier of the Jail
Division and asked that a running log of defendant's requests
and activities be maintained during this trial.

✳ ✳ ✳

Made in the USA
Lexington, KY
09 October 2011